FILM FREAK

www.transworldbooks.co.uk

FILM FREAK

Christopher Fowler

Doubleday

LONDON · TORONTO · SYDNEY · AUCKLAND · JOHANNESBURG

TRANSWORLD PUBLISHERS
61–63 Uxbridge Road, London W5 5SA
A Random House Group Company
www.transworldbooks.co.uk

First published in Great Britain
in 2013 by Doubleday
an imprint of Transworld Publishers

This book is a work of non-fiction based on the life, experiences and
recollections of the author. The author has stated to the publishers that,
except in such minor respects not affecting the substantial accuracy of the
work, the contents of this book are true.

A CIP catalogue record for this book
is available from the British Library.

ISBN 9780857521606

Addresses for Random House Group Ltd companies outside the UK
can be found at: www.randomhouse.co.uk
The Random House Group Ltd Reg. No. 954009

The Random House Group Limited supports the Forest Stewardship
Council (FSC®), the leading international forest-certification organisation.
Our books carrying the FSC label are printed on FSC®-certified paper.
FSC is th   ding
environmenta   :urement
policy   it

*For Peter, who missed the start of the movie
but not the end.*

MARGARET RUTHERFORD *(watching Joyce Grenfell thrash the school dinner gong)*: You don't have to hit it so hard, Miss Gossage, you're not introducing a film.

The Happiest Days of Your Life (1950),
Dir. Frank Launder

VICTIM *(who has come to have her palm read, suddenly suspicious)*: Is there someone else here?
SHEILA KEITH *(clearly mad)*: Sometimes the little woodland animals come to visit me. There's one peeping at you now.
(Victim reacts in shock.)
SHEILA KEITH *(laughing coquettishly)*: Not really.
(Keith kills girl with flaming poker.)

Frightmare (1974),
Dir. Peter Walker

Foreword

With the arrival of digital cinema, the first age of film came to an end. The projection of fierce light through speeding triacetate stock by a chain-smoking technician, who was keeping one eye on his audience and the other on the two projectors he was required to shuttle between every twenty minutes, is over; now there's just you and the computer.

And the days when a writer could hawk a dog-eared filmscript along London's Wardour Street and get it made a few weeks later have also gone. The drive to produce purely domestic fare is as strong as ever, but the system for making it has vanished, along with the likelihood of getting it shown on screens. The majority of popular UK films were shot on shoestring budgets for big working-class audiences, and this market is now catered for by television. 'English' films are now largely made by and for the middle classes, and have become multinational productions: talent is lured away by Hollywood and routinely destroyed.* The remainder offer nostalgic views of our heritage or provide

---

*I always felt that Dudley Moore's talents were frittered away by Hollywood. Thirty years later Russell Brand followed in his footsteps with the appalling remake of *Arthur*.

arthouse glumfests for international film showcases. Popular film is no longer a provincial medium. The time is fast approaching when films could be simultaneously released in all formats on the same day, all around the globe.

What constitutes a British film now? It's a complex equation of finance deals and creative talent. Once, it meant anything with Sid James in. I turned up just at the beginning of the end for popular English cinema. What I got was a glimpse of a world that has now completely vanished.*

While this book is horribly true, a couple of names have been changed so that I don't get beaten up, some events are not in chronological sequence (simply because I can't date them exactly) and an awful lot has been left out. Rather, it's an accurate but selective memory, and I subscribe to Katherine Whitehorn's belief that you can remember things that didn't happen to you without lying. Time is a great confuser, and an anecdotal memoir does not have a logical plot.

I've consciously attempted to avoid name-dropping, because when you've worked in film for a long time you become allergic to people who bounce the names of the famous about like tennis balls. I could tell you some stories about celebrities that would make your hair fall out, but that would be another book, and bad behaviour is fundamentally predictable. For anyone who is even tangentially connected with the film industry, information is currency and not easily surrendered. Besides, most stars are as interesting as wool.

*Having said that, there's not a huge difference between *Lesbian Vampire Killers* (2010) and *Oooh . . . You Are Awful!* (1972), in which Dick Emery chases after a bank account number tattooed across four sets of buttocks. They both bombed, funnily enough.

Throughout the text I've mostly used the term 'English film', because that's what it was. With the exception of the Mancunean Film Company, nearly every studio – Amalgamated, Bray, Denham, Ealing, Elstree, Gainsborough, Goldhawk, Pinewood, Spitfire, Camberwell, Twickenham, Shepperton, Boreham Wood – was based in London or its environs.*

The footage that didn't make the final cut in these pages also included lots of scandalous, appalling and hilarious stuff about my fellow workers, which would have been too much information – but the personal side of the journey isn't complete without them. Mike Devery, Sarah Fforde, Martin Butterworth, Mia Matson, David Coultas, Graham Humphries and Jim Sturgeon lived it. And they watched all the movies, too. As for the rest of you, you know who you are. And what you did.

Finally, a word of warning. This is not a nostalgic memoir. It's about films and friends, the seventies and cinema, and is a mirror-maze of mercifully forgotten entertainments.

*Many have now gone. Twickenham was the largest studio in the UK. It produced now-forgotten films like *Sherlock Holmes and the Missing Rembrandt* (1932). The 1960s saw it involved in many of the world's most popular English movies. Titles such as *Alfie*, *The Italian Job* and Roman Polanski's *Repulsion* went there as well as *Help!* and *A Hard Day's Night*.

1

Obsessive

Setting the scene, Victorian values, early entertainments, lists, books and talking rabbits

I'm sitting in a run-down, soon-to-be-demolished cinema in London's Wardour Street with a tiny group of paying customers, some of whom don't look very savoury. The walls are covered in peeling crimson paint with filigreed gilt mouldings. There's a nostril-stinging smell of mildew. The screen is stained and has a rip in it. The ceiling leaks. If there is a quiet bit in the film, you can sometimes hear the toilet being flushed in the Gents.

I am desperately trying to follow the on-screen action, but I'm so upset that I start crying. In fact I become so noisy the handful of punters in the cinema are turning round to stare, but it makes no difference. I try to concentrate on the screen, but the figures shake and dissolve in front of me.

It seems as if I have been coming to this place for ever, but I know this will be the last time. The world moves fast, but its changes are incremental. Film records those changes, locking them into a specific timeframe. Somehow it makes even recent movies look as dated as your nan's old photo albums.

The film unspooling in front of me has already become a piece of history, and will soon be forgotten. Outside, the old Wardour Street – the centre of the British film industry for decades, London's own Hollywood – has gone for good.

Nothing shows the passing of the years quite like a favourite film. If I could send the projector into reverse, rushing back through time, I would arrive at the terraced red-brick house in Greenwich, south London, where I grew up, and where my fate was sealed . . .

When my father decided to cut the canary's toenails, he pretty much signed its death warrant. Canaries have veins running down into the claws, and he cut them too close. After a few minutes of wavering about on its perch it fell off and bled to death in its cage, and we guiltily flushed it down the toilet.

Most people bought pets before they had televisions because they were something to watch, but we were never very good with them. Tropical fish boiled because the thermostat was set too high, and tortoises failed to wake from hibernation, or were lost somewhere in the garden. A ginger tom died in the kitchen and my father forced me, at the tender age of seven, to carry out the stiffened corpse and bury it in the garden in order to 'toughen me up'.

One spring I found a tortoise we had completely forgotten about, and realized it had been in the back of the shed for a long time because when I looked into its shell I could see out through its leg-holes. Cats choked to death on chicken bones, gerbils dehydrated because we forgot to put water out for them (why did we ever keep them in the greenhouse that hot summer?), budgies got stepped on* and dogs were

*My father had an apocryphal story about a local carpet fitter who discovered a lump under the Axminster he'd just laid. After finding his cigarettes missing, he hastily hammered the lump flat with a mallet. He was confronted by the lady of the house looking for her budgie.

returned for being faulty, like toasters. Nothing was ever thrown away, but was instead half-heartedly repaired. One Alsatian was sent to police training school and came back with permanently bared teeth.

Unfortunately, this satisfaction-guaranteed-or-your-money-back deal didn't cover members of the family. My father couldn't return his wife for belatedly realizing that she was unhappily married to the wrong man. The warranty had expired, so now they were forced to stay together for the sake of the children and communicate via a complex series of misunderstandings. It was like sharing the house with The Two Ronnies. This was what lower-middle-class families did in the sixties, respectability being more highly prized than airy notions of passion or free will. It was very important to present the neighbours with a portrait of familial bliss in the front room, even though you were throwing dishes at each other in the back.

Perhaps because he descended from a family of Victorian Londoners, my father had a distinctly Steptoe-ish attitude to life. Despite being a white-collar professional, Bill insisted on doing everything in the most awkward and working-class way possible, in some kind of misplaced homage to his roots. At Christmas we would never shop in department stores to buy gifts for each other – that would have been too easy. Instead, we had to trot off up freezing, run-down East Lane, behind the Elephant & Castle, to buy suspect tat from market stalls.

My brother Steven and I were made to drink a glass of scalding sarsaparilla* to keep out the cold. After this we were taken to watch a man stacking dinner plates and cups in great fans, elaborately tucking them into each other before throwing the whole lot into the air and catching it.

*A biting sweet drink that had ceased to be popular around the time *Oliver Twist* was first hitting the shelves.

While he did this, he would keep up an interminable flow of patter along the lines of: 'You'd think this lot would set you back at least a carpet* but I'm not asking that, I'm not even asking for fifteen nicker, not fourteen, not thirteen, not twelve, not eleven but ten sheets, that's right missus, which is less than you're getting from your old man these days, ain't it? I'm talking about housekeeping, love, you want to watch her, sir, she's got a dirty mind.'

At the weekends I was forced to wear scratchy woollen short trousers and a school cap, or, if it was raining, a gabardine mackintosh. I looked like a street urchin from a 1920s novel until I was eleven years old, and this was in the sixties; everyone else was in dayglo orange nylon with Velcro fastenings. I had to endure a short-back-and-sides while they looked like backcombed mops in turtlenecks. Seven years before I was born, bankers could still be seen wearing top hats in Threadneedle Street. Seven years after, hipsters were wearing cowboy hats in Portobello Road. What had happened in that schismatic interim? The wartime baby-boomers had come of age.

Sundays with my father were like being on the set of *Bedknobs and Broomsticks*, all rumpty-tum fake cockney bravado as Bill got down with the lads from the 'hood, ignoring the fact that he'd not been born within the sound of Bow bells. Also, because the markets were like open-air auctions, you might scratch your ear and, before you knew it, become the proud owner of a 'Balmoral' fluted floral dinner service that looked as if it belonged on a funfair bingo display in Cardiff.

My father had two modes of speech: Mock Posh, a clipped, stilted, vaguely army-officer accent he'd adopt

---

*£30, as opposed to a monkey, which was £25, supposedly because soldiers returned from India with 500-rupee notes, which featured monkeys.

when confronted by anyone he considered to be from the Lower Orders, and Mock Common, an uneasy mateyness he used to prove that he knew what garage mechanics were talking about. Class is a serious and complicated issue in England, and the middle classes traditionally do most of the soul searching. Alan Clark famously defined the bourgeoisie as people who bought their own furniture, but it was more than that: it was a schizophrenic status, simultaneously aspired to and frowned upon.

It wasn't Bill's fault; his generation had been hurled through a period of change that went from Edwardian prudery to post-Wilson swingers' parties without an instruction manual on correct behaviour. Like many of his contemporaries, he felt confused and short-changed by a post-war evolutionary system that had switched from advertising 'Rooms To Let – No Blacks' to renaming streets in Urdu.

He valiantly tried to adapt to changing styles and eventually did so, although his experiments with hair gel met with limited success. He was a man who used a razor strop and got through a jar of Brylcreem every two months, so working out what to do with 'Intense Fibre Matt Hair Product' was the most minor of his adjustment problems. And because he was a scientist he broke down the component parts of household products to make them at home more cheaply, more out of curiosity than meanness. He would only belatedly realize that his version of Fairy Liquid took the skin off your hands because he had combined lethal industrial strengths.

But at least we went and *did* things as a family, even though my father chose our activities from an incredibly limited menu. I hated having to take the obligatory Sunday trip to the coast armed with windbreak, mallet, Primus stove, sliced Sunblest loaf, hard-boiled eggs, pickled onions, gherkins and beetroot (jars), trips which involved endless consultation of the weather forecast via a faulty barometer and radio reports of 'South Cones Being Hoisted', whatever that meant.

Staying in meant reading books or listening to *Two Way Family Favourites*. We went out because our TV never worked properly, and even if it had, there was nothing on that I wanted to watch apart from *A for Andromeda* and *Doctor Who*. My maternal grandmother had refused to have a television in the house, fearing it would ruin the art of conversation, and when she finally succumbed she hung a green baize tasselled vase-cloth over it whenever there were visitors so that they would be tricked into thinking it was some kind of giant ornament.

My mother wasn't actually ashamed of owning a television, she just thought it was common, but she had an exaggerated idea of what was common anyway, and said she could judge the class of a woman by how she sliced her toast: corner to corner was correct, across the middle was working class. She wouldn't watch *Coronation Street* because it revelled in commonness, and featured women who wore curlers in public and men in string vests who didn't own their own homes. Like all soap operas, *Corrie* remained stuck in a time-warped alternative universe where the English resolved their problems by thrashing them out, as opposed to hiding them behind net curtains, fences and false cheerfulness. English television, like English theatre, is an entertainment that still resists evolution. Almost everything on it is at least fifty years old, and is part of a government plan to get us to go out more.

What Old Shows Turned Into
Opportunity Knocks – The X Factor
Come Dancing – Strictly Come Dancing
The Brains Trust – Newsnight

Watch With Mother – CBeebies
Sunday Night at the London Palladium
   – *Britain's Got Talent*
No Hiding Place – *Morse*
Simon Dee – Jonathan Ross
Fanny Cradock – Nigella Lawson
Dixon of Dock Green – *The Bill*
Larry Grayson – Graham Norton
Emergency Ward Ten – *Casualty*
The Archaeology Show – *Timewatch*
Upstairs, Downstairs – *Downton Abbey*

The television wasn't on very often. It took ages to warm up and we always turned it off before the *Epilogue*.* Our world was settled, and had space and silence around it. People spent a lot of time just thinking. The sound of a car horn was enough to bring them out into the street.†
Even so, the orderly calm of a sixties suburban childhood that allowed a child room to flourish and ruminate was counterbalanced by an equal number of negatives.

Childhood Things I Was Happy to Leave Behind
Having to stand up in a cinema while they played the
   National Anthem
Crockery in the shape of thatched-roof cottages
Briar pipes, and all council officials who smoked
   them looking like Arthur Lowe

---

*A nightly charade nobody watched in which a weak-minded man of the cloth trotted out vague, indecisive tosh about being nice to your fellow man.
†Cars backfired too. They sounded like gunshots. Now, most kids know what a gunshot sounds like, but not a car backfiring.

Vaccinations that left marks on your arm like radiation burns

The idea that every man should know what to do with a carburettor cap

Dr Finlay's Casebook

Simon Dee: foppish, unfunny, self-absorbed TV presenter who set the pattern for all chat-show presenters to come

The fete being opened at short notice by the Deputy Lady Mayoress because Dickie Henderson pulled out

Braces under a decent winter overcoat

Amber ceramic storage jars

Wicker

Pink medicine that smelled like sick and came in a peculiar 1940s bottle, and was called something like 'Dr Parsnip's Miracle Dropsy Curative for the Elimination of Watery Bowels'

Fuses you had to fix by threading a copper wire through a ceramic block

Britain closing down at 10.30 p.m. every night

Thinking that G-Plan chairs and wire fruit baskets were the shape of the future

'Short-back-and-sides'

Not being allowed to get your ears pinned back, like the boy down the road who looked like a taxi with its doors open

Cilla Black's high notes

Getting Green Shield Stamp Tongue

Waiting for photos to come back from the chemist

Tomato juice or half a grapefruit as a starter in a restaurant

Classmates who mysteriously vanished halfway
   through term due to whooping cough or polio
*Emergency Ward Ten**
The chorus of coughing and expectoration that
   greeted dawn in our street because everyone
   smoked. A lot

Childhood Things I Sensed I Would Miss
Radio Caroline
Getting cocaine and a boiled sweet at the dentist
Being allowed to carry a knife, glue and matches
   because it showed you were practical
Site-specific smells: railway compartments,
   tobacconists, hardware stores, sweet shops and
   cinemas
Free Jet Screamer Inside This Week's Issue of *Buster*!
Letters arriving in time to be read over breakfast
Being able to walk down the middle of a street
   knowing you couldn't get run over because no one
   in the neighbourhood could afford a car
Robot bartender ('He mixes martinis!') sold by local
   toy store, on display next to the sweet cigarettes
   and rifles
Unironic hats (i.e. worn to instil dignity and respect)
Model boats! Model planes! 'Comes With Free Razor
   Blade'

---

*While the BBC thought of itself as brain tonic – foul-tasting but
good for you – ATV dumped any pretence of worthiness and targeted
bored housewives with Britain's first hospital soap, in which nurses in
black stockings, funny hats and with cut-glass accents fell in love with
doctors who disappeared behind pipe-smoke.

A for Andromeda*

'Ten Senior Service, please.' 'Certainly, young sir.'

Cinema double bills you could sit through as many times as you liked

Heinz Kidney Soup

Pubs with smoky children's rooms

Tubes and post offices without tannoy systems

Dangerous funfairs that always played the Everly Brothers on the Waltzer

Singing bus conductors. 'Hold very tight, please! And everybody join in the chorus this time!'

A deckchair on a silent sunny pavement

Finally, like the disappointing weather, the ravens at the Tower and cheaply priced ginger nuts, part of our shared national past managed to survive the decades, and there were living treasures who continued from my childhood, including Tony Benn, Stirling Moss, Bobby Charlton, Sir Cliff Richard, Michael Caine,† Bruce Forsyth, Vera Lynn, Rolf Harris, David Attenborough, Lulu and Alan Bennett.

The innocent pleasures of rolling Plasticine and building model planes slipped quietly away to be replaced by

---

*Brilliant 1961 adult SF TV drama in which aliens instructed us how to build a super-computer, which in turn created the stunning Julie Christie, causing my flustered father to head for the shed and hammer things for a while. Typically, the BBC only has eleven minutes of it left in the archives.

†When Sidney Furie made *The Ipcress File*, deliberately distancing Harry Palmer from James Bond, a movie executive told him to dump Caine's spectacles and make his girlfriend do the cooking because Caine 'looked like a faggot'. They didn't care for Caine's culinary skill of breaking two eggs with one hand, either, which gives you a good clue as to why Hollywood gets so much so wrong.

more sophisticated obsessions. Everyone will tell you that they're unhealthy and irrational* but they can also do you good. My mother had warned me that 'nobody loves a good all-rounder'. She felt it was better to have one intense passion than to chase a dozen half-heartedly until they fizzled out like cheap fireworks on a wet night. Her advice was sound; I eventually parlayed mine into a career.

My passion had always been stories. I didn't care what form they came in, they just had to be good ones, with characters you cared about and surprises and twists and terrific endings that made some kind of organic, truthful sense, and some kind of a point. When you start work, you often have to abandon your passion and concentrate on bringing home the coal. I didn't dare allow myself the dream of becoming a writer, so I decided to get into film, however obliquely. Unfortunately I should have been in Hollywood instead of London, where I emerged at a time when the only English film in cinemas was *Mutiny on the Buses*.† This, then, is about my journey through the arse-end of the English film industry, of what I found there and the peculiar, life-changing friendship I made.

Sickly children often fall in love with words. I suffered regular bouts of pneumonia through my childhood, and as a consequence read far more than the average kid. If you want to change a young boy's life, give him Ray Bradbury when he's not feeling well. If he doesn't fall in love with the words, you can safely assume he won't

---

*My pal Martin became obsessed with *The Poseidon Adventure* and repeatedly visited the Leytonstone Odeon with a reel-to-reel tape recorder up his jumper to record the soundtrack. The usherettes knew what he was doing and indulged him. Now they have night goggles.
†Sample review: 'Will fail to provoke a smile even with fans, if there are such people.'

ever be much of a reader. Stephen King once admitted that he would try to read even when he was peeing; I still read when I walk to the shops. This is tricky, as it involves cutting through London's busiest station, so you develop a sixth sense about hurtling objects, particularly if they're on fire.

Above all other obsessions were the words, most in English, some in French, a few in Latin,* but right at the top beside words cunningly arranged into books were films, the double bills, triple bills and all-nighters, many appalling, many enthralling. It's no fun going to the cinema by yourself (I'd had enough of that in my childhood), but when I left home and started work I made a friend who shared my fanaticism, someone who eventually passed through the screen with me, to emerge shocked and delighted in a world far, far removed from the placid English suburbia of our childhoods. He became my best pal, the other half of my head, and from the day we met it was obvious I would lose him.

In the sixties everybody seemed to be reading, partly because the end of the war meant the return of cheap paper. It was the golden heyday of the Pan paperback, of Puffin and Penguin and Picador and Panther, and besides, there was nothing on TV before seven o'clock except talking rabbits† and elderly gentlemen in armchairs discussing

---

*To this day I struggle to use the phrase *ad hominem* in a sentence, although a theatre critic friend of mine casually used it the other evening without batting an eyelash. Ponce.
†What was the sixties obsession with puppetry? You couldn't turn on the TV without stumbling across Muffin the Mule, Rag, Tag and Bobtail or the Flowerpot Men. Worse still was *Tales of the Riverbank*, in which Hammy the Hamster – a real live one – drove a motorboat. Presumably the wranglers glued his little paws to the wheel.

nuclear disarmament.* I was able to find cheap editions of Anthony Burgess, Joseph Heller, Doris Lessing, J. G. Ballard, B. S. Johnson and John Fowles.† The 1960s was a time of innovative, bravura experimental literature.

Unfortunately I didn't leave school until the 1970s.

*Now daytime TV is entirely given over to people having vases valued and bedrooms badly renovated with chipboard.
†Oddly, all unfilmable authors (although *Catch 22* is underrated).

2

Dead Novelist

Conformity, being raised conservative, careers advice, advertising and being careful not to mention S-E-X

You know me. I'm the boy who carried a briefcase to school every day of his academic life. The early riser, the fretter in the sweater, the one who always turned in his homework slightly ahead of time, who had his hair cut in the same style every three weeks for ten years, who worried what the teachers thought and never gave them any trouble.

The one who got beaten up a lot.

Those ingrained habits never died. Even now, I'm unable to miss a meeting and always arrive at airports too early. In a child, such traits are attractive. As an adult they're vaguely pathetic, and invoke the same feeling I get when I see a grown man struggling to decide which sandwich to buy in Pret-A-Manger.

We are who we were at seven. On holiday recently, I put a towel on a vacant beach seat and a sclerotic fifty-year-old Englishman came storming up to me. 'Look here, you,' he shouted in my face, 'I just bagsied that chair for my lady wife!' Childhood leaves marks on us all.

It seemed that every child raised in the southern half of England in the 1960s was a small 'c' conservative, and that Labour supporters were all from up north. We were Janets and Johns, they were Stans and Enas. We were private and self-effacing, they were public and abrasive. My father read the *Daily Express* until I went to the newsagent and stopped it from being delivered. Being a good liberal, I was very keen to halt everything I didn't agree with.

Even though they were transparently free thinkers, my parents insisted that they were conservative, but then nothing our family did made any sense. We had inherited so many mistaken beliefs that hardly anything my parents said ever proved to be correct. Our conversations were peppered with catchphrases that were patent gibberish. To this day, if I lose something and it turns out to be right in front of me, my mother says: 'What's that, Scotch mist or a packet of Woodbines?' Other phrases would only have worked in a wartime context. She'd say, 'He's as dim as a Toc-H lamp', because wartime Nissen hut lamps were indeed dim.*

We good grammar-school boys grew up shuttling between two institutions: the municipal public library and the ABC cinema. The former gave us literacy and the latter gave us lurid dreams. The posher West End cinemas had liveried staff and sold big glossy programmes for their films, aligning the experience with theatre-going; they were heading for a rude awakening.

When I was twelve I earnestly believed I was destined to write fiction and everyone told me, in the nicest possible way, to stop being stupid. At sixteen, my hopeless

---

*Toc-H was short for Talbot House, headquarters of the International Christian Movement. 'Toc' signified the letter T in the signals spelling alphabet used by the British army in the First World War.

enthusiasm undimmed, I explained this to my careers advisor and he looked at me as if I'd announced that I was planning to become a shepherd.

By the time the 1970s arrived writing had become an unusual career choice once more, and when you make an unusual choice, people try to be kind to you by completely putting you off the idea. But to give up in London is to admit that the city has defeated you, so it was a matter of pride to keep going. It takes many years to become an ingénu. Soon after that you become a veteran, then you die, and then they republish your backlist. Writing is a way of passing on your knowledge if you're not going to have children.

As a matter of record, my careers advisor was a small, bald, rumpled, nicotine-stained man who worked in an office off Charing Cross Road without any natural light, beside a single window that overlooked a litter-filled open stairwell. I can see now that he wasn't qualified to advise me on the purchase of a sardine sandwich, but at the time I hung on his every word because I had been indoctrinated to believe that every adult's advice was right, no matter how ridiculous it seemed.

I knew my strategy was going to be risky. The plan was to train as a copywriter, write some award-winning ad campaigns, hone my literary skills and become a successful author. I haven't a clue what inspired this plan of attack. I knew that popular writing was considered to be a vaguely disreputable pastime unless you were in advertising, where it was inexplicably glamorous. I would have to learn to type and like the taste of whisky, that's all.

Advertising looked easy: all you had to do was throw away your moral compass, buy an unstructured linen jacket and set aside a few hours each day to sell cigarettes and dried milk to poor people. To give you an idea of the exaggerated esteem in which ad-folk were held in the late sixties, consider this: Michael Winner made a film about advertising called *I'll Never Forget What's 'is Name* in which no less a personage than Orson Welles* was the scheming creative director and Oliver Reed was the hot-shot account exec applauded for chopping up his desk with an axe. Advertising was sex. It was fast cars, sheath dresses, pastel cigarettes, shiny suits, jazz, cocktail bars, brittle laughter and nervous breakdowns. I was a clueless suburban nobody in a Burton's mackintosh and a Tootal shirt that came with a matching top-pocket handkerchief that had a piece of cardboard inside to keep it neat. Quite how I was going to achieve this leap of cool was not something I had considered.

The careers advisor looked blankly at me when I mentioned advertising. His mind was geared around insurance and quantity surveying.† I hit him with Step Two: Bestselling Novelist. He could see that there was some cachet in being a dead novelist, but I could hardly have put Dead Novelist on my Career Choices form. To him real writers were Robert Louis Stevenson, Charles Dickens or slightly hysterical women with too much time on their hands. They weren't Daphne du Maurier or George Orwell (both of whom I admired) and he certainly couldn't see me as the next Georgette Heyer. So he did what he'd been trained to do: he dumbly agreed with my plan and signed off my form, which he followed up with

---

*Welles ended up playing Unicron in the animated version of *Transformers*, and was commonly thought to have lived his life back to front, although artists are generally best remembered for their early work. 'You were at your peak five years ago. You were very funny in those days' – Kenneth Williams complimenting Tony Hancock.

†My best mate Simon wanted to design cars, but the careers advisor suggested he should join the army. These days he's a car designer. He built the Atom, *Top Gear*'s highest-rated English car.

an ancient mimeographed list of contacts before shooing me out of his funereal office.

Creativity is nurtured by the right time and place. I wasn't born in either. I had been raised in Greenwich, south-east London, which was the furthest our family ever managed to get from the city centre. We once had an aunt who moved to Reading and we always acted as if we were going to Sweden when we visited her. My mother: 'Have you got your scarf and gloves? Because it's going to be cold over there.' Real Londoners pack food when they go to the country, just in case there's nothing to eat. My mother could rustle up a full Sunday dinner on the beach, and we were always safely back home before nightfall. Perhaps she thought we would be attacked by wolves or sold into a gypsy slave ring if we stayed on after dark.

My family fought themselves to a standstill, but I like to think I grew up pretty well adjusted. At seventeen, during my girl-dating period, I decided I was probably gay.

ME: That's a very attractive dress.
GIRL: Really? No boy has ever said that to me before.
ME *(thinks)*: Uh-oh.

In our house sexuality wasn't really an issue because no one ever expressed much of an interest in the subject. It was unmentionable, but so was the word 'underwear' – we always said 'nether-garments'. My mother once snogged the captain of the royal yacht *Britannia* by mistake (a long and somewhat unlikely story) but all forms of intimacy were taboo and anyway, nobody had the energy to think about intimacy after they'd finished a day's work. I can hardly remember a time from my childhood when my mother didn't have two jobs, so I imagine sex appeared on her agenda somewhere below rinsing the nets* and repairing the Ascot.† We had 'bachelor' family friends, and it was always assumed that if I didn't follow in their footsteps I would at least help out when they were busy. Your body was considered such a private thing that revelations of a personal nature from homosexuality to verrucas were all regarded with equal horror, thus creating a strangely level playing field of acceptability for pretty much everything so long as you jolly well kept it to yourself. Sexuality was neither very important nor interesting, because we were English and therefore above discussions about gusset-bothering. This ability and the presence of a good navy were what made our island great.

The twin taboos of sexuality and career occupied my waking mind. I finally decided the former when I snubbed my school's rugby final to go to *Die Fledermaus*.‡ I couldn't do anything about that, but at least I could continue reading and help advance the latter.

I was a child of the sixties, a time of intensely original London writing that was closely tied to experimentation. Some authors experimented so much that they actually dropped dead, which made the career choice even sexier. Before I could experiment I wanted to understand the city of my birth, starting with the London of books, bombs and the first baby boom. The London just before me.

---

*All houses in the sixties had net curtains in case anyone looked in and caught you off-guard, enjoying a relaxed moment.
†Scary water heater whose pilot light inexplicably went out sometimes, creating panic as everyone rushed around looking for matches before it blew us all to Kingdom Come.
‡There's a litmus test for finding out if your son is gay: did he enjoy the 'Can You Read My Mind' flying sequence in Richard Donner's *Superman*?

3

Ghosts

Ghosts, London, society, a detour into vulgarity,
punks, disco and the end of innocence

I had always been drawn to ghost stories because I instinctively understood why they worked. I knew that the streets of ancient London followed the lines of hedgerows and underground rivers. The lowlands were poor areas largely because they were damp. Water and fog brought illness, and early deaths created superstitions; that's why ghost stories were more associated with, say, the poor East End than the city's prosperous raised-up north. The sooty, partly derelict London of my early childhood was a city of ghosts.

If you want to see how London looked then, don't read about it in a book, watch the title sequence of *Steptoe and Son*, the saddest and most disturbing sitcom ever written.*

---

*This beautifully scripted two-hander was never meant to be a series, but began life as a single play. The Steptoes' painful, antagonistic relationship was not mirrored off-screen, as the BBC would have you believe. Ray Galton and Alan Simpson, writers of the show, told me that its leads Harry H. Corbett and Wilfrid Brambell were professionals who generally got on very well.

Beneath the titles and behind the jaunty Ron Grainer music, the misted streets look full of ghosts. Everything was grubby. If you leaned on a fence, you usually had to have your coat dry-cleaned. It was as if the spirits of the war dead had left their residue behind as a reminder for the next generation.

Where there are ghosts there are stories, and where there are storytellers there are actors. The London theatres kept late hours and bred their own special late-night venues. Inevitably, some catered for a largely gay clientele. When I was seventeen there must have been about thirty tiny theatre bars in the West End, each with its own over-dramatic personality: the Festival, the Cabal, the Rockingham, Chaguaramas, several in every main Soho street. This would have been the clubland of John Gielgud and Kenneth Williams, and it was dying just as I arrived. I thought that if I frequented them, perhaps something dramatic would rub off on me, but the first Soho bar I dared to enter alone was the A&B club, and the only thing that rubbed off on me were the hairs from the monstrously fat cat that slept on the counter.

The A&B stood for Arts and Battledress. It was a schizophrenic place struggling to cope with the changing standards of the 1970s. On the one hand it wanted to be a gentleman's club which required jackets and ties, and it had stained-glass crests in the windows and the evening papers neatly laid out, but it was up a disreputable red-light alley off Wardour Street and the barman had a taste for Carmen Miranda headgear.

There was something reassuring about being in a club swathed in red velvet curtains, surrounded by ladies and gentlemen who had all been in the same production of *Aida*. Entire conversations still took place in Polari, the peculiar slang created by actors, gypsies and queens. You could be mentored by classically educated older men without worrying if they were paedophiles, and drugs had yet to rob night society of intelligent conversation. There was no binge culture. Everyone got quietly pissed and wobbled off home.

But there was a painful stiffness to the London of the sixties and seventies. Swinging London looked like your father trying to dance. I saw it in documentaries about Soho coffee bars, where a disapproving patrician would interview defensive floppy-haired chaps in rollneck sweaters and nervous girls in thick black mascara whose parents obviously didn't know they were out drinking strong coffee after nine o'clock. London might have had Chelsea and the West End, epitomized by grainy footage of a few neon signs shot at jaunty angles, but the rest of the city consisted of misty suburbs, empty roads, boarded-up lots and grimy alleys. I remember walking along the Regent's Canal and passing an upended Robin Reliant* sticking out of what appeared to be a rubbish-filled swamp; a far cry from the neat apartment-lined waterways that occupy the same spot today.

London existed in schizophrenic polarity. One tiny, privileged part attended parties in the Post Office Tower's revolving restaurant while the rest watched the coverage on minuscule monochrome tellies in hundred-year-old slum terraces. If you'd like to witness the nightmare of a country trapped in two distinct time zones, go back to your episode of *Steptoe and Son* and watch the rest. The series was shot in the derelict backstreets of White City. London looked wet, sooty and abandoned. The vestiges of wartime chaos lingered everywhere. The signs of the past, of war damage and waste ground and dingy Victorian

---

*An embarrassing three-wheeled car you could actually tip over if its driver cut you up in traffic.

warehouses, were not easily shaken off, and did not truly start to disappear until the early 1980s.

In the popular culture of the sixties, flower power had created a graceful marriage of Edwardian aesthetics and dazzling psychedelia,* gentle, lyrical, but defiantly experimental, revealing a variety of influences from Greek sculpture to the posters of the First World War. Theoretically, the seventies should have built upon this blend of old and new to create something even more interesting, but something went horribly wrong; the nation took a detour into vulgarity. The sleek, cleanly painted lines of the sixties were replaced with beige wallpaper, lychee-shaped lamps and brown-glass coffee tables. Victorian pubs, much prized by sixties hipsters, were inexplicably made over with plastic fascias in circus colours and Double-Diamond serif typefaces. A succession of terrible prime ministers turned the SS *Great Britain* into a clown car. The ensuing rampage of strikes and protest marchers became the trudge of a country mired in such economic doldrums that the Prime Minister actually suggested emigration might be best for everyone. As productivity levels plunged, workers and management looted what was left, and a stale-tobacco aura of dissatisfaction settled over us. Everyone acted as if they had been short-changed.

Where had the rot set in?

After its efflorescence of creative glory in the previous decade, the country had jellified under three dismal leaderships: one Conservative and two Labour. Despite the fact that his catastrophic clashes with unions led the country into a three-day working week, at least Ted Heath never spoke to Enoch Powell again after Powell made his

---

*A style that manifested itself in rotating oil discs, Zapata moustaches, split ends, collarless shirts, Velcro and an over-reliance on mauve.

infamous 'Rivers of blood' speech damning immigration. Wilson and Callaghan were the down-at-heel fag end of Old Labour, and the useless trio reversed the clock of progress, turning Britain into an embarrassment of failed industrial relations, missed opportunities, bad service and lousy culture.

Mods and rockers were replaced with skinheads, a gormless, bulldog-racist style born of inner-city poverty and disillusionment. One would like to think that punk evolved to oppose this movement, but the streets weren't filled with skinheads and punks attacking each other's ideologies. Punk was primarily a fashion fad centred around Chelsea, seized upon by a handful of nihilistic trustafarians who talked of revolution without ever fomenting it, feared by everyone except music critics who were desperate for something new to write about and art teachers who vicariously lived their rebel lives through their pupils.

Based far more on clothes and attitude than on actual music, punk was set in motion in London partly by a series of photographs taken in the King's Road outside Vivienne Westwood's streetwear shop BOY. The shop was owned by the talented fashion designer who, together with her partner Malcolm McLaren, was busy creating costumes for films like *Mahler*. McLaren often quoted his grandmother as saying: 'To be bad is good . . . to be good is simply boring.' But McLaren came from a background of resolutely middle-class factory-owners, while the former primary teacher Westwood seems perhaps a tad disingenuous when describing herself as working class.*

Like the beatniks before them, many of the early punks were middle-class dropouts seeking to annoy their parents

---

*She is now a Dame and something of a national treasure. She lives in an eighteenth-century house that belonged to the mother of Captain Cook.

and be noticed; the small movement was helped by two factors – outrage in the gutter press, and support from genuinely working-class kids who would soon charge American tourists to have their photographs taken in the King's Road. How did they come to choose mohawks as the archetypal punk fashion look?

Well, one explanation comes from 1712, when a gang of marauding posh boys caused trouble in London. It was said they were rebelling against the status quo, which was putting pressure on them to conform to a moral code. They were called the Mohocks, and had modelled themselves on the visiting Iroquois chiefs who had recently dined with royalty in London. Native Americans had yet to be romanticized as 'noble savages' and were thought to be childlike and uncivilized. The Mohocks capitalized on this fear, attacking pedestrians at night and causing panic. Although rewards were posted nobody ever claimed them, because the Mohocks were rich and well connected, and their friends didn't need the reward money.

In the middle of this uncertainty, English pop culture fell over and died. The rococo artistic renaissance of the sixties had been a largely upper-class revolution, and a fairly limited one at that, but by the time the next decade arrived everyone wanted a slice of the new modernity, and the simple truth is that democratization ruined it. The *Monty Python* cast might have been singing songs about philosophers, but Beverley was sticking Beaujolais in the fridge and playing Demis Roussos.

The sixties had bowed out on a grace note with the Beatles* performing on the roof of Apple Records, and

---

*There's a reason why artists like George Harrison and Cat Stevens went off to explore world religions: the megabuck sixties had left them spiritually bereft. They weren't simply trying to be annoying.

the ensuing silence was filled by tacky lounge acts from the end of the pier. As the icons of our youth vanished we were left sandwiched between Morecambe and Wise* and the sweetly shambolic Johnny Rotten, who looked as if he'd never drunk a glass of water in his life.

Without role models, it's no wonder we jumped at the chance of leaping about in satin shorts to Donna Summer. The youth of the seventies had been driven into a corner, and remained trapped there by disco, which was invented solely for the purpose of allowing a DJ to put on a twenty-minute track while he went out for a snout and a wee.

Disco didn't exorcize London's ghosts (the Conservative 'no such thing as society' policies did that some time later), but it made it harder to hear them. Watching colour footage of London in the 1920s and the 1950s that has recently surfaced online, one is struck not by the change in the city between the two decades, but rather by the sheer lack of it. Despite the Blitz bombsites and the blackened buildings of post-war London, it's clear that the capital's interior life had hardly altered at all. Hemlines were higher and there were a few more cars, but city chaps still wore bowlers, working-class men wore flat caps, and the social order sought to remain in place. Everyone is proper, self-conscious, thin-faced and a little awkward. 'We're going about our business and keeping to ourselves, and we're making a jolly good job of it,' the men and women in the films seem to be saying; but the sixties shook them about and changed them for ever.

Change, it seemed, was a good thing. It was portrayed on film as an effusion of youth and energy – the Beatles running towards the camera laughing, the flower-power

*Old-school comedians so innocent that they shared a bed in their sketches.

girls in daisy-coloured dresses, swinging their arms in the sunshine – but creeping cynicism and complacency undid all the good, and this delicate soap-bubble soon popped, leaving me to arrive in Wardour Street with the kind of hopeful smile that crosses someone's face just before they have their pocket picked for the first time.

4

Past and Present

Living on your nerves, clubs, hedonism, talking to
people, nostalgia and coming down to earth

'Margaret lives on her nerves, poor soul,' my mother told
me in confidence. Margaret was our thin, whey-faced
neighbour, a woman palely glimpsed behind net curtains.
She had her shopping delivered and only opened the door
a crack to callers.

'What does that actually mean?' I asked. I was in the
final days of living at home, the brief confused period in
which all fathers call their sons layabouts.

'Well, she lived through the bombs and after that she
could never have intimacy again without crying for a day.
Her husband left her, her son died of polio and she stopped
going out.'

'Has she been to the doctor?'

'He says she's just over-sensitive. He told her to pull herself together.'

For my generation, childhood was much as it had
always been. There was little sympathy for weakness.
Psychological problems were always seen as symptoms
of poor breeding. This had reached a level of horror in

1917, when a Canadian neurologist, the Frankenstein-like Dr Lewis Yealland, tortured shell-shocked English war veterans by stubbing cigarettes out on their tongues and frying their throats with electric shocks to make them behave like real men again.

At school I'd been considered 'sensitive', but in a different way. I spent too much time reading, writing and painting, and defied all manner of peculiar attempts on my father's part to toughen me up. Teachers had a battery of expressions with which to describe their charges. The terminology has become less euphemistic, but the conditions are still there.

Psychological Terms Now	Psychological Terms Then
ADD	Fidget
OCD	Little Miss Neat
Autistic	In a world of his own
Hyperactive	Class clown
Learning Disability	Slow on the uptake
Anger Management Issues	Stroppy
Eating Disorder	Likes his food
Tourette's Syndrome	Potty Mouth
Sex Addict	Popular
Clinically Obese	Big-boned
Lesbian	Tomboy
Hypertense	Chatterbox
Oppositionally Defiant	Bloody-minded
Gender Identity Dysfunction	Loves the dressing-up box
Dyslexic	Outdoorsy

Manic Depressive	Sulks if he doesn't get his own way
Bipolar	Moody
Conduct Disorder	Keen on sport
Anxiety Disorder	Lives on her nerves
Dissociative Disorder	Easily led
Processing Disorder	Chooses what he wants to hear
Social Anxiety	A bit shy
Separation Disorder	Mummy's boy
Borderline Psychotic	Natural leader
Panic Disorder	Excitable
Dissociative Fugue State	Keeps to himself
Anorexic	Fussy eater
Rumination Disorder	Needs to pay more attention
Narcissistic Personality Disorder	Well turned out
False-Belief Deficit	Always looks on the bright side

One of my teachers wrote in my report that I was 'a joy to have in class', which is probably diagnosed as a severe mental illness now, and remedied with Ritalin.*

The BBC has seemingly adopted the premise that you can summon up the past by sticking everyone in bonnets and top hats – I heard one of their designers naively promise that if you got the shoes right you could get the rest of

---

*People of my age have no time for faddishness, having been raised in an atmosphere of common sense. I have a tendency to think that people who say they are gluten-intolerant are just attention-seekers.

the period – but the past and the present are separated by much more than shoe fashions.* The informing mindsets are so radically different that if you could step into a time machine and go back fifty years, you'd probably be threatened with a punch in the face within fifteen minutes of arrival. There's a good chance that the most strait-laced twenty-first-century person would have been seen as a dangerous radical.

In the UK, the civil right to vote was changed in 1970, and voting age was reduced from twenty-one (when you got 'the key of the door') to eighteen.† If you're attuned to such things it generally represents your passage into the horrors of adulthood. Certainly, it was the first time I felt alone. With parents who were too busy considering divorce to remember birthdays, and school friends dissipating to the corners of the world, I had grown into the kind of gawky semi-adult who was suddenly about to get a building society account and two weeks' holiday a year.

To celebrate my coming of age, I hit town with the rest of the suburban kids and was photographed in Mayfair's Blitz Club simply because I had ill-advisedly dyed my hair prostitute yellow and was wearing roller skates. I had suddenly started dressing like a clown. Years of attending school in black regulation trousers with turn-ups that were measured by teachers for their correct height from the ground will do this to a boy.

---

*If there's one gruesome fashion symbol of the seventies that stands above all others (literally) it's the stacked boot. Suddenly you no longer had to go to Chamonix to break your ankles. You just had to slip off the kerb outside the Dog & Duck.
†During the two years before you reach eighteen you can freely choose to marry and bring children into the world, but you're not allowed to decide which council should dig up your road.

When the picture appeared, I found that make-up and eyeshadow had been added by the newspaper's retouchers in an attempt to suffuse me with an aura of unbridled London hedonism. It made me look like the love-child of Gary Glitter and Barbara Cartland. The picture is supremely awkward. I'm spinning a girl in a silver leotard, and it doesn't look like we're having fun, it looks like I've broken her back.

The pupils of Colfe's, my alma mater, found their way to London's West End like baby turtles rushing for the shoreline, and we were just as easily picked off by predators.

London's creeping air of desperate seventies sexuality was summed up by the arrival of a gay nightspot called Adams, which hosted London's first back-room and was next door to the Odeon Leicester Square. This in itself was shocking because the Queen attended Royal Film Performances in the cinema with which it shared an adjoining wall, and her proximity to men having sex must have unwittingly duplicated life at the palace. Adams appeared at the height of the moustache-and-parachute-trousers period in male fashion history.* Everyone had to act as if they were in the infantry. To prove the point, the club had a camouflaged army jeep sticking out of the wall in its lobby and phallic rockets poking up from the floor. If Donna Summer had ever appeared in an army recruitment video, she would have shot it here.

Soon the superclubs arrived in their first incarnation and threw endless fancy-dress parties, as if they couldn't believe their luck at being allowed to open without police invasions; it was still a novelty to be stuck on Tottenham Court Road at 2.00 a.m. in thick snow dressed only in

---

*I want to think that men were keen to prove a level of masculinity, but suspect they liked the fabrics.

Speedos, body glitter and workboots. Wild times were nothing new in London, though. I have this on reliable authority from my mother, who says that if you wanted to get high in 1959, you drank three Babychams* and sat through *Fantasia*.

Not long after, I found myself writing for an advertising agency, but also running a company, trying to write my first novel, working as a freelance cartoonist for a lifestyle magazine and opening a catastrophic Soho nightclub. In the evenings we argued over the meanings of books, films, plays and art exhibitions. At weekends we went to protest marches and discos. Our lives were a mix of darkness and light, in the way that Linda Blair could star in both *The Exorcist* and *Roller Boogie*.

This leap from buttoned-down conservatism into lunatic intemperance was a rite of passage I barely noticed. Being invisible suited me because I lacked confidence, despite the Speedos and body glitter. I was fascinated by London, its underground rivers and lost theatres, its mob politics, its secret societies and newly forming tribes. A little digging produced massive results – everyone wanted to talk about their particular kingdoms. I found I'd stumbled on a goldmine for my budding fiction.

In the years to come I met some astonishing people, simply because I had got up the courage to go and talk to them. There was an ancient archivist from the Palace Theatre who had lost the key to a room full of props used by the Marx Brothers and Fred Astaire when they'd

---

*The story goes that after the war a Devon farmer came up to London with a strong sparkling cider that he wished to market. The adman he visited realized that females had not been in pubs during wartime and no longer knew what to order, so he removed most of the alcohol, put the drink in tiny bottles labelled 'Champagne Perry', made women memorize the slogan 'I'd love a Babycham' and insisted on serving it in gold-rimmed champagne glasses. He made a fortune.

performed there. The guardian of Goldsmiths Hall showed me the throne of a Roman goddess and expressed surprise that anyone should be interested. A security guard guided me across the rooftops of Soho, revealing how cat-burglars came in from above instead of street level. I met a WPC whose north London beat took her through the site of a lost pagan temple. Londoners possess a fantastic amount of strange information about their home city, but you always have to ask them; they never simply volunteer their knowledge.* Eventually, the city's peculiarities were sprinkled through my books as seasoning.

In the years that followed I became another of the city's resident biographers in hiding – hiding behind zeitgeist novels, thrillers, mysteries, anything so long as it told you nothing about me. I wrote a Faustian novel called *Spanky* with a cover that looked like porn and nobody batted an eyelid, because I remained concealed – as I still rather think authors should – and let the writing speak by itself.

Having started out with a plan to become a Dead Novelist, I finally ended up becoming a novelist of the dead – or at least, a chronicler of that part of the country which was disappearing fast. It became very important to write down people's thoughts about their identity and use it in some imaginative way.

When I considered London's murky mazelike history and overlaid it on my own, the soot-stained buildings and afternoons spent diving into theatre stage doors, the fights about politics in smoky West End pubs, the London of mass rallies, flying pickets, barricades, student riots, IRA bombings, and more-or-less peaceful continuity, I was

---

*Shop assistants are good because they know the habits of the public and are often too smart to be on tills, so they're happy to chat. People smoking outside offices are more wary, and if you approach them with a question they assume you're about to ask them for money.

not nostalgic so much as anxious to keep a time-line that might explain who we once were and who we became. It's a resolution brought about by the quiet revolution of passing time. That time began when my childhood ended, in the seventies.

The previous decade had promised much that it could not deliver. As a result, we hoped the seventies would become like those science fiction illustrations from the 1950s of how the future should look, with flying cars and anti-gravity walkways and air-tubes. We had been offered a grand vision of society where young liberals would rout the old guard. There would be equality, creativity and sexual freedom, or at the very least, flat TVs you could hang on the wall. Instead, the country bumped down to earth in a reality that was unimaginably horrible. And for anyone seeking a creative career, it was not even a question of compromise: the opportunities had entirely evaporated.

5

Goodbye-ee

Leaving home, being creative, Tony Hancock, saying goodbye, going out and sailing into a storm

I was wearing a grey suit, a white shirt and a grey tie. I looked like a less wrinkled version of my father. He was managing a gas showroom in the Elephant & Castle shopping centre, an embarrassing descent for a former experimental scientist, and was giving me a lift to work on my first day.

'I'll go almost as far as London Bridge but no further,' he announced, rather like those carriage drivers who refuse to take foolhardy travellers up to Castle Dracula. He dropped me off on a street corner at the end of the Old Kent Road. I turned back to wave but he'd already driven off.

Greenwich was technically part of London, historically vital because of its naval connections, but separated from the city centre by a long, broad road that had been used by the Canterbury pilgrims, the only way out of the city to south-east England. If you were searching for a street that embodied everything that was wrong with seventies Britain, the Old Kent Road would have fit the bill nicely.

Bombed and battered, chopped about by traffic planners and built upon by social reformers intent on battery-caging the low-waged, showered with soot from passing lorries, its run-down shops were let and sublet, its pavements littered and unsafe at night. You couldn't hail from south London and not be deeply ashamed of it. The road passed through the most deprived areas of the city, which allowed property developers to treat it in a way that would have outraged the residents of any wealthier neighbourhood. Carpet-bombed with discount barns and giant American junk food outlets, it is now being rehabilitated with regiments of 'luxury loft-style apartments', or 'future slums'.

I didn't fancy seeing its spray-painted façades every working day, so I decided I'd move out as soon as I had accumulated a few pay cheques. I still had no clue how to go about being a writer, but with the arrogance of that period's ignorant young I assumed that the career would somehow find me. Meanwhile, I was ready to join the workforce in Prime Minister Edward Heath's disastrously grounded Britain. I wanted to be creative. I didn't want to wear a suit and work in the kind of office where everyone kept one eye on the creeping clock hands through the day.

Unfortunately, there weren't too many role models to be found in the shabby gentility of south London's suburbs. It seemed there was no one who could advise me on my choice without revealing the bitterness of their own failed aspirations. Everyone was too busy hiding, like schoolchildren pressed close to their desks with their arms thrown around their heads to prevent others from copying. Disappointment in life is something you don't want to share; the British have an unsettling habit of always putting on a brave face.

I assumed that London's creative heart, then centred around Soho, would yield expansive teachers who would airily provide encouragement and support to a gormless teen without wanting anything in return. It goes without saying that this was the kind of hilariously naive world-view sported by young models who discovered that men who they hoped would advance their careers merely wanted to do weird sex stuff to them.

A few weeks later, with my first wages banked, I left my parents' house with a holdall of clothes, dragging a vast box of books to the open front door. My mother was in the kitchen listening to Joan Turner* on the radio. My father was burning a large chest of drawers in the garden. Turner was hitting high Cs and telling corny jokes. The air was acrid with scorched varnish. It seemed important for everyone to act as normal as possible. Kath concentrated hard on the radio. Bill shoved another stick in the flames. As a consequence, the scene was as bizarre and forced as everything else that happened at home.

My parents left the radio permanently on so that they didn't have to talk to each other. For years I had been aurally drenched in radio entertainment, my favourite being the doomed Birmingham comic whose scripts explained so much about life's potential disappointments. I came to believe that the Hancock radio shows could teach you everything you needed to know about people. They captured the full horror of post-war Britain, a country that was always shut or just about to close.

Those who bemoan the ubiquity of tourism might have enjoyed the strange becalmed privacy of Sundays, but for us the Sabbath dragged by on feet of lead, enlivened

---

*Joan Turner, brilliant four-and-a-half-octave soprano who mixed knockabout comedy into her act. I once heard her break off a Puccini aria to tell the audience about going to the seaside. 'The beach was so crowded that if the woman in front hadn't had her ears pierced we'd never have seen the sea.' She then finished the aria with a flourish.

only by Sunday lunchtimes with Hancock. 'Do you want to take the clock to bits?' Hancock asks Bill Kerr in one particularly depressing episode, when they've completely run out of things to do. Bill admits that he's suicidally depressed and would drown himself if he lived near the river, to which Hancock drily replies, 'I've got a car.'

Like all great comic writers, Galton and Simpson were masters of darkness – or rather, masters of dampness, for they captured the penny-pinching, clock-watching, barrel-scraping state of the nation more perfectly than any monochrome documentary.

Hancock played a failed comic who lived on borrowed time and self-delusion. Thinking about his own un-desirability in one episode, he complained, 'When the petals begin to fall from the rose, the bees don't come round so often – strike while you've still got some hair.' But it was already too late for him. 'People respect you when you don't get laughs,' muttered the fictional failed Hancock, possibly forced by the writers to comment on his own state of mind. Like all of Galton and Simpson's great creations, Hancock was locked in a spiral of self-loathing and delusion that paradoxically kept him alive.

Typically, Hancock's finest moment never actually materialized. Galton and Simpson had written him a second film after *The Rebel* called *The Day Off*, which he turned down for being too parochial. The comic headed for Hollywood, where he was fired from Disney's *The Adventures of Bullwhip Griffin* for drinking, and by the time he returned his writers had moved on to *Steptoe and Son*. *The Day Off* has Hancock playing a bus driver, arguing with his landlady and various people around Hammersmith, meeting a girl in a dance hall, messing up the date and going home.

The filmscript is virtually plotless, sad and very funny indeed. In it, Hancock meets up with another bus driver, and argues with his bank about the pointlessness of saving and withdrawing the same amount each week. He tries to bully a man on a park bench into admitting he feels insignificant, and fails. He loses an argument about wasps and bees. He meets Charlotte, a girl who works in a dress shop, and pretends he's an architect building a cathedral, which makes her pretend to be a model. He forces her to have a dessert she doesn't want because she says she needs to stay model-thin. Finally, he gets found out just before a touching goodnight kiss, and the romance turns sour. The film ends as it begins, with Hancock alone. One of the delights is the way in which Galton and Simpson continually undercut expectations.

There's a painful moment at the close of the script where you think Hancock and his girl will be reconciled in the rain. As he leaves he pauses, and you think he's about to say he loves her, but his pride won't let him.

HANCOCK: Charlotte, there's something— I'd like to say . . .
CHARLOTTE: Y-yes?
HANCOCK: Dior doesn't like fat birds so stay off the spuds.

After over a hundred radio episodes, which Hancock himself analysed in painful, self-flagellating detail, he should have come to realize that he was intelligent but not an intellectual, and that he actually needed great writers to put wonderful dialogue in his mouth. That he didn't, and took his life because of the fateful, fatal choices he made, is his great tragedy, and why he came to represent an entire archetype of post-war man. He was replaced by the satirical surrealism of *Monty Python*, and in the decades that followed, in-quotes irony overtook uncomfortable truths. Comedy is a cyclical thing, and truthful humour eventually returned to fashion, but Hancock continues to fascinate because of the uncomfortable assonance between his life and his scripts. Neither of his films captured his peculiar genius, although the first twenty minutes of *The Rebel* came very close.*

Although critics disagreed at the time, Galton and Simpson were the perfect choice to adapt Joe Orton's black comedies for British screens. Their version of *Entertaining Mr Sloane* neatly elided sixties hedonism into seventies tat, perfectly capturing the mood of the time. If Orton had lived, I wonder if he would have managed to realign his career in time for the shock-proof eighties.

For decades, English comedy centred on a unique archetype: the annoying bumbler. From the chinless wonders of *Bulldog Jack* to the blustering union officials of *I'm All Right, Jack*, we displayed a fondness for inept and wrong-headed anti-heroes, whose journeys were the antithesis of those proposed by screen guru Joseph Campbell in his rules for Hollywood. Instead of action, we had inertia; instead of leadership, gormlessness. Perhaps we should blame Evelyn Waugh and P. G. Wodehouse for creating comic novels that featured a parade of hopeless buffoons who couldn't be put in charge of a banana trifle, let alone their own destinies.

Comics like Will Hay, the Crazy Gang, Charlie Drake, George Formby, Norman Wisdom, the *Carry On* regulars, Harry Worth, Arthur Haynes, Michael Crawford, Marty Feldman and John Cleese knew how to draw laughs while setting our teeth on edge. This archetype reached its apogee with *The Brittas Empire*, an astonishingly

---

*Asked by a pretentious art critic how he mixes his pigments, the bogus painter Hancock replies: 'In a bucket with a big stick.' The joke works because of the single-syllable words, delivered bluntly and without comprehension.

subversive mainstream TV show in which Chris Barrie played Gordon Brittas, the well-meaning, incompetent head of a health centre who destroyed everyone with whom he came into contact. From his irritatingly nasal admonitions to his ability to misconstrue situations in the most offensive way possible, Brittas blundered blindly through seven nightmarish seasons in the 1990s, leaving a trail of mishaps that included murder, madness, blackmail, trauma, drug abuse and mental cruelty of every hue.

Here, of course, was the key to the show's success. Creators Andrew Norriss and Richard Fegen had produced an extreme example of English comic irony: everyone could see the surreal havoc unleashed by the lead character but was powerless to prevent past mistakes from recurring. The result was like being trapped in a weekly depiction of Parkinson's Law scripted by Franz Kafka and Brian Rix, the trouser-dropping, vicar-bothering farceur whose ludicrous comedies once occupied the Whitehall theatre.

I had bundled up my Hancock LPs, and as I opened the front door to leave my parents' house for my first flat, Peter Cook and Dudley Moore came on to the radio singing their appropriate signature song, 'Goodbye-ee'.

For me, these comedians represented a future of cynicism and satire, a world so mysteriously closed to my father that he would change channels whenever they appeared. He didn't like people who made fun of his values, and I could hardly blame him. I no longer wanted to hear his speech about surviving the war just so that we could have *Monty Python* making fun of it. Pete and Dud told a joke about the three Grecos, Juliette, Buddy and El – and I got the punchline, which made me as smart as them. That was how sophomore humour worked. But the smarter I thought I got, the less I could talk to my parents.

I left because it seemed likely that my father would kill me if I stayed – not with his fists but with the string of bitter sarcastic remarks and silences that would eventually drive my mother into a breakdown – and it would be easier on everyone if I went. I never returned to live at the house. When my parents finally moved they took nothing with them, leaving furniture, clothes, even boxes of old photographs behind, shedding the past as easily as they changed address. It was the best thing they ever did, as if they knew that bad memories resided in abandoned belongings. They walked away from their own ghosts, and after that, their lives became incrementally happier.

'Well, I'm going then,' I called out, unconsciously mimicking a Tony Hancock scene in which he insisted on being left alone to live in the woods, but actually hated seeing his friends leave.

'So you said, dear,' my mother replied absently. Our family had always displayed a refreshing absence of sentimentality. They failed to honour birthdays and Christmases because to them the celebration of such anniversaries seemed trumped-up and false after the deprivations of the war.

'Well, I'm going now,' I called. 'I'll be back when—' but my voice was drowned out by the whine of my father's power drill. I had twenty-two pounds in my pocket; I hadn't actually got a flat but was sure I would find one. Things would probably work out. London was filled with cheap lodgings. The lodging-house was a staple of most post-war English films, a melting-pot where you could make friends and find dubious job opportunities you'd never known existed.* Most seemed to be filled with bogus colonels and

*In some episodes, Hancock lived in a lodging-house, whose landlady disapproved of renting to a low comic. 'I don't want you going out and coming in all the time,' she told him, 'going out' being regarded as a suspicious thing to do in England. 'I went out and now I've come back in,' Hancock tells her angrily. 'I don't call that going out and coming in all the time.'

alcoholic spinsters, but these residents were soon replaced by the first generation of single professionals.*

A few days earlier I had read a story by Daphne du Maurier in which an unhappy man sails off in a hand-built boat, abandoning the status-conscious family who frown upon him. In a typical touch, he heads straight into a thunderstorm but refuses to turn back, and there the author leaves him, ploughing on into roiling darkness with a smile on his face. You didn't have to go to sea to embark on such a stormy voyage.

*Films like *The Ladykillers*, *The Lavender Hill Mob* and *The Lonely Passion of Judith Hearne* make capital of their lodging-house settings.

6

Darling

Patriotism, sprocket holes, site-specific London,
the romance of hackery, Bohemia

Recently I watched a TV programme called *The World's 100 Greatest Movies*, featuring clips from Hollywood films and interviews with surgically enhanced actors tanned to the consistency of flayed cows. When the unctuous voiceover asked: 'Can there be anyone in the world who isn't familiar with "Moon River"?', I thought: well, you could whistle it to people in Libya and get a few blank looks, and realized that the desert town of Harleywood had somehow confused itself with the main part of the planet, where people actually live, where a Mexican might not automatically be taken for a gardener.

For decades, Hollywood mistook itself for the world.* This was how England still saw itself after the war: we were plucky victors who once ruled the planet, and we could trade on the image for decades to come, eventually persuading everyone that we were still top dog, mainly by

---

*Not any more. The chastening economic downturn meant that Hollywood films now make more of their profits overseas.

selling them Union Jack tea caddies. My parents thought of the two world wars as a pair of football matches that the English side had won by drafting in a couple of expensive American players during extra time. My mother always looked puzzled when Americans banged on about their involvement; as far as she was concerned, they arrived at the party in time to do the washing up, then stuck us with the catering bill.

There was a resentful undercurrent to our patriotism; everyone was still moaning bitterly about Germany, how they had lost the war but won the peace. Beset with bedrock management problems, Britain's manufacturers were floundering. There were only the faintest shreds of dignity left; 'Swinging London' and 'I'm Backing Britain'* had arrived to bolster dented egos. James Bond was still arching an eyebrow in the cinema.† The Beatles were separate but individually intact. Big events, however – Watergate, Kent State, Vietnam, the space programme and the Cold War – were profoundly affecting American confidence, and Britain's irrelevance on the world stage was increasingly obvious.

At the age of eighteen, having been fast-tracked to sit two sets of A level exams in the same year and cram in some basic knowledge at art college, I had set out to try to find a job. Although I had been accepted for university, the family was stony broke, and I convinced them I should find

---

*A failed campaign created in December 1967 by five suburban secretaries who offered to work an extra half-hour a day to boost company productivity. The next PM, Harold Wilson, used the campaign to hide labour-relations mismanagement, and Robert Maxwell tried to hijack the whole enterprise, flogging Union Jack T-shirts that were manufactured in Portugal.

†As Simon Winder points out in *The Man Who Saved Britain*, Bond existed as a collection of attitudes shaped by English military and colonial contact with the rest of the world.

employment. Throwing away the careers advisor's contact list I checked the phone book and, putting on my poshest Received English voice, began making appointments.

Just one week later, I started work as a courier at a Charlotte Street advertising agency that granted copy tests to employees who wished to become writers. The tests were full of exercises like: 'A manufacturer has accidentally produced two thousand asymmetrical clear plastic boxes and wants to get rid of them. Create a campaign to sell them.' My father had previously championed every dodgy gadget from the Home Soda Maker (Save a Fortune on Soft Drinks!) to the Rolf Harris Stylophone,* and would have definitely been in the market for a room full of asymmetrical boxes, so I didn't find this much of a challenge. My mother was just as bad. Kath once bought a pair of gold plastic inflatable pants that were supposed to 'sweat away the pounds', but the first time she put them on we all laughed so hard that they were quickly folded away in a cupboard, never to be seen again.

My copy test was well received because, despite unemployment topping one million for the first time since the 1930s, I was apparently the first person ever to bother taking it seriously. There was little sense of determination among job-seekers in the creative industries back then, because the general public hadn't cottoned on that it was a good way to make easy money, and media studies had yet to bring popularity and pretension to the field. You could get a job in advertising just by turning up and looking vaguely keen.

On my first day as a courier I was sent out by sniggering producers to buy a box of sprocket holes, but just six weeks later I became a fully fledged copywriter on

---

*An electronic keyboard played with the aid of a plastic stick, that emitted a high-pitched wailing noise like a child trapped in a cupboard.

two conditions: that I could learn to type in a week and would be willing to paint my own desk. This might come as a shock to the Tory fundraisers who, in February 2010, raffled off a two-week media placement as a tea boy for £3,700.

Delivering film cans had given me a crash course in memorizing London streets. The London of the early seventies was still site-specific. Films unspooled in Wardour Street, the press hogged Fleet Street, fruit and veg sprouted in Covent Garden, fashion strutted the roads north of Oxford Street, hippies lounged in Camden, finance accrued around the Bank of England, art was garreted in Soho, and photographers flashed in Fitzrovia. Within these catchment areas were subdivisions: Newman Street was filled with photographers' file libraries and Broadwick Street was the home of art supplies.

In Tudor Street, vast rolls of newsprint had always been delivered by barges. The newsrooms and printing presses were here, so that the entire process of producing a newspaper took place in one tiny neighbourhood. You could feel the pavement trembling with the thunder of the great steel rollers. The very air smelled of ink and warm paper. This closed world spawned pubs and restaurants filled with a single profession, so that feature writers knew typesetters, printers knew photographers, and if you didn't have experience in a particular field you could hang out with those who did.

In a short period of time you could gain an understanding of how a newspaper was produced. Junior journalists were required to handle court reporting, which taught discipline, accuracy and an instinct for investigation. This was the old school of journalistic training, before reporters were turned into sentient chairbound PR-sponges. I didn't want to be a reporter: it was a hard life that turned you into a strawberry-nosed alcoholic, and if you were stuck in the provinces you spent most of your time reporting things that didn't happen:

> After 75 years of motoring without an accident or conviction, Muriel Gladwin has decided it is time to give up driving, at the age of 94!
> – *Gloucestershire News Service, December 2007*

I settled on copywriting because it had an interesting pedigree. P. G. Wodehouse, George Orwell, E. M. Forster, E. F. Benson, Somerset Maugham, Salman Rushdie, Fay Weldon and many others had started their careers by dabbling in advertising. It taught succinctness, respect for the correct use of words and, most importantly, the art of communication. I had read a quote: 'The steps between thoughts must be cut shallow in order to travel from one mind to the next.' It seemed the kind of advice I might not have got if I had chosen only to study the classics, and became a mantra for writing ad copy.

I arrived for my first proper working day at my Charlotte Street office wearing the grey off-the-peg suit* my father had picked for me, and sat in front of a Selectric Golfball typewriter at my still tacky crimson-painted desk, wondering what to do. The first person in – a full hour after I had arrived – was Jeff, a hairy, thug-browed man with huge unruly sideburns and a forest of chest hair sprouting from his floral nylon shirt. 'Sorry to sling shit at you on your first day, darling,' he said, chucking me a sheet of paper; 'can you whack this out?'

No one had ever called me darling before, although I had seen John Schlesinger's film of the same title, about London in the grip of its first celebrity cult. In one second

---

*'We very nearly fired you when we saw the suit you turned up in,' said my boss some time later. 'We'd seen better dressed crabs.'

the suburbs fell away, to be replaced by what I assumed was Bohemia.* I had read a bit of Plato and Aristotle, some Milton, Keats and Wilde. I had an unprecedented knowledge of the films of Norman Wisdom. I felt I could probably handle a two-inch recruitment advert for a tyre company.

*A Hapsburg principality that became part of Czechoslovakia (and now the Czech Republic) after the First World War. The name and its adjective came to denote 'having an unorthodox lifestyle' because it described any place where you could live and work cheaply, and so attracted artists.

7

Wardour

Boredom, nuns, dynamite, *Jason King*, strippers, Aqua Manda and a total lack of style

As a step towards fulfilling my fantasy of writing films, it wasn't much. The creative team sleepily assembled as the day wore on. Our sexy account director Vicki chain-smoked and was married to a Trinidadian trumpeter. Our ethereal copywriter Kevin was permanently clad in midnight-blue corduroy and drifted about warning everyone of bad times ahead, like Banquo's ghost. Stefan, our dedicated typesetter, sat on a high stool gloomily arranging letters like a Victorian accountant. Our creative director, Mick, was full of jargon and jealousies.*

It was the world of advertising, but nothing like the one represented in the cinema. I had seen several movies set in ad agencies, all of them filled with beautiful women and ugly morals. In *The Rise and Rise of Michael Rimmer*, oleaginous PR man Peter Cook insinuated himself into an

---

*Years later I bumped into him in the South of France. 'What on earth are *you* doing here?' he asked, as if he had reserved the entire coastline for himself.

outdated banking institution and destroyed it from within. In *Every Home Should Have One*, Marty Feldman struggled to come up with a sexy campaign for porridge, and Penelope Keith played a dominatrix. A groundswell of tutting had been started by tabloid journalists who wanted their readers to disapprove of easy money. Advertising was obviously the place to be.

Our creative department did not have ergonomic furniture, bean bags and a stripped-pine boardroom. It looked like a Welsh post office. The staff were sweet and drippy, and couldn't have schemed their way out of a moist paper bag. We had a tea lady who came round with an urn and a limited selection of Peak Frean biscuits,* and an ex-army lift man with one arm. We weren't even quite in Soho, where the trendy offices were. Soho in the seventies was an uneasy mix of wholesale haberdashers, sweatshop tailors, model agencies, Sicilian coffee stores, film companies and strip clubs. The villains fell into two categories: Maltese gangsters and a new breed of property developers seeking to terrify the area's few remaining elderly residents into selling up.

In the afternoon, things were so quiet that we played Cow Gum† cricket, a game which required you to manufacture a ball from layers of rubbery clear glue and rolls of toilet paper. Some of us slept. Others went to an illegal afternoon drinking club run by a vicious old gin-bag who was always going on about how much she'd enjoyed the war because she liked a *man's man*.

The work was low end and stultifying: trade ads for tyre

---

*One of my favourite moments in British film occurs in *The Bliss of Mrs Blossom* when James Booth explains to Shirley MacLaine why love and loss are so important to understanding the world, using the example of discontinued Peak Frean biscuits.
†The EU finally banned Cow Gum in the late 1990s for health and safety reasons.

companies, catalogues for sanitary engineers, a flyer for fishing bait (basically, an ad for worms), leaflets for insurance firms, charity ads that consisted of a blank space.* One day I was asked to write a recruitment brochure for a convent, and travelled to the end of the Northern Line for a meeting with a superfluity of very sweet nuns. I asked the Mother Superior what she had in mind for the front cover. After thinking carefully for a while, she held up her hands to help me visualize the concept and told me, 'I thought we'd have a cross.'

I loved my job. After living in the suburbs I would have found a milk round exciting, but the work was hilariously, embarrassingly, painfully simple. My colleagues were adorable in a bored, unambitious, derailed way. It was like being on a branch line Dr Beeching had forgotten to close down. And I was being paid, which meant that I was able to leave home and escape my father. No one had explained to me that the art of constructing fake dreams would quickly prove spirit-crushing, and if they had I probably wouldn't have believed them, but after six months of swearword bingo, charity ads and afternoon naps I was bored enough to look for another job. Luckily, work was absurdly easy to find. While Doncaster miners tried to figure out how to feed their families as the pits closed down, I walked down Regent Street and picked up a new 9–5 the day after I started looking.

I moved into a Soho agency sandwiched between a run-down boozer and a strip club called The Dolls' House. I'd picked it because the creative department was four times bigger and they had nice furniture, but soon discovered I

*We put them next to crossword puzzles, the idea being that people would work out anagrams in them and remember the charity while doing so. If you tell someone to 'Send £2.57', that's exactly what they'll send.

would be working on some of the worst accounts in the world.

My creative director was a smarmily handsome American called Temple Wilson whose catchphrase was 'Dynamite!' He winked and gleamed his teeth at us, snapped his fingers and said 'Gotcha!' and we thought he was adorable in the way that some people take to small, useless dogs. Our boardroom had black and gold furniture. There was an aura of thwarted ambition about the place, as if nobody had expected to wash up here. Suddenly the job didn't seem so bohemian. It was more like an episode of *Jason King*.* Looking back, it seems obvious now that the 1970s were spent in training for the gaudy excesses of the 1980s.

London was entering a state of flux from which it would never entirely emerge. In *Sparrows Can't Sing*, James Booth comes back to the East End after a two-year absence and finds his house gone, and nearby flats occupied by the first wave of Caribbean and Indian immigrants enthusiastically seeking a better life. But those who had stayed on had watched the idealistic visions of the sixties wither into selfishness and cynicism. The country was visibly crimped by recession and dulled by the rise of corporate culture. Everything about the seventies was as cheap and fake as the glittery strip-club sets I could see from the back of my office.

Except Soho's Wardour Street. That was real. It had been there since Elizabethan times, and was named after one Sir Archibald Wardour. There had been a windmill, a church and a gaming house, a combination that perfectly

---

*Queasily awful detective series starring Peter Wyngarde, the model for Austin Powers. The actor sidetracked his career by being convicted for gross indecency with a truck driver in the toilets of Gloucester bus station.

captures the confusion of seediness that always marked the area. In the late nineteenth century it was famous for second-rate furniture shops. Peculiarly, it was also known for tinned food. Wardour-brand tinned fruit and veg was still available in the 1970s. From 1964 to 1988 it was the home of the legendary Marquee Club. A pub, the Intrepid Fox, had been founded in 1784 by the Whig leader Charles James Fox, who promised free beer and a kiss from the Duchess of Devonshire for anyone offering him electoral support during his campaign. The Duchess showed her own prowess by drinking a yard of ale and dashing the empty vessel into the fireplace. The Fox became a Goth pub and was eventually closed down, the meaning of its elegant sculptured friezes lost to future generations.

Sandwiched between Dean Street and Berwick Street, the thoroughfare was lined with film offices on either side, from huge international outfits to tiny two-man operations. Rank Films had their artists' studio here, and it now seemed as if every room of every building was exclusively filled with film and post-production companies. Runners dashed in and out of the traffic delivering film cans to projection booths, and the entire street had a manic energy similar to that of Fleet Street, with its copy boys racing to meet editors' deadlines.

The windows of all the old buildings from Hammer House to Warner Brothers were filled with poster displays, so that walking from one end of the street to the other was like ambling through an art gallery of popular culture. Beneath the road were the screening rooms, boxy, smoke-filled joints that brought all of the publicists together in one spot to watch movies at six o'clock each evening. Afterwards they would gather in the Ship, the smoky, sepia-ceilinged Wardour Street institution where everyone went to discuss films with directors, writers and producers.

Underneath Wardour Street was a chain of tunnels that

led to, and linked, the viewing theatres. Many of these had been dug out from the original causeways of the Fleet River, and their entrances stood on opposite sides of the road in pairs.*

There were once dozens of strip clubs dotted all over Soho. Girls in pink baby-doll nighties would stand in the doorways, beckoning punters and separating them from twenty-pound notes before ushering them down the steps. Once inside, the marks found themselves in tunnels that led across the street and back out of a different doorway, with no club in sight. The strippers who worked the clubs would perform at fifteen-minute intervals in different venues, and it was not uncommon to see them dashing from one club to the other dressed as giant butterflies or Viking women.

Meanwhile, the rest of the country was stuck in the time that style forgot, with TV sitcoms like *Love Thy Neighbour* and *Are You Being Served?* and variety shows that featured smutty comics telling smirking jokes about 'darkies' and 'nig-nogs'; with Budgie jackets and wet-look shirts that fell apart; with patch-pockets and plastic shoes; with budget aftershaves like Brut Splash-On and Aqua Manda;† with red plastic Wimpy Bars and chemists that sold 'surgical appliances' and Scandinavian porn; with Farmer Joes, clogs and matching knitted beanies; with

---

*A lot went on under London: there was an excellent port and oyster bar beneath Piccadilly Circus, and for years one heard rumours of a Masonic lodge in the basement of the old Café Royal. Nearby was a vast underground bar called Mr Fogg's, each of its rooms based on a different scene from *Around The World In Eighty Days*.

†Aqua Manda was one of the few aftershaves that ever attempted to make men smell like oranges. It was mysteriously popular. Brut smelled like something you'd use to freshen a drain, and was advertised by Henry Cooper on the assumption that we'd all want to smell like a sweaty middle-aged boxer.

the Ford Cortina and the Hillman Imp, cars that were positively Balkan in their ugliness. Half the streets in London were boarded up with corrugated iron, and the other half were having yellow plastic fascias tacked over their Victorian brickwork. The English were shabby and behaving more shabbily than ever as town councillors sat behind their leather-topped desks, pocketing contractor bribes and making smutty suggestions to their mini-skirted secretaries. Advertising seemed an almost virtuous profession in comparison.

As I trudged to Soho each morning from a miniature flatshare in Belsize Park where my outstretched arms touched both walls of my bedroom, I set aside my dream of becoming a proper writer, and started spending my evenings studying other people's work at the cinema.

Specifically, as Londoners do in their early twenties, I discovered the National Film Theatre.

8

Double Bills

Iambic pentameter, Consulate, English films,
stiff upper lips, fleapits, Franz Liszt and
the National Film Theatre

In our school Shakespeare was administered like a polio
vaccine; early exposure prevented you from catching it for
real. I was made to see *Hamlet* at the age of eleven, when
I was still having trouble with basic concepts like theft
and shame, let alone duplicity, insanity and allegorical
playwriting in the service of exposing murderous complicity, performed in iambic pentameter. But I could
sense the stories inside, a bit like imagining the skeleton
beneath the skin. And iambic pentameter suddenly got
easier after a teacher explained that Shakespeare was
simply leaving breaths in the spaces as an instruction to
his performers.

By the time I was fourteen I had sought out the Olivier
film version of *Hamlet* in a screening at my local library
and I fell in love with the language, even though the projectionist panicked and substituted one reel from *The*

Dam Busters in the middle of it.* Teachers knew what
they were doing with Shakespeare. For every ten pupils
who yawned and grew bored, there was one who said 'I
don't understand it, but I feel something . . .' This is how
such seeds are planted.

On a similar principle, we were dragged complaining
to mystifying concerts and performances, just to see what
would stick in our brains. The music teacher herded us
into the Royal Festival Hall to hear *The Young Person's
Guide to the Orchestra* and *Peter and the Wolf*, handing
every child a Hacks cough sweet with a solemn warning
not to make a sound. The art teacher had us looking at
Rothkos before we'd even covered figurative art, just
because he wanted to go himself. Best of all, the sports
master was given no budget to take anyone to sporting
fixtures because healthy outdoor activities were treated
with utter disdain by the majority of pupils.† You can love
a school for that.

The result of all this forced artistic input was that I had
grown up loving stories, and wanted to be somehow connected to them in my day job, which meant the choice had
come down to copywriter or confidence trickster (which
amounted to the same thing). Every young copywriter in
London secretly wanted to be a scriptwriter. Most of the
ones who were my age had grown up through an astonishing decade of English film.

It came as a shock to be flicking through a copy of *BFI*

---

*He also showed Powell and Pressburger's *The Red Shoes* without the
reel that contained the ballet. Nobody noticed. Most of the audience
was sheltering from the rain, the way Edith Evans does in the library
in *The Whisperers*.
†Mind you, that master did seem to enjoy looking over the tops of the
cubicles when we were showering after PE. We got to practise flirting
and he got a dream job – it seemed like a fair deal.

Monthly (now called *Sight & Sound*) and discover that the first English colour feature film was made just sixteen years before I was born. *Wings of the Morning* was lensed by Jack Cardiff, possibly the greatest cinematographer of all time, but that didn't let him off the hook for making me feel ancient. What next? Would I discover I was born before the invention of the kettle? There were still a lot of films to catch up with, and the NFT showed most of the ones it thought worth remembering. But there was something indefinably poncey about seeing films there, so I tried to catch them in real cinemas, where they showed in scratched double bills, sandwiched between ads for Consulate cigarettes ('Cool as a mountain stream') and Gordon's Gin.

Despite the offensive but accurate remarks French director François Truffaut made about English cinema,* we had an illustrious history of actors and technicians, including brilliantly idiosyncratic cinematographers, art directors and composers. Even before the Second World War the English film industry had attracted extraordinary talents. In the 1941 film about the Salvation Army, *Major Barbara*, the following names could be found attached to the production: George Bernard Shaw, William Walton, Deborah Kerr, Rex Harrison, Wendy Hiller, Robert Morley, Robert Newton, Ronald Neame, Jack Clayton, Arthur Ibbetson, Emlyn Williams, Michael Anderson and David Lean.

In particular, the musical scores of John Barry, William Walton and Ron Goodwin and the cinematography of Freddie Francis and Geoffrey Unsworth were synonymous with entire eras of English film. The jewels in our crown, the big three, were Alfred Hitchcock, David Lean and Michael Powell. But there were a great many less heralded (and often less expert) directors like Anthony Asquith and

*Truffaut said there was 'a certain incompatibility between the terms "cinema" and "Britain"'. Rude sod. He was right, of course.

E. A. Dupont who became interesting with the passing of time, because they offered glimpses of a country that had vanished from sight.

In the fifties, the Boulting Brothers and Launder and Gilliat had produced chains of sharp, satirical monochrome comedies featuring casts so familiar that it was possible to name every actor with a speaking part in them. In the sixties, directors like Tony Richardson, Richard Lester, John Schlesinger and Ken Russell caught the kinetic energy of the era. But the broadsheet English critics sought to reduce the visibility and importance of homegrown films, and routinely dismissed all those without overt socialist agendas or auteur tics. Films could be about the working class, provided they were presented in a certain way, but never for them. French cinema, to which the general public had extremely limited access, received endless column inches in the so-called quality press while popular releases were blanked. At the point of their demise, a few *Carry Ons* and Hammer horrors were partially rehabilitated to be ironically included in the critical pantheon. However, class snobbery clung to English film like a nylon chemise. If the general public went to see it, surely it had to be lousy.

Having grown up watching homegrown hits, I found adjusting to arthouse fare was not easy. While I appreciated Bresson, Ozu, Truffaut and the New Wave auteurs, I didn't really enjoy them. However, I resented the automatic charge of philistinism in English film from critics who were more interested in innovative technique than the pleasure of being lost in a story. Why should we be told to love films because they reflected real life? Why was escapism so frowned upon?* What I failed to see was that critics were fascinated by the global development of a virtually

*Of course, this argument has come back to haunt me in a modern cinematic landscape that mainly consists of films about flying teenagers.

dialogue-free film language, while at home we were still presenting ideas through clever wordplay.

Many successful English films from the past were erased from the nation's collective memory, but I could still sometimes catch them at one of the many repertory cinemas that peppered the capital – there were at least seven fleapits in Oxford Street alone. But who now remembers films like *The Passing of the Third Floor Back*, *The Stars Look Down*, *The Man in Grey*, *Passage Home*, *Live Now Pay Later*, *I Believe in You*, *The Seventh Veil*, *Tiger in the Smoke*, *Woman in a Dressing Gown*, *I See a Dark Stranger*, *Odd Man Out*, *The Fallen Idol*, *The Rocking Horse Winner*, *The Holly and the Ivy*, *King and Country*?

On Sundays, English cinemas always double-billed prints that had been in circulation for years, looking as if they'd been dragged through a sandpit with hooks. But a big screen changes everything. It wasn't until I saw the Academy Award-winning thriller *Seven Days to Noon* revived at the Everyman Cinema, Hampstead, that I had any real sense of its power. This Boulting Brothers film depicts the full-scale evacuation of London as a pacifist prepares to detonate a devastating bomb in the city centre, in order to shock the world into disarmament. It remains a source of fascination both as a social document and for a plot that feels prescient. Similarly, *Hue and Cry* was enjoyable on a big screen because of its Blitz-bombsite landscape, and a climactic trawl through the London sewers that was obviously shot on a real location.

There were much stranger films about.

'By the pricking of my thumbs, something something this way comes.' The deranged Miss Honey starts the quote, and Mr Pastry forgetfully finishes it. The pair are climbing a wall, covered in doves, intent on stealing a secret formula for an alcoholic brew. Making their getaway through foggy London streets with a knitting-obsessed cab-driver, Mr Pastry, wearing a false nose, realizes he has bitten off more than he can chew . . .

This was a deeply peculiar English comedy full of non-sequiturs and recurring strange images, and felt like being trapped in a bad dream. It featured the nation's most sinister copper, creepy children, a man wooing his girl with quotes from the *Encyclopaedia Britannica* and lots and lots of white birds. It starred Margaret Rutherford* and was called *Miss Robin Hood*. In films like this the English played to their strange strengths, but nobody recognized them. We had no European film language, but there was something in our odd little films that gave the game away about our national identity.

The films I had grown up with as a child were self-effacing tales of stiff-upper-lippery, but the English hero I most admired was the back-room boffin, the quiet little chap who got on with the job and looked sheepish when you congratulated him. It took an actor like Alec Guinness to truly get the measure of such men, playing one with a glinty-eyed streak of madness in *The Man in the White Suit*. Powell and Pressburger tackled the character even more directly in *The Small Back Room*, which featured an embittered alcoholic bomb-disposal expert.

Since the 1950s there had been renewed interest in the lives of working-class Londoners, evinced in the low-life novels of Roland Camberton, Gerald Kersh and Alexander Baron, and the theatre of Joan Littlewood, and it had spread on to the screen in films like *The Small World of Sammy Green*, *It Always Rains On Sunday*, *Pool of London* and *The Yellow Balloon*. When you looked into it, English cinema history became far richer and stranger than expected.

---

*On train journeys to the film studio or theatre she used to get her teapot filled by the engine driver. So civilized.

I worked my way through the English films I hadn't seen,* then plunged into their continental counterparts. In a cinema your attention is drawn into a skewed dimension where the director controls your peripheral vision. I soon realized that Jacques Tati's *Playtime* played differently according to where I sat in the auditorium. Set in an ultra-modern Paris, with the city's architectural antiquities seen only as reflections in glass, much of the action was staged at different depths on the wide screen, and minor characters told their own stories depending on how close you were to them.

By this time London's great cathedral-cinemas were reduced to running European exploitation double bills. I saw the gory Italian exorcist sleazefest *The Devil Within Her* (together with *Tentacles!*, the giant killer-octopus movie) on a football-pitch-sized screen at the Dominion, Tottenham Court Road, in earbone-rattling, seat-wobbling Sensurround. Modern cinema-goers are denied the chance to enjoy the sensation of your trousers shaking as Juliet Prowse spews green vomit over appalled family members.

London's repertory cinemas were not so much fleapits as armpits. They didn't serve organic apple juice and carrot cake, they served Fanta and wafers, and smelled of warm tramps. They were upholstered in flesh-scorching purple Dralon. Their seats were split and the floors were sticky. A half-hearted attempt to ban smoking resulted in a ludicrous commercial in which a stern voiceover warned: 'The seats on the RIGHT-hand side of this cinema are reserved for smokers only', as if the smoke wouldn't drift over.

I spent night after night in these dumps, unaware that they would all soon be gone. It made a change from writing

---

*The films I had seen – and loved, like every other schoolboy of my era – included *Jason and the Argonauts*, *Goldfinger* and *First Men in the Moon*.

TV spots for polyester sheets. Without realizing it, I was extending the loneliness of my childhood into adult life, avoiding any kind of human connection or commitment. Films had always made better friends, and were there for ever.

The National Film Theatre held a Ken Russell season, and I bought a ticket to every screening. Russell was a TV arts director who successfully transferred to mainstream movies, finding audiences for films which often showed his love of maverick artists and composers. He was an impassioned speaker, although with his round red face and white hair he looked like a deranged archery target. He fought the tide of homegrown kitchen-sink dramas with bombastic, lurid imagery that incensed Britain's literary purists, splitting critics and audiences, but at least he was never boring, and he understood cinema every bit as much as David Lean, who was feted for making the more conservative 'classic' adventures that later inspired Steven Spielberg.

Russell was branded a bottom-waggling bad boy, and when he failed, he failed spectacularly: *Lisztomania* represented some kind of all-time cinematic nadir, and was probably the only musical drama ever to feature Frankenstein, Chopin, the Pope, Hitler, Thor, and Franz Lizst riding a giant penis. Although it was truly awful, even this had a scale and grandeur of vision that, no matter how absurd and misguided, still deserved to be called a cinematic experience. Oddly, Russell seems to have had no awareness of what he did that was good. He dismissed *The Boy Friend*, his multi-layered, backstabbing reinvention of a dried-out old theatrical workhorse, as mere hackery.*

As the decade ground on, English films were described

---

*'Let's face it, darling, the closest you got to the West End was Harrow on the Hill' – Madame Dubonnet in *The Boy Friend*.

with increasing frequency as 'better suited to TV'. With the shrinking of screens came a matching reduction in ambitions. Big cinema auditoria had demanded powerful emotional displays, but small screens meant you could keep slobs happy with TV spin-offs.* The English creative movement snapped at scraps and floundered about as the financing pond dried up.

Now that I had a bit of money in my pocket and was free of my parents' control, I had chosen to behave like a ten-year-old boy again. This was akin to keeping a bear captive for years then releasing its ankle chain, only to find it returning to shamefacedly slip the chain back on. It was the period when I was meant to be experimenting with drugs, sex, travel and minor criminal acts. Instead I worked like a dog and went to the flicks.

The National Film Theatre was a building designed to punish people for liking films. It had a meeting area that looked like the bar of a German cultural collective and an auditorium with no centre aisle, so that in order to take a bathroom break you had to squeeze past at least twenty tutting people in goatees and berets. The consequence of this was that you'd become paranoid about needing a wee halfway through a four-hour Russian odyssey, and would barely be able to concentrate on the film. The audience generally consisted of autistic loners and art teachers on their afternoons off.

Worse still, there was an exaggerated reverence about this temple of celluloid that rendered films joyless, as the fish-eyed audience analysed the jokes when they should have been laughing and studied the lighting when they should have been experiencing dramatic tension. Many

---

*They're still here with us. *The Inbetweeners*, basically *Carry On Abroad* with fanny jokes, proved a popular hit in the cinematic wasteland of 2011.

years later, just after the smoking ban, I went to the NFT with a friend who forgot herself and actually became so involved in the film that she lit a cigarette. The audience reacted as if there had been a sarin gas attack, screaming and falling away from her, so in panic she dropped the lit cigarette into her handbag, closed the clasp and sat anxiously staring at the film as if nothing had happened while a smell of smouldering plastic pervaded the auditorium. The National Film Theatre always had that effect on you.

I knew I shouldn't be spending so much time in darkened cinemas. I needed to get out there into the light and make some friends. Just one friend, I decided, would do.

9

'A Bit Camp'

Head of Television, doing nothing, *Witchfinder General*, rubbish films, and what we lost in Wardour Street

Assuming Europe to be the home of historical veracity, the Canadian actor Donald Sutherland apparently immersed himself so deeply in the title role of Fellini's *Casanova* that he had his teeth filed, only to discover that Fellini wasn't that fussed about details. In fact, he was quite happy to have Sutherland make up his dialogue on the spot, and instructed him to count aloud from one to twenty, so that he could dub whatever he liked into the appalled star's mouth afterwards.

I suspect the English find this story funny, Canadians less so, because we're not terribly detail-oriented. We're not like those Chinese kids who stand up and recite prime numbers for two days. We'd be lucky if we could find the building where the event was being held.

However, we were rather good at lateral thinking and the broad strokes of creativity, and the advertising agencies of the sixties built their reputations on big ideas. Commercials directors like Ridley Scott, Hugh Hudson and Alan Parker started to become more famous than the products they peddled, and formed their own production companies. More interested in the look of a film than how it sounded, they broke the middle-class old-boy network, then began making features. As a result, advertising was eventually seen as the cineaste's career choice, a stepping stone to a bright future in English cinema. And for a very short time, it was.

My agency, Allardyce Hampshire, was painted entirely in blue and green, so it was a bit like working in an aquarium. Our creative director, the endearing American cheeseball Temple 'Dynamite' Wilson, felt we were getting complacent, so he poached a new Head of Television from Ogilvy & Mather to come in and give the place a lift. 'His name is Jim Sturgeon and he's a bit camp,' he told us, 'but he's a very smart cookie.'

I was dying to find out what Temple's idea of 'a bit camp' was, seeing as he himself was off the scale when it came to heterosexual campery. The advertising industry was surprisingly straight in every sense of the word, despite the orange trousers, flapping wrists and everyone calling each other 'darling'.

The gentleman who joined the following Monday was short, creased, paunchy and prematurely bald, with a snubby nose and poached eggs for eyes. He chain-smoked Rothmans and coughed every second time he opened his mouth. He looked about fifty, but was, incredibly, twenty-eight. 'I look like my father,' he'd say with a shrug.* He wore canary-yellow loons and matching yellow love beads,

---

*Physical changes in the human face mean that period dramas now never feel right when it comes to portraying the working classes: poorer nutrition and chain-smoking affected facial shape, and women routinely used to have their teeth removed, as false ones were deemed healthier.

but he had an involving, innocent smile and an aura of quiet authority that made everyone assume they knew him.

Charisma is a very peculiar quality that has no correlation with beauty and very little with brains: there are people who can turn heads in any restaurant and make bank managers beg for friendship. Throughout the years of our partnership there was a constant refrain from those Jim passed. They would turn to me and demand to know 'Who *is* that man?' Jim favoured Cecil Gee blazers and walked around with one hand in his pocket like an incognito millionaire. He always managed to look as if he were sizing everything up before deciding whether or not to buy it, but in a benign way. He hardly ever spoke unless he had something important to say, and remained the silent heart of every hurricane. Years later, Pierce Brosnan told me how director Martin Campbell instructed him to play James Bond. 'Restrict your movements, be still inside and show people very little of what you are thinking. Only speak when you're going to inform someone of your decision.'

This indefinable ability to pique interest by doing almost nothing drove me mad. The world is divided into those who look, and those who are looked for. I spent the next three decades trying to locate Jim while he blithely went on his own way, unaware that he was being sought out. I would follow him into a room and become so invisible in his wake that he jokingly called me Mr Cellophane, after the sad nobody in *Chicago*, which had just completed its first, most Vaudevillian incarnation on the London stage. Mr Cellophane sang, 'You can walk right by me, look right through me, and never know I'm there.'

'Hello,' said Jim, holding out his hand. 'My name's Sturgeon. Where the caviar comes from. Do you want to come to the bank with me?'

It was a funny way to get to know someone, accompanying them to make a deposit. I tagged along and discovered that he banked in a grand Old World edifice beside the Savoy Hotel. Despite being permanently in debt, he had chosen it because he liked the building.

'Surely they won't let you stay if you're in debt,' I wondered.

'They wouldn't let me stay if I wasn't,' he said, 'and besides, banks look after your money all your life, so it's only right that you should occasionally look after a little of theirs.'

I hadn't encountered this kind of radical thinking before. Nobody in my family had ever owed a penny, with the result that we passed through life entirely unnoticed. My father thought this was a good thing, and encouraged invisibility at every turn so that we wouldn't prove an embarrassment to anyone. Our family mottoes were 'Keep your voice down' and 'People are looking'. Jim took a different approach. He had the self-confidence not to care what others thought. 'They're strangers,' he would say. 'You'll never see them again. It doesn't matter what they think.'*

'I won't be long,' said Jim, 'why don't you take a look around?'

Feeling increasingly uncomfortable in a hushed marble-and-mahogany hall housing the kind of London bank that still closed its doors so that the directors could go grouse-shooting, I was sure some uniformed guard would realize I didn't belong and throw me into the street. Jim took his time, strolling through the ground floor with a vague smile in his eyes, like a shareholder who had come to check up on his investment. Everyone stopped for a word with him.

---

*Needless to say, this was a very un-English attitude, as the opposite is usually true. We know this from seeing Hyacinth Bucket touch a national nerve in *Keeping Up Appearances*.

'How do you know them all?' I asked, awed.

'I don't,' he replied. 'They know me.'

I watched how he drew them in without doing anything. It was an extremely odd talent. I was so nervous and eager to please that people actively avoided me, and here was this man who attracted people because he was visibly uninterested in them. Yet it turned out that our hot new producer was broke and still living with his parents.

Sensing that I could learn a lot from him, I began hanging around his desk after work, hoping to pick up some knowledge that would stop me from being thought a total fool.

The following week, we were teamed together to create some of the world's worst commercials.

Brentford Nylons was a chain of super-cheap linen stores that had begun on a market stall in London's East End, although 'linen' is technically inaccurate as they sold the kind of sheets that electrocuted you with static and clung to your body like an ugly, grateful sex partner. Nylon was big in the seventies. The great USP* of nylon shirts and sheets was No Ironing! To which it was tempting to add No Warmth! Nasty and Shiny! Will Give You A Chinese Burn During Sex! But the company spent heavily on television, so we loved them.

Of course, it wasn't what either of us wanted to do, but you have to start somewhere. The nadir of these early collaborations was the use of ageing, nervous BBC radio DJ Alan 'Fluff'† Freeman to flog nylon sheets. These ads dug so irritatingly under the nation's skin that when Brentford Nylons went bust after its owner suffered a

---

*'Unique Selling Point' – eight points in Media Wankword Bingo.
†So called because he could never remember his lines. He lived in fear of being outed and losing his fanbase – he would not have done, because everyone respected his integrity.

stroke from overwork, the *Daily Mail* ran the jingle's sheet music across its centre spread. Writing commercials taught concision and memorability, if nothing else.

With my mother's unconditional encouragement, I had grown up with an egalitarian attitude to storytelling that allowed me to nip between Shakespeare and Superman without a flinch. Snobbery is rife in the creative arts, and if you suggest that a comic can be as powerful as a play, writers will behave like housewives being asked to switch from Waitrose to the Co-op. I happily trawled the outer reaches of bad cinema, but counterbalanced each find by seeking out a masterpiece.

Like me, Jim was a film freak, but in a gentler, more traditional way. Lovers of cult film tended to be intense, analytical and exhausting. Often prepared to champion badly made B-movies over beautifully constructed classics, they revered irony, seeking out fifties SF for camp value, swinging sixties fare for groovy fashions, and seventies grindhouse flicks for unreconstructed machismo and outrageous gender politics. There were plenty of film freaks who had seen *Faster, Pussycat! Kill! Kill!* and *Plan 9 from Outer Space* who hadn't seen *The Thomas Crown Affair, Picnic* or *The Pumpkin Eater*. In the same way, musicians may champion assonance over complex rhyming schemes because it's somehow more real, whereas a beautifully constructed rhyme creates its own internal truth. Writers replace rambling natural conversation with tightly constructed dialogue in order to produce insight. So, too, carefully planned and constructed films offer pleasures that B-films may only uncover by accident.

Jim's relationship to cinema was simpler than mine. One of four children, he viewed cinema as the soothing hobby of a prematurely middle-aged man, like repairing classic cars. Despite being bright and fairly bursting with ideas, he was a curious mix of naivety and quietly informed opinion. He had grown up in the pleasant Thames Valley town of Hampton, with gentle, sweet parents who were married for over sixty years, whose house always seemed filled with sunlight, who kept a vegetable garden and rarely went further than Cornwall for their holidays. They were everything my parents were not. There were never recriminatory arguments that left a fractious atmosphere for months; Hilda Sturgeon ran the household and her husband Tom was happy to stay in an armchair and keep the peace. It seemed to me that, as a consequence, Jim gravitated towards films with truthful, calm, unironic central performances from actors like Peter Finch, Dirk Bogarde and Anne Bancroft.

My upbringing had created the opposite: I was nervous, fidgety, brittle, sharp-witted, often exhausting to myself and others, and chose my films accordingly. By hanging around with Jim I had found someone who could give me confidence and calm my fears. In return, I could articulate his thoughts and act as his public face.

For Jim, there were less desirable concomitants of unconditional friendship that included trips to horrible fleapits, being forced to listen to pub diatribes on the misunderstood merits of *The Wicker Man* and becoming a one-man audience for script read-throughs. He had inexplicably missed some of my favourite films from his 'must-view' list, so I quickly rectified the situation by trotting him off to catch my great obsession: *Witchfinder General*.

I had first seen this film when it opened in 1968, and it haunted my dreams. It had been made for peanuts, scripted from a rather stodgy book and mismarketed to audiences as a horror movie, but the barely experienced director, twenty-three-year-old Michael Reeves, had transformed the mundane material into an elegy for a lost country.

Styled as an English western, the film showed how witch-craft accusations arose from the chaos of an England riven by civil war, to break society down at its most fundamental level. Evocative and devastatingly moving, it existed in two cuts – one with carousing topless pub wenches for European distribution.

The film had caused a critical outcry against violence* and was condemned by the tabloids in one of their periodic shrieking fits of moral hysteria, which naturally made it essential viewing. With atmospheric settings, an elegant score that quoted 'Greensleeves' and a mythic sense of tragedy, it had a sense of time and location few have captured since. Later, critics, ever the seagulls trailing behind the trawler of public consensus, swiftly U-turned and rechristened Reeves a major talent, calling his premature death a tragic loss to the film world.

It had originally been written to star Donald Pleasence as the Witchfinder, which would have made the source of evil banal and barely visible; Vincent Price, however, rose to the material and, although he never ceases to be himself, brings out the grandeur of the state-approved inquisitor.

Reeves's on-screen alter ego, Ian Ogilvy, was one of the few actively vengeful English heroes, although in true English style he gets hopelessly sidetracked on his quest and goes mad in the process. Hilary Dwyer, his ethereally beautiful, strangely mournful love interest, vanished from films soon after. Decades later I met her at a party and found that she still had the same luminous, melancholy quality.

You can't break the kind of friendship made by two

---

*The most rabid criticism came from Alan Bennett writing for *The Listener*, who described the film as 'morally rotten'. Mind you, he also used the word 'autochthonous', which said a lot about his readership (it means 'indigenous').

people who love the same films.* Jim understood this film's eerie beauty at once. *Witchfinder General* had made me desperate to be involved with cinema, and after leaving work at night I lurked around the fringes of the dying industry, wheedling invitations out of projectionists, thrusting badly written scripts at the wrong people and making small talk (intense on my side, desultory and inattentive on their side) outside poky Wardour Street screening rooms that bore absurdly regal names like the Baronet, the Crown and the Coronet.

The producers of Wardour Street worked in attic rooms at the tops of rickety staircases, in shoebox offices with inappropriately huge desks and onyx ashtrays filled with cigar stubs. If they were elderly, they were lost in dreams of the happier times, better budgets, bigger stars. They had failed to realize that British screen history had faded from national consciousness like degrading film emulsion. I was desperate to meet them, but their time was already passing, and they were losing their passion for film.

The few features from their glory days that survived were locked away in BFI vaults or owned by Burbank companies. The handful of forgotten stars who lived on were stashed in county nursing homes with scrapbooks of memories, the time for salvaging their stories almost past. I wanted to hear the backstories that began when the studio lights were turned off, but it was simply too late.

---

*There should be a special word for the awful feeling you get when you revisit an old film that's a personal favourite and realize for the first time that it has dated so badly you can never share it with anyone.

10

The Decline

From the bountiful richness of English cinema
to its last sad gasp, including scruffy writers,
burned-out stars, down-at-heel producers,
smut, freaks and ultragore

Gentility had been English cinema's biggest curse, but perhaps its greatest blessing as well. Our scandals were more low key, our falls from grace less steep, and they have now been scrubbed from Wardour Street's collective memory.

The story of English film was one of shameless neglect. Just as features from the 1920s were melted down by scrap dealers to make aircraft resin, so their legacies were ignored. Besides, everyone knew that English directors secretly wanted to make ersatz Hollywood films. There was a move to rechristen our industry 'Jollygood', and we couldn't stop making fun of American stars. Rudolph Valentino had been sent up in the UK as Rhubarb Vaselino.

Pompous critics preferred continental art pieces, so

who, other than the 'Bakelite-sniffing nostalgist',* was left to wonder about the homegrown talent that once adorned billboards and broadsheets? By the time the 1970s arrived, who cared that the sensual star Lillian Hall-Davies had slashed her own throat, or that Ivor Novello had had an affair with Siegfried Sassoon, when monochrome English films had managed to vanish so entirely from our lives?

We now know that the history of English film didn't deserve its reputation for stolidity and conservatism, on-screen or off. Although too in love with the spoken word, such films could be passionate, permissive and enthralling. Scenes of sexual ambiguity, degenerate glamour and perverse psychological cruelty were unhampered by a Hays Code, and performances were often a reflection of our stars' lives.

Novello's sexuality certainly didn't damage his career, nor did the unorthodox sleeping arrangements of a dozen other early British stars, grouped together as 'ambisextrous' social radicals. Films were produced with great speed and little thought. The smutty double entendre became a venerable tradition which meant that desperate lines like 'Ooh, what a lovely looking pear' (Barbara Windsor to a man holding fruit) provoked laughter, not outrage. Without such quickies churned out to fill quotas, directors and cinematographers would never have honed their craft, and ultimately there would have been no Guinness, Olivier, Powell or Lean. Thus, the gory melodrama of Sweeney Todd and crass cross-dressing antics of Old Mother Riley paved the way for *Lawrence of Arabia*, but critics could not see beyond the idea that English films were merely music-hall rubbish for proles.

*Matthew Sweet's term from the excellent *Shepperton Babylon*.

Even more surprisingly, I discovered that English back-stage scandals sometimes rivalled anything Hollywood produced. Tremulous actress Meggie Albanesi's death occurred from abscesses caused by multiple abortions. Comedian Sydney Chaplin's career was destroyed by accusations of a horrific rape in which he bit off an actress's nipple. Hitchcock actor Donald Calthrop's adultery resulted in the object of his desire being immolated backstage in her costume crinoline. Victoria Hopper was moulded in the style of an earlier gifted actress by the lover who was responsible for her death.

Although their antics didn't make the papers (we had few scandal magazines in Blighty), cuckolded performers slapped their spouses' faces in fashionable restaurants or lived in blatant *ménages à trois*, while their lovers snorted cocaine off the glass dance floor of Jack May's nightclub under Maidenhead Bridge. Rampant hedonism filled the lives of these neurasthenic, needy players, and the result was often adultery, underage seduction, abortion, alcoholism and suicide. Gossip columnists were wittily savage about performers, but abstained from commenting on their off-screen relationships.

This was the background of the industry that had come to roost in Wardour Street. Hollywood quickly stamped its mark on English cinema, using our theatre network to shovel US product on to local screens, a hard-nosed but vampiric practice that continues today. Consequently, our inferiority complex remained in place through the decades, despite the fact that our stars projected wonder-fully complex personalities, from the smouldering silken sadism of James Mason to the selfish amorality of Alec Guinness.

While Hollywood retreated from adult themes, many of our writers and producers rushed to meet them. Michael Balcon's early Ealing films sought to project an image of Britain as a leader in social reform and a champion of civil liberties, yet many still considered the Ealing comedies to be snobbish and insular. This is nonsense, and if we really want to remind ourselves of backward-looking arrogance we should watch the James Bond films, exercises in self-congratulation that reimagined the failure of empire in more acceptable terms. Cinema is best when it's not obviously preaching, and British hits were often the results of accidents. Their directors remained less known, even reviled. Some were so inept that they would have been better off repairing buses than trying to fix stories; it doesn't mean they didn't sometimes produce glorious cinematic moments.

At the start of our film development there was a rush to shoot the classics and the great historical stories; after all, the nation was steeped in the theatre. Arguably, the first great English sound film is Alexander Korda's *The Private Life of Henry VIII* (1933). It was followed by films about Nell Gwyn, Rembrandt, Queen Victoria, Henry V, Caesar and Cleopatra, Isadora Duncan. Between them were social comedies, morality plays, dramas, musicals, filmed versions of the great Dickens novels, of the plays of Oscar Wilde and Noël Coward, of work from Shakespeare, D. H. Lawrence, A. J. Cronin, Graham Greene, Terence Rattigan, John Braine, H. G. Wells, Nigel Kneale and Joe Orton.

The casts and crews of such films were roll-calls of the world's greatest cinematic talents. It wasn't all good, of course. British film had some inexplicable stars. Gormless, spoon-faced George Formby had a wife who was paranoid about his leading ladies making passes, as if anyone would consider such a thing. Wartime audiences had to settle for the shrieking jollity of Gracie Fields and the mugging of 'Two Ton' Tessie O'Shea (who now looks positively svelte compared with modern bodies).

Meanwhile, the Rank Organization's unerring ability to finance inappropriate productions – from Dirk Bogarde's leather-trousered gay western *The Singer Not the Song* to the Nic Roeg arthouse doodles that horrified their executives – proved the shiniest nail in British cinema's coffin.

Even after this, though, there are delicious tales of the industry in decline. Nudism films like *Naked as Nature Intended* featured unappetizingly bare performers wandering around Cornwall eating ice creams and gazing at donkeys, while the relaxed new attitude to horror films led to Scottish actress Sheila Keith making a career-switch into heavy gothic gore at the age of fifty-five. British actresses presented themselves as self-deprecating throughout, dismissing their films and treating the idea of the Rank charm school as risible. They were unconsciously sexy: Patricia Roc's sultriness surfaced even when she was sawing at a loaf of bread with a fag in her mouth, and Kay Kendall won hearts by drunkenly playing the trumpet in *Genevieve*.

The best thing about English film was that we saw a reflection of ourselves, our women, our homes, our jobs, our lives. American movies had the glib talk and guns, but we recognized English behaviour when we saw it, and couldn't help but empathize. When Celia Johnson fell in love in *Brief Encounter*, she merely felt cheap, and a million middle-class English ladies would have agreed with her. With the passing of time, Hollywood films came to bear less and less resemblance to anything we could relate to.*

---

*Except Tobe Hooper's UK effort *Lifeforce*. In this film a beautiful naked alien woman is lured out of a building with the offer of a biscuit.

Hollywood Film	British Life
Man on phone to girl says, 'Meet me at the Plaza.'	Man fails to get through on phone. On successful third attempt he is forced to explain which Plaza, what time will be convenient and then give poorly explained directions how to get there.
Man looks into girl's eyes while driving car.	Man looks into girl's eyes and drives into back of van.
Boy climbs in through girl's bedroom window.	Boy attempts to climb up drainpipe, which comes away from wall. Is arrested.
Man takes out huge gun.	Man looks for something with which to defend himself, comes up with a magazine and an orange.
Man's boss says, 'Shape up or I'll fire your ass.'	Man's boss makes withering remark about class.
Teens find abandoned cabin in woods.	Teens find abandoned cabin in woods is now next to Tesco.
Man enters fabulous neon nightclub filled with gorgeous dancing girls.	Man waits outside club while bouncer cleans sick off steps.
Man goes on picnic with girl. They make love in a sun-filled dell beneath drifting blossoms.	It rains. Couple get soaked, look unappetizing, don't meet again.

This, then, was the world of English film that had passed, and now all that was left were a few scraps from the feast. At the tops of those wonky Wardour Street stairs were young men, too – but they were now scrabbling about for a few thousand quid to make films about psycho killers, rubber monsters and randy stewardesses.*

If it was a bad time to finance films, it was an even worse time to try to sell a script. I might as well have been attempting to flog them in a hospice. I was overbearingly keen, annoyingly geeky and generally offputting to the hard-drinking, chain-smoking men (there being virtually no women) who picked through the grubby leftovers of the English film industry. I had chosen the wrong time to try to enter the business. Video recorders were arriving, film sales had collapsed and, just around the corner, Margaret Thatcher would hammer a stake into the industry's coffin by removing its tax breaks.

After work and at weekends, Jim and I took to haunting the baroque red and gold cinemas that were soon to become DIY showrooms, discount carpet warehouses and theme pubs, feeding our taste for English B-movies. These were the films that were made because somebody had a bit of dodgy money to dispose of quickly, because somebody had become possessed by the flickering light of the projector, because somebody's girlfriend wanted to be a star, because a country house was available for a long weekend. They were made without the fuss and self-importance of committees. They were made with envelopes-full of grubby notes. They were made simply because their makers didn't mind losing money on a passion.

---

*Comics and character actors from my childhood were reduced to appearing in soft-core porn: Terry-Thomas starred in the gruesome smutfest *Spanish Fly* and Ronnie Corbett turned up in *No Sex Please, We're British.*

We trotted off to see *The Mutations*, a ludicrously tasteless monster throwback featuring Donald Pleasence, a man-eating plant-person – half serial killer, half lettuce – and several real-life 'freaks' including a gentleman who could pop his eyes out on stalks by suddenly concentrating. We sat through *Twisted Nerve*, starring baby-faced Hywel Bennett and Walt Disney's own Pollyanna, Hayley Mills, a film which ran into such trouble for suggesting that psychopathic behaviour was genetically connected to Down's syndrome that the producers were forced to bolt a hilariously dramatic disclaimer on to the feature. And we saw *Psychomania*, with mysticism-spouting Beryl Reid and a visibly un-interested George Sanders* reviving lame-looking elderly Hells' Angels from the dead.

Many of these films featured psychotic dancing at brightly lit parties by people with unfeasible sideburns who wore woven leather belts over huge-collared paisley shirts. They provided essential study material for anyone majoring in haircare and minidress design in Baby Boomer England.

Failing to appreciate that I had nothing to offer the industry except enthusiasm, I was frustrated and angry: with the times that lowered everyone's aspirations, with the capital's shrinking outlets for creativity, with the blatant class discrimination that shut me out of decent assignments. The BBC was still an Oxbridge sinecure for the tweeds-and-cravats brigade, whose numbers were swollen by an army of tea ladies, janitors, lift men and union officials who had nothing to do except sit around

---

*Soon afterwards, Sanders became so uninterested that he killed himself, leaving behind a note that read: 'Dear World, I am leaving because I am bored.' He had presumably been watching his own late film output.

the studio telling people it wasn't their job to tighten a nut or change a lightbulb.*

Wardour Street was tottering on its last legs. A handful of scruffy writers and producers worked the pubs, buying beers and bumming fags, trying to raise money for zero-budget sex and horror films, but the well had dried up even for them. 'English film' had become an oxymoron, the punchline to a national joke on a par with 'English car industry'.

At least advertising agencies treated their writers well, paying them huge amounts of money for doing virtually nothing. Bad behaviour was condoned so long as it attracted unimaginative clients who thought their lives might be enriched by hanging around with louts who knew long words. We had all heard stories of copywriters who'd driven motorcycles into boardrooms, set fire to presentations and hurled typewriters out of windows in fits of creative pique; it had become expected of them.

The prevailing moral vacuum also meant that it was fine to sell your soul so long as you got a good price for it. Our agency made its money by creating campaigns to flog sugary junk to children and getting busy mothers to replace fruit with bags of crisps in lunchboxes. The only account the management checked you had no problem working on was the pariah-like British American Tobacco, which was run by a sweaty account manager with a stutter, whose unappetizingly visual catchphrase

---

*In *Sparrows Can't Sing*, creepy Stephen Lewis caught the zeitgeist in his playing of a caretaker revelling in the zealous application of Health and Safety laws. His yell of triumph when a car is finally towed away probably landed him the role of the grimly proscriptive Blakey in *On the Buses*.

was 'Well, f-f-f-fuck me sideways.' Moral discomfort can be eased with a fat pay cheque, but as we lurched from one shockingly crap campaign to the next, Jim and I both felt there had to be something better for us, like grave-robbing.

To me, Jim was proof of what you could do with foresight and fearlessness. He had taught himself to draw and applied for work as a storyboard artist at Ogilvy & Mather, swiftly graduating to producer. The new PA he employed was a former Mayfair Playboy bunny girl* who possessed sizeable charms but no secretarial skills of any kind. Maggie would stare at a ringing phone until it stopped and breathe a sigh of relief, saying, 'Thank God for that, I thought they'd never go away.' She told clients things like 'They can't pay you because, frankly, I don't think they've got any money', and once told a client, 'Jim can't come to the phone, love. He's on the toilet and I can't interrupt him because I imagine he's already started.'

Many of our TV campaigns involved hiring actors by slipping them envelopes stuffed with cash. There was nothing dishonest about this: it was virtually the only way you could get anything done at that time. The *Goodies* comedian Tim Brooke-Taylor recently dismissed his involvement with Brentford Nylons by admitting, 'I was a whore.' Everyone talked about the power of the unions, the dues, the demarcation lines, the penalties. It was the true era of the jobsworth.

From those days on, my name was inextricably locked in with that of my producer. In the modern parlance

---

*She can still do the 'Bunny Dip' which prevents you from being pinched on the bottom, only now she has to be helped up.

of 'Brangelina' and 'Jedward'* we would have been
'Fowlgeon'. We were so much like Bialystock and Bloom,
the tawdry theatrical agents from *The Producers*, that
we even attempted to register their name as a company.
Considering Jim left school at sixteen, he had great respect
for the written word and particularly loved good scripts,
citing the first twenty minutes of *The Producers* as his
favourite sequence in film.† There was hardly a day when
we didn't share each other's thoughts, to the point where
we used to perform a mind-reading act at parties, and
we only stopped because eventually Jim was smoking so
much that he was unable to remember the master code.
Hothousing is a process whereby like-minded people leap-
frog off each other's ideas, reaching levels they would not
have managed alone. We were hothousing naturals and
loved working together, but although we both enjoyed
stories Jim was no reader, so we lived increasingly at the
movies. In every relationship you care about, sacrifices have
to be made. Besides, I was passing through a succession of
claustrophobically tiny flats, and found it better to sit in
a roomy cinema than go home. As Jim still lived with his
parents, he usually came along with me.

'They think you're a bit camp, you know,' I told him,

---

*Twins who achieved a nanosecond of entry-level fame for having
identical silly haircuts. They accidentally reversed the traditional role
of singers – that of delivering the joy of music – by making people
grimly aware of the sheer pointlessness of human existence. By the
time this book gets published you'll stop at this page, scratch your
head and fail to recall them unless they've become serial killers or won
the Eurovision Song Contest.
†Nervous accountant Gene Wilder attempts to do the books of sleazy
theatrical agent Zero Mostel, who terrifies him into the creation of
a scam, the entire scene conducted in an office just like the ones in
Wardour Street. 'You're going to jump on me. I know you're going to
jump on me – like Nero jumped on Poppaea!' – Wilder.

as we settled down to a double bill of *It's Alive!* (killer mutant baby)* and *Squirm* (the best killer worm movie in an admittedly limited subgenre).

'Maybe it's the beads,' he said, trying to get them off his wrist.

Maybe it's because everyone else knows you haven't come out yet, even to yourself, I thought, but decided to say nothing as I settled down to watch killer worms drill holes in the face of a howling hillbilly.

---

*Incredibly, there were two sequels. Scripter Larry Cohen was all story, no style, which is sometimes preferable to the reverse, although his film *The Stuff*, about murderous yoghurt, was a step too far.

11

The End

Shooting, acting, apologizing, reading, writing,
and watching celluloid vanish

'Quiet on set. We're rolling.'

The director turned round and glared everyone into silence. I had just walked into the hangar where we were shooting and, having gone from bright sunlight to penumbral darkness, couldn't see a hole in a ladder.

As my eyes adjusted I saw a kitchen set with a very large boiler, and the actors being filmed by a director who was in turn being filmed by another director. The first director was played by mincing seventies comic Larry Grayson, the latest in a long line of limp-wristed stereotypes beloved by the English Saturday-night TV-watching public. Grayson was smart, though. Quick-witted and gentle, he knew his limitations and exactly what he was doing. The second director, the real one – for this was a comedy about the making of a film – was a smooth-talker called William G. Stewart, who later perfected his smarminess by becoming a game-show host. I had written a half-hour comedy script for Potterton Boilers. Just about everyone in the cast was a showbiz name working for peanuts. We had assembled them here for one afternoon only, and could afford no mistakes.

I desperately peered about for Jim, who was producing, trying to locate his canary-yellow loons. There's nothing more redundant than a writer on a set. If the director's any good, the words have long been locked in place and all you do is get in the way of people who have proper jobs to fulfil.

In the distance I could see John Cleese, Graham Stark and Aimi MacDonald delivering their lines. Jim found me and whispered in my ear, 'Find yourself somewhere to sit and be very quiet.' I looked about. Behind me a large Victorian oak writing desk stood against a wall. As quietly as I could, I swung myself up on to it.

But it wasn't an oak writing desk. It wasn't oak at all. It was two sheets of polystyrene joined together with gaffer tape and spray-painted to look like a desk, a prop that had just been removed from the set. There wasn't a wall behind it, either.

I fell backwards through the prop and through the blackout psyche, and watched in horror as it tore at the top and continued tearing all the way round the studio to the rear wall of the set, which in turn fell over, landing on the actors.

I was thrown out of the sound stage. 'I'm doing this,' said the director, 'so that you remember and never do it again.' My first time in a studio put me off them for life. Whenever I went on to a film set after that, my stomach always turned over.

'You made a mistake, get over it,' said Jim. 'And stop saying sorry all the time. Remember, they're all here because of you. You're the one who puts the words in their mouths. If people want to grow trees they first have to do the watering, and you writers are in a great position, because you own the well. Remember that.'

'The actors were very upset,' I pointed out.

'Oh, *actors*.' He waved his hand dismissively, wafting clouds of Rothmans smoke over me. 'Remember what Zero Mostel said.'

I thought back to a scene in *The Producers*:

GENE WILDER: You can't treat actors like that! They're not animals!
ZERO MOSTEL: Yeah? Have you ever eaten with one?

Despite the fact that we were only making a crappy short film about boilers, there were some fairly good jokes in the script and I was excited about working with great comedians at such an absurdly young age. It took Jim many years to break me of the habit of always saying sorry. It was ingrained within me. I had been raised by parents who constantly apologized for being a nuisance when they should have been the ones being apologized to. There's an annoying English response that drives me crazy.

'Would you like a cup of tea?'

'Well, only if you're making one.'

How did we become so cowed? Was it something to do with the seventies, a time when so many people appeared to have caught disappointment as if it were the measles? All I heard around me was people saying sorry. Parliamentary speeches were either filled with toothless union bile or the damp drizzle of appeasement. Fire and pride and joy had been misplaced. In smoky bars and steamed-up buses, downbeaten individuals couldn't wait to offer up an apology. When served inedible food – 'Sorry, but this chicken seems to be frozen in the middle'; when poured a bad drink – 'Sorry, is there any chance of an ice cube?' It was a triumph of environment over heredity. Overseas visitors still acquire the habit of English apology within seconds of arrival, but in the seventies it felt as if some kind of shame peak had been achieved. John Cleese caught the mood perfectly with *Fawlty Towers*. In his 'Waldorf Salad' episode, he shows how the unctuous hotelier is unable to provide a difficult American customer with even a basic salad.

The only people who didn't believe their own apologies were those based in corporate headquarters, which had begun to spring up across the nation, ugly blocks painted in circus colours, with the reek of burgers in the lifts and muzak in the canteen. Companies had been thrilled to discover that we were only vaguely disgruntled when service deteriorated and promises collapsed. We had come to expect failure, because we no longer believed in the future. Fractured and disjointed by the very processes that were intended to make our lives easier, we found ourselves behaving like Russians in the 1950s, half-heartedly patching and repairing just enough to see us through, without a thought for anyone coming after. Even the Chancellor of the Exchequer admitted that he woke up every morning wishing that he lived in another country.

My father said, 'The trouble nowadays is that nobody wants to do any bloody work,' but as usual he was wrong. The workforce was being rendered powerless no matter how many hours they put in, because, for the first time, all major decisions were being made somewhere else by people whom they would never meet.

If the archetypal hero of the 1950s was Alec Guinness, eccentric post-war boffin, and the hero of the 1960s was David Hemmings, coolly arrogant fashion photographer, all the seventies had to offer was whiny Laurence in *Abigail's Party*, dying from stress in his cheap suit on the living-room floor, unnoticed and unappreciated.

The fifties had been frumpy and the sixties were psychedelic, but the seventies were cheap plastic, its population full of beery swagger, alternately picking fights and saying sorry. The music was rubbish: the Bay City Rollers, the Osmonds, Gary Glitter,* Slade and the New Seekers. TV was even more dire: *The Des O'Connor Show, Miss World*, Cilla Black and Benny Hill.† And I was part of a team proudly helping to make matters worse.

So, after turning the kindly, closeted Radio 1 DJ Alan Freeman into a national figure of ridicule with the Brentford Nylons commercials, we had switched to making short films for Potterton Boilers, famous for being one of the dullest accounts in the country. Using the wad-in-hand approach to casting, we ended up shooting surrealist promos for brain-flatteningly boring clients who wanted to brush – just brush lightly – against the magic of the silver screen, no matter how tawdry and distant the connection had become.

Thanks to such accounts we worked with most of the *Monty Python* team, Boris Karloff, Peter Sellers, Larry Grayson, Kenneth Williams and Terry-Thomas, all paid in grubby used fivers. I loved working with John Cleese, who proved to be consistently charming and filled with smart ideas on how to improve my dismal scripts. Martin Campbell,‡ the director who had taught Brosnan stillness, was drafted on board to direct our commercials. With the English film industry in dire straits, overqualified

---

*A singer who not only became a byword for paedophilia, but also entered the lexicon with an unfortunate piece of rhyming slang which will probably survive his own demise, like Ruby Murray.
†America still has a peculiar notion that the English love Benny Hill, in the same way that they believe the French love Jerry Lewis; but all anyone over here vaguely recalls is speeded-up footage of portly girls in Union Jack bikinis running around to the Yakety Yak track, and a song about a milkman called Ernie.
‡Campbell once stormed across a film set, seized an actor by his lapels and shouted 'Act *better!*' in his face. That did the trick.

professionals were mucking in and staying busy on lousy jobs and lousy money, just to continue working.

How bad was it? Well, in 1974 the big English cinema hit was the joke-free smutfest *Confessions of a Window Cleaner*, featuring Cherie Blair's father Anthony Booth as Sid Noggett. It was popular enough to spawn a series, and made the *Carry On* films look like the collected works of Pasolini. Against this, my boiler script looked like *Some Like It Hot*.

It wasn't just what we were watching and listening to. The popular literature of the seventies was appalling. There are certain books only college students have the patience to read. *Everything You Always Wanted to Know About Sex but Were Afraid to Ask* and *Zen and the Art of Motorcycle Maintenance* were romping up the charts in university towns. It seemed that students were prepared to read a novel exploring the life philosophy of an avian parasite: Richard Bach's *Jonathan Livingstone Seagull* smashed the bestseller records. The slender square tome was to be found poking out of backpacks all over the country. It concerned an anthropomorphic bird that yearned to fly higher instead of just worrying about where its next whiting was coming from. Millions swallowed the inspirational Christian parable which, at 120 pages (heavily illustrated), was faster to digest than a small pellet of white bread. It was so successful that it became a film consisting of shots of seagulls floating about to wiffly Neil Diamond songs, the overall effect of which was like lapsing into a coma caused by getting a paper cut from a Hallmark card.

Bach followed this bestseller with *Illusions* and *One*, the message being that we transcend the gravity of our bodies and believe in ourselves, or something. Claiming to be a direct descendant of Johann Sebastian Bach, the former-pilot-turned-novelist loved to explore the metaphysical aspects of flying. Bach's books were fictional versions of moments in his life that illustrated his philosophy. I liked to think that his books fell from popularity because students became too cynical to swallow this kind of tendentious, artery-hardening new-age sputum.

Of course, it's easy to think this now. At the time, I was writing scripts for boilers, pipe lagging, tyres, nylon sheets and car exhausts. With Jim as my producer I began churning out commercials for everything from department stores to crisps using every cheap, awful cliché I could think of involving comedy Santas, tightrope walkers, beauty queens, old ladies on roller skates, fat ballet dancers and people falling into wet cement. The great thing about exploring clichés is that you quickly learn never to go near them again.

Every week I checked the pages of *Screen International* for job opportunities. England's version of *Variety* was so thin some weeks that it barely needed staples, having become a parish magazine for a church without a congregation. I hung out with the few remaining Wardour Street writers I knew who were trying to get films off the ground, and they all looked used up by their efforts, like drug addicts who no longer enjoyed getting wasted.

We were two years away from the all-time rock-bottom for English cinema, a year which saw the release of *The Boys in Blue*, a grimly unfunny Rank comedy starring an end-of-the-pier comedy duo nobody even liked, and yet even in 1982 there were standouts: Richard Loncraine's period charmer *The Missionary* with Maggie Smith, Richard Attenborough's epic *Gandhi* and Peter Greenaway's oblique and haunting *The Draughtsman's Contract*. The following year there would be *Heat and Dust*, *The Dresser*, *Educating Rita*, *Eureka*, *Local Hero*, *Merry Christmas, Mr Lawrence* and *Monty Python's The Meaning of Life*. All of these came from well-established industry figures working hard to secure smart production and distribution deals. None were sequels, reboots or franchises (the Python film was unlike anything they had done before, and was entered at Cannes, where it won the Jury Grand Prize). What had changed was that the staple diet of English film-goers had vanished – the long-running stories and stars who had kept companies like Rank afloat through the decades had evaporated, and would never return.

My careers advisor had been proved right: jobbing screenwriters had become as much use in England as shepherds. I packed up all my scripts in a box and left them out for the dustman. I kept no copies.

12

On the Inside

**Writing, flirting, acting, old folks and standing
in the background fondling fruit**

One day Jim introduced me to some actors who had a
tenuous connection with the BBC. 'Well, I needed to do
something before you became suicidal,' he said. They invited me to join them on the writing of a comedy radio
show, a poisoned chalice if ever there was one.

There were six writers, and we were to be paid by the
number of minutes of material we provided, recording
in a mildewy basement studio in the Euston Road. It
looked to be about two weeks' work, but Jim wasn't on
hand to provide a level of quality control. Instead, I was
given a producer who had no sense of humour whatsoever.
(Surprisingly, quite a few BBC comedy producers wouldn't
have been able to pinpoint a joke with an electron micro-
scope and a mint pair of surgical tweezers.) He took out
all the laughs and put in his own terrible old-fashioned
puns, laughing noisily through his nose and showing his
work around while we all smiled, nodding and calling
him a wanker behind his back. I wrote all night several
days a week and delivered my scripts, only to have them

turned down and rewritten. I rewrote, and rewrote again, then discovered we were being paid per minute of material broadcast. The job took eight weeks and I eventually earned £32 before tax. The show was mercifully cancelled after being on air for just two weeks.

I was now on the inside, although only just. Through the BBC I met a theatrical agent called Derek who lived and worked in an extraordinary penthouse at the top of Baker Street, overlooking Regent's Park, and who acted as an old-fashioned mentor/den mother to a Fagin's gang of young writers and actors.

Derek was the type of theatrical agent who has now completely disappeared from London. Obese, screamingly camp, dressed in a bewildering array of awful Hawaiian shirts, leaking sweat from beneath an orange wig that looked like a dead marmoset and fooled no one, constantly pushing his glasses back up his piggy nose, he took all manner of waifs, losers and strays under his voluminous wing. Sweat trickled beneath his bulging eyes so much that his clients were misdirected into believing that news of their backstage woes had moved him to tears.

Armed with the world's largest gin and tonic, Derek nightly held court at his desk until far past midnight. 'Well, I have to be there when they come off stage, my dears, they need the *reassurance*, you see,' he explained.

These days he would be suspected of being some kind of sinister sexual predator, but in fact he was the opposite: harmless, kind and endlessly supportive. Every night his flat would fill with broke actors and writers who were between jobs, arguing about theatre, television and film until they were so plastered they could hardly stand.

'You can't go home in that state, love,' Derek would say, 'you'd better have another large gin while I call you a cab.' He fed them, lent them money, read through their lines with them and bolstered their deflating egos. We, in return, were flirtatious and amusing as we emptied his liquor cabinet and kitchen cupboards.

Most actors and writers remain invisible. When you look up their life's work, you realize you haven't seen or read any of it, unless you had perhaps caught *The Caucasian Chalk Circle* in Leeds Playhouse during two weeks in November 1979. A very small handful break into the general public consciousness, but most of the heavy lifting is done by these phantom toilers who stay cheerful in the face of poverty and virtual non-existence.

I met actors who performed on cruise liners, in prisons, on piers, in old people's homes and hospitals. There were girls who specialized in playing maids and waitresses, and boys who only ever got cast as policemen, standing silently in the background while an Agatha Christie detective reeled off his list of suspects in the East Sussex Playhouse. A girl I knew, Amber, briefly specialized in performing pantomimes in old folks' homes. In one such place in Sevenoaks she played Cinderella. During the intermission she waited in full ballgown costume at the foot of the stage because there were no changing rooms, and a very old lady approached her.

'I know who you are,' said the old lady, pointing at her clothes. 'You're Cinderella.'

'Yes, I am,' said Amber.

'Well, Cinderella, could you answer a question for me?' the old lady asked.

'I'll try,' said Amber.

'Cinderella,' said the old lady, 'where the *hell* am I?'

These performers appeared in dreadful old warhorse plays by Brian Rix and Francis Durbridge, usually at the ends of piers. They would leave a country house scene by climbing out of the window if they found the door stuck, or they would cover for Ophelia's late arrival onstage in

Hamlet by saying: 'That blasted girl's never on time – I bet she's been down by the river again.'

Regional theatres were minefields where at any given moment anything might go wrong. Sofas weren't secured and went rolling off sets by themselves. Windows fell out, boats jammed and trees stopped several feet off the ground. Curtains dropped and revolves froze, telephones rang too early and orchestras struck up the wrong songs. Amidst the upstaging and forgotten lines (sometimes entire pages were played in the wrong order and whole scenes missed out) someone would occasionally appear on stage who had nothing at all to do with the production. One of the actors, Jeff, told me about a woman who appeared on a chaise longue halfway through the big whodunnit reveal, thinking she had wandered into the lounge bar. The actors would soldier gamely on, through the empty houses and inattentive matinees, spending their lives away from home, never forming emotional ties with anyone but the company with whom they were engaged for this particular week.

Like the jobbing writers, these stalwarts were also under threat as provincial theatres lost money in the economic downturn. Many had been able to rely on film work to see them through years of dark theatres, but now they took early retirement, and entire generations of character actors were lost. The alternative was appearing in *Adventures of a Taxi Driver* or *Confessions of a Driving Instructor* and then never working again.

Even further down the ladder of celebrity were the non-speaking artists. I remember sitting on the floor of Derek's flat talking to a group of 'background actors' (extras). One complained: 'I hate early starts. I live in Barnet, in north London, and the travelling does me in. There aren't many showbiz types where I live. You can't buy *The Stage* in Barnet.' He told me they were experts at five types of scene:

1. Squeezing fruit and pretending to talk to stall-holders in market scenes, or slowly pushing trolleys in supermarkets, admiring shelves with unnerving intensity.
2. Chatting at restaurant tables behind the one where the main actors are sitting, but not looking animated enough to draw attention from the leads.
3. Appearing shocked in high streets when the hero passes them chasing someone, and staring after the hero tutting until the director calls 'Cut'.
4. Storming a building with placards and shaking their fists to protest about something, or besieging the hero for a quote as he leaves a courthouse.
5. Waving goodbye with little flags from the decks of ships, or, in cheaper productions, waving on railway station platforms as the hero leaves his girlfriend.

Some did modelling work for the Ugly agency. One quite elderly but very elegant lady told me: 'Once a model, you're always a model. You always find work but as you get older the kind of work changes. In my teens I advertised party clothes. In my twenties I did swimwear. In my thirties I played mums. Since then I've done irritable bowel syndrome, constipation tablets, slippers, colostomy bags and coffins. You take the work where you can find it.'

Another of the extras chipped in: 'Do you know what the worst part of this job is? The dry-cleaning. The casting director tells you to bring your own clothes, but the director wants you to run up and down a hill on Hampstead Heath half a mile away from the camera; it's been raining overnight and after two hours of running your trousers are ruined. And you end up not even being in the shot.'

Would they be happy to run up and down a hill in the background of a commercial for boilers?

'Oh yes,' came a chorus of prompt replies. They were just happy to be on the inside.

13

All Night

A full brain, *Tales from the Crypt*, sleazy
producers, drains, *Death Line*, all-nighters,
Diana Rigg and the noisiest film ever made

'Come on,' I said to Jim, 'let's go to the pictures.'

'That'll make a change. What do you want to see this
time?' he asked, attempting to blow smoke rings.

'How about a double bill of blaxploitation horrors?
Scream Blacula Scream and *Blackenstein.*' We'd just
covered Douglas Sirk and Federico Fellini, and needed
something trashier.

'Yes, I suppose so.' He never expressed annoyance with
my choice of films, although sometimes I caught him looking at me in vague wonderment. It seemed that nothing
ever surprised or dismayed him. Sometimes, when our
assistant Maggie was rambling theatrically, in the way
women who were once sought-after beauties tend to do,
he would smile and raise his eyebrows very slightly. It was
the closest he ever got to offering criticism.

It appeared that Jim had once had a girlfriend, but
nobody had ever seen her except his friends Ronnie and

Marcia. They had known him longer than me – the only friends I ever met who had – and had an equally mysterious relationship with him. When they married, Jim was the Best Man and held the groom's hand all the way to the church, to his future wife's great annoyance. When I asked them about this odd situation, they laughed. It made me realize that truly interesting people should always hide something of themselves from view.

One day we were walking through Soho and I was blathering on about obscure films as usual, and caught Jim looking at me.

'What?' I asked, stopping.

'One day your brain will be full. Then what will you do?' he asked.

'We could go and see a repertory film,' I said hopefully. 'There are plenty of English ones around at the moment.'

There were, too. Vincent Price was starring in the sardonic *Theatre of Blood*, a double bill of *Don't Look Now* and *The Wicker Man* was doing the re-run rounds and Alan Parker's *Midnight Express* was still playing in an Oxford Street armpit. One of Hammer's last films was the most successful in its history: *On the Buses* showed the way forward, and the sight of ugly Brylcreemed bus-conductors standing with their hands in their pockets, going 'Phwoar' at strutting miniskirted birds, wasn't one to inspire budding film-makers. Ever gluttons for punishment, audiences would then queue for the sequels, *Holiday on the Buses* and *Mutiny on the Buses*, also based on the cancerous bus-driver sitcom. This was what the public elected to see: sex farces about two gargoyle busmen trying to shag hefty 'dollies'. It was the end of the line for Hammer Films, and good taste in general. The studio had been brought low by its failure to appreciate the changing times. Its horror films were elegant fables

of good and evil, and because good always triumphed*
they were not taken seriously, never threatening the status
quo, whereas films by Michael Reeves and Peter Walker
usually ended badly by exposing the inherent venality of
humans, and had to be suppressed for the sake of common
decency.

After 1968, there was never again a time when the
English film industry was thought to be doing really
well, even if it was. When Colin Welland, writer of the
earnestly patriotic *Chariots of Fire*, stood on the stage
at the Academy Awards and announced 'The British are
coming', he unknowingly sealed off any future for us as
originators of great stories and reduced us to the status
of Hollywood employees. Hollywood does not appreciate
the strength of its competitors being announced from its
own stage.

Ever since the mid-seventies, people had been starting
to feel that the great era of cinema-going was over. Huge
advances were being made in video equipment, cinemas
were turning from cathedrals into crypts, and it seemed
that the two approaches would neatly converge in a new
small viewing format designed exclusively for home use.
Meanwhile, English films were consigned to grubby little
porn-houses off Piccadilly Circus.†

For those seeking a career in the industry, the times
paralleled the present – with one noticeable exception.
Nobody was coming out of college with a media degree
expecting to walk into films, because Wardour Street had
become a laughing stock and no one wanted to touch
English film-making with a bargepole. As city property

*The end shot usually featured the hero and his girl watching as an
evil building was cleansed by flame.
†To see one of the last Piccadilly newsreel cinemas in action, watch *An
American Werewolf in London*.

prices climbed, the seventies brought about the final desperate fling of the picture palace, and those huge valuable spaces were inexpertly carved into tiny screening boxes with lousy sightlines and sound that bled from room to room.

Traditionally, English films had fallen into two camps: those that were meant to be good for you, like church, and ones with jokes about faulty lavatories. Generally, it might be argued that English films were only ever about class, and that the concept extended to both sides of the camera. The cap-and-monocle directors of the forties might have chosen vehicles about the cheery poor, but upper-middle-class directors from Lindsay Anderson to Guy Ritchie were always careful to cultivate a laddish attitude for their not-terribly-daring capers. BBC directors were the worst: uniformly white upper-middle-class men who made jokes about having to put a penny on the licence fee if there were budget overruns.

All in all, it was a bad time to become obsessed with the idea of writing a portmanteau horror movie. Since the wonderful *Dead of Night*, these collections of mini-films, usually four of them inside a wraparound tale, had become an English staple, proving popular with audiences but especially with producers, because the episodic screenplay structure meant that they only had to hire guest stars for a few days apiece.

The Amicus film *From Beyond the Grave* proved an outstanding example of the genre, even though the stories, from veteran chiller-writer Ron Chetwynd Hayes, were pretty simplistic. The second tale, in which Ian Bannen becomes involved with unctuous old soldier Donald Pleasence and his real-life daughter Angela, is imbued with a creepy, mildewed seventies melancholia that's hard to shake off. An echo of Pinter can be felt in the Pleasence performances, and the low budget worked in the film's favour, depopulating London's narrow streets to the point of appearing post-apocalypse.

Portmanteau films of every kind had a happy history in England, from trios of tales by Terence Rattigan to the fondly remembered but risible *Dr Terror's House of Horrors*. The latter featured our man at Brentford Nylons, Alan 'Fluff' Freeman, terrorized by plastic weeds in a performance that, in all honesty, has not entirely stood the test of time. EC comic adaptations spawned movie versions of *Tales from the Crypt* and *Vault of Horror*, *Asylum* featured tales about patients in a mental hospital, while *Torture Garden* showcased the patchy post-*Psycho* stories of Robert Bloch. The portmanteaux were easy to shoot in segments, and although quality control of scripts clearly remained a problem, performances from reliable stalwarts including Herbert Lom, Joan Collins, Glynis Johns, Ian Ogilvy, Ian Carmichael, Margaret Leighton, Terry-Thomas, Peter Cushing and Roy Castle were never less than full-blooded. I went to see them in double bills and took notes in the cinema before rushing home to type everything up.

Stuffed into the world's mankiest flat (orange hessian walls, brown woven-straw lamps, stripped-pine louvre doors) in a then-unfashionable part of Kensington, I finished my portmanteau script and set off to hawk it around Wardour Street. The producers I managed to dig out sported corduroys and comb-overs. Some smoked roll-ups. They would seem strangely excited, and make rash promises about shooting my film in just a few weeks' time. Then they would go off the idea after a few meetings in grim Soho pubs. The awful truth dawned when I discovered one producer walking his nicotine-stained fingers up my inside leg under the table in The Ship, the Wardour Street pub. I was young, hungry and suddenly a bit less ugly than I had been as a child. It simply had not occurred to me that anyone would try to parlay my second-rate scripts into casting-couch shenanigans.

If this is film industry networking, I thought, *they can stick it. I'm only the writer – what on earth do they do to the starlets?* If I was going to sleep with anyone in the film industry, they had to be under fifty and not look like an ashtray in a jumper. I went home to see my folks.

It seems all women of a certain age can remember where they were when they first saw *South Pacific*. I know my mother could, because she sang selections from it for the rest of her life. Whenever I came home, I would find her by listening out for the chorus from 'Bali Hai'. Given her relationship with my father she should have been singing 'Gonna Wash That Man Right Out Of My Hair'.

'I can't stay long,' I called out to my mother as I came in through the front door.

'Never mind,' said Kath, unfastening the apron she always removed whenever the front door opened, 'it's nice to see you. If you need any books I've a roomful. Margaret next door died. I suppose it was a blessing, poor soul. What brings you over here?'

'Nothing, I was just passing by and thought I'd drop in.'

'But you live on the other side of London.'

'Yes. Can I use your washing machine?'

I went home at the weekends to do my laundry and listen to the latest skirmishes between Kath and Bill, usually only managing to last until halfway through the dry-cycle before shoving damp clothes into a bag and beating a retreat. Their fighting now seemed sad and pointless. It was obvious they would be together until one of them died. My brother was usually out with friends, so they had no one left but each other.

My father had broken his nose several times in his rowdy youth, and to me, with my newly acquired fancy Soho ways, he looked more and more like a street labourer, even though I knew he had been a scientist. To my horror I found myself becoming ashamed of him. There was a Peter Cook and Dudley Moore sketch that mirrored our relationship.

MOORE *(as father)*: My father went down the drains and I go down the drains. Our family has always been down the drains. But you, you're too big.

COOK *(as son, drily)*: Yes, Father, that's right. I'm too big to go down the drains.

And my father could not begin to comprehend what I was doing for a living.

'But what do you actually *make*?' he would ask. 'I mean, what is the point of it?' He would have been happier if I'd said I was being paid to build stocks to lock children up in, because at least he would have understood the problems of working with hinges. I got the same blank looks then as teenagers get now when they tell their great-grandfathers they want to build websites for a living.

'Your clients should spend their money making better quality products instead of hiring actresses to con gullible people,' he said, though this was a man who owned a gadget that cut the tops off wine bottles to produce cheap water tumblers. They cut your lips when you drank from them. He'd bought it after seeing it advertised on TV.

There is an age through which you pass when you simply don't want to be near your parents for a while. For all my mother's well-meaning help and good advice, I could not remain to hear the tally of slights and recriminations each time I visited. 'I have to go,' I'd say. 'There's an all-night horror movie bill I really need to see.'

'You're always going out,' said my mother with more than a twinge of envy. She had forfeited her teenage years to the war, which had begun when she was fifteen and ended when she was twenty-one. 'When are you coming back?'

I mentally calculated how many pairs of pants I owned. 'Oh, in about nine days.'

Dumping my laundry, I would race to one of London's many all-night cinemas. First up was Gary Sherman's cult classic *Death Line*, which really caught the shoddy mood of the seventies. Here the police were corrupt (and half-cut), politicians spent their nights seeking out Soho sleaze and teenagers were ridiculed by sneering members of the establishment, although the leads deserved opprobrium for their taste in big-collar shirts, wiggy hairstyles and moulting Afghan coats.

Death Line, so the story went, had originally been suggested by a copywriter who discovered that there existed a tube station called British Museum between Holborn and Russell Square stations. An old photograph of the tube station showed men in top hats sitting on the edge of a wooden platform, which was later replaced when they realized that it was a fire hazard. The station opened in 1900 and was closed in 1933, but was used as an air-raid shelter during the Second World War.

The story of *Death Line* assumes that early tube stations periodically caved in during construction, imprisoning the men, women and children who worked on them, and that the survivors at the British Museum became cannibals in order to survive. In addition to drunk coppers, perverted civil servants and faux-youthful protagonists in retina-searing clothes and flowerpot hairdos, *Death Line* offered class conflict, government complicity and a very uncharitable look at the tatty remnants of 'swinging' London. It appeared to have been shot on greasy paper, like so many films in this cycle, making you want to have a wash after seeing it; even now it feels horribly seedy.

English horror films did not strive for the gloss of

US products. Apart from anything else, they didn't have the budgets. Interestingly, the hero of *Death Line* is the tragically noble cannibal with higher morals than the politicians; he's motivated by love and loyalty.

The notorious poster for *Death Line* featured my artist friend Vic Fair's version of the London Transport roundel, redesigned as a skull. It was promptly banned (making fun of the logo was considered blasphemous) but the film remains a wonderful example of the morally ambivalent anti-establishment attitudes of the time. The first time I watched it was in a cinema in Russell Square, near to where the story is set – just for the verisimilitude.

Next up on my all-night bill was *The Abominable Dr Phibes*, directed by Robert Fuest, himself a graduate of *The Avengers*. This art deco high-camp gothic romp had Vincent Price avenging the death of his wife by gorily dispatching the guilty in accordance with the plagues of Egypt. The writing was sassy, the direction slick, and the film's structure had an appealing circularity that proved popular enough to warrant a sequel entitled *Dr Phibes Rises Again*. Unusually, the sequel proved as smart as the original, and felt like a logical extension of the story.* Phibes's success paved the way for this sub-species' crowning glory, *Theatre of Blood*, in which Vincent Price's ham actor destroys the critics who have ruined his career by slaying them in manners corresponding to Shakespeare's greatest stage deaths.

Requisite rules of these films included loopily inventive murders and mysterious, glamorous female sidekicks. In the latter film Diana Rigg took the sidekick role, playing in huge shades and a male-drag curly wig that made

---

*A third film, either *The Son of Dr Phibes* or *Phibes Resurrectus*, in which Dr Phibes took on the Nazis, was apparently turned down by Vincent Price. A dropped hurdle, I fear.

her look like a Newcastle dopehead. By now, the old trick of gradually shifting from mundane reality to a world of dark magic had been dismissed. As in *The Avengers*, no attempt was made to ease the viewer into a fantastic realm – they were simply dropped into an alternative England, in the same way that Harry Potter could not exist in a real English town where the most popular restaurants are Balti houses and Chinese takeaways.

The cinemas that ran all-nighters were little more than reeking doss-houses. They rarely screened arthouse movies, but settled for quintuple bills that drunk tramps could enjoy – for example, all of the *Fistful of Dollars* films shown out of order – or random programmes that could only have been put together by a partially sighted manager armed with a bottle of gin and a pin: say, *Carry On Up the Khyber*, *Frightmare*, *South Pacific*, *Driller Killer* and *Last Year at Marienbad*.

This was a step too far even for Jim. Faced with such fare, my producer would offer up the sort of sad smile you'd save for a cat you were about to put down, then spark up a snout and stroll off to the Captain's Cabin pub, leaving me to face eight hours of pick 'n' mix films, watched through gritty eyes in a cinema full of snoring, farting, homeless drunks, before I staggered back into work in the morning.

I had a high tolerance threshold for bad camerawork, hopeless continuity, amateurish lighting and lousy acting so long as the story was halfway decent, because I thought that for writers the story was everything. I loved English films packed with pages of dense dialogue, and especially liked plays that had been adapted for the screen, including Oscar Wilde's *The Importance of Being Earnest*, Noël Coward's *Blithe Spirit*, Peter Nichols's *The National Health* and *A Day in the Death of Joe Egg*, Peter Barnes's *The Ruling Class* and Galton and Simpson's canny adaptations of Joe Orton's *Entertaining Mr Sloane* and

Loot. These were the very films critics found uncinematic, claustrophobic and stultifying, but sometimes you just resent being told what to like.

With the exception of Barnes and Nichols, these playwrights had all written for the printed page. Joe Orton had taken his cues from the strange literary style of Ronald Firbank, a sickly child-man whose prose condensed whole worlds while leaving much unsaid. Asked for his opinion of literature, Firbank admitted that he adored italics: a typically oblique Firbankian remark. His books contain party chatter consisting of disconnected words and phrases, much as we might actually perceive them. Infamously, one chapter comprised nothing but eight identical exclamations of the word 'Mabel!' Firbank's novels were scribbled on postcards in hotel rooms heavy with flowers, but at a dinner party given in his honour he consumed a single pea. Strange plants can bear wonderful fruit.

However, you can't build a national cinema industry on films of people hermetically sealed in heavily draped drawing rooms, having peculiar conversations. The Japanese, Brazilians, Swedish, Cubans, French, Italians, and to some extent the Americans, were exploring space and light, silence and sound.

Then I saw a film that crystallized the problem, and changed my mind about film for ever.

The ABC New Oxford Street showed double bills of movies no one in their right mind would want to see. One Bank Holiday Monday, Jim had gone home to visit his phantom girlfriend and to see his family – the Sturgeon males were all the same: short, bald, snub-nosed and stocky, with identical friendly faces, as if they had been stamped out in pastry – and I went to the pictures. Sitting in the front row of the empty auditorium for the next three hours, I nearly lost my hearing. The double bill was

Genesis In Concert and Dario Argento's first UK screening of *Suspiria*. Genesis turned out to be an appalling synth-rock band I had never heard of, and presumably the projectionist was some kind of head-banger, because he'd cranked the volume to eleven.

Suspiria is still the noisiest horror film ever made. Nothing in it happens quietly. Doors shriek, girls scream, rain hammers down, glass smashes, and even the sighs of the title sound like hurricanes. Argento's *giallo** films – murder mysteries with sinister and increasingly supernatural elements – made less and less sense as he blundered erratically through his career.† For *Suspiria*, though, he was at the height of his powers. The astonishingly lurid set pieces tumbled one after the other, to the point where I finally realized something that had never occurred to me before.

In film, a story doesn't have to make sense if you're enjoying it from one moment to the next.

The plot of *Suspiria* is almost coherent until you start to examine it from even the most careless perspective, at which point it falls apart like Greek lamb.

Giallo films only ever made sense in the loosest possible way. Usually a black-gloved killer would murder several busty semi-clad victims in inventive, colourful ways before being unmasked as an outside suspect who had been traumatized as a child. The arcane methodology of stalk-and-kill was the point of interest, not the motive. Whether Argento recognized this or simply couldn't tell a story to save his life is still a matter of debate, although I strongly

---

*Italian for 'yellow', it comes from the origin of the genre as a series of cheap paperbacks with trademark yellow covers.
†Years later, I had dinner with him. He didn't speak any English and I didn't speak Italian. I remember nodding and smiling a lot. I think he asked me to pass the pepper.

suspect the latter. This narrowness of interest means that the genre must conform to a strict set of conventions, making it similar to locked-room mysteries or road movies, and therefore cultish. Argento's films used chiaroscuro colour schemes and lavish set design to release the images from the constraints of plot, making them almost freeform art pieces.

An essential element is the fetishizing of certain objects – the gloves, the weapon, the girl (nothing if not objectified), even childhood toys that sparked the trauma. These play roles every bit as important as the actors.

Suspiria starts with a young girl, Jessica Harper, leaving a red-and-blue-lit Milan airport in a thunderstorm. As she walks towards the glass exit doors with apprehension suddenly crossing her face, there's a close-up of the doors' pistons bursting apart, and as she steps into the maelstrom the ends of her scarf sweep up around her neck like a strangler's hands. The music ramps up, Jessica's white dress is lashed by rain as she tries to hail a cab, and suddenly all hell has broken loose. There are close-ups of woodlands strobed with light and water thrashing into drains, and an arrival at a baroque pink dance academy just as a girl is running from it in terror.

The next twelve minutes are virtually dialogue-free as broken glass, rope, knives, a gloved killer, a bleeding throbbing heart, a whispered secret, a soundtrack on which the metal band Goblin screams 'Witch!', disembodied eyes and screaming fill the art deco landscape. The sequence is so audacious that I watched it sensing that Argento had just killed his career. Nothing he could ever do would top this moment, although a few bravura sequences came very close. In the sequel, *Inferno*, an astonishing sequence featuring a flooded ballroom, a lost necklace, a chandelier and a corpse is inserted into the plot for absolutely no reason at all, other than to look cool.

Suddenly it was clear that story wasn't everything after all. The cleverest plot twists and the most controlled dialogue could never top the extraordinary experience of feeling something strange and beautiful, whether or not it made any sense. David Lynch later became a genius in this field, allowing himself to be guided by a dream-logic that shredded up the need for logical plot development and replaced it with powerful, irrational emotions.

It was the moment when I knew I would never write a film.

Suddenly it was obvious where English cinema had been going wrong, and why it had died. We had treated cinema as clever filmed plays, when we should have been marrying sight and sound to create visceral emotions. This meant that directors would always be the best writers from now on. And so, I believe, it has largely proved to be.

I staggered out of the ABC New Oxford Street feeling as if I had seen the future, and it didn't belong to me. Shattered, I returned to the agency to work on an ad campaign for strawberry yoghurt, but my head was filled with blood and screaming.*

---

*It would be interesting now to see what work I produced that day. I don't think anyone would have wanted to buy strawberry yoghurt from a shrieking female presenter in a bustier with a knife in her chest.

14

Really Mad Men

Going broke, sex on desks, mentoring, Morecambe
and Wise, Kenneth Williams and the concept of shame

'I think we're in trouble,' said Jim one afternoon.

'You may be right,' I agreed, watching as a pair of work-men lifted up the sofa in the reception area of Allardyce Hampshire and walked out of the door with it. Two more went past carrying the light fixtures.

When you start work, you think you're finally free and independent right up until the first time something goes horribly wrong, at which point it dawns on you that power was an illusion created to keep you working hard. Things were going wrong now. Temple 'Dynamite' Wilson, our superstar creative director, had vanished. One day he went to the shops and never came back. Rumours abounded. Somebody had seen him in Denver, Colorado. He'd been fired, he'd embezzled from the company, he'd seen it was going bankrupt and fled. I thought he'd probably had enough and found himself a better job. Whatever the truth was, his dream of setting up a hotshot agency that would stand the world on its ear was over. Brentford Nylons was the account that had kept us afloat, but it was crashing into insolvency. Ping went the strings of the owner's heart, and there had been no one around to succeed him. The agency was falling out of a plane without a parachute.

The staff kept poking their heads out of their offices, looking to see if it was safe to come out without debt collectors walking off with their desks. A couple of blokes wandered past with a hat-stand. Maggie, our ex-bunny PA, looked up from painting her nails in alarm, as if she'd finally been caught skiving. 'Is there something going on?' she asked, touching her hair into place just in case it was a stunt someone was filming.

An emergency meeting was called. There were no board directors to be found anywhere. It suddenly felt like being in the bunker with Hitler and finding out he'd shot himself. 'The phonelines are all dead,' said one of the art directors, panicking that the Accounts Dept had found out about his long-distance calls to his girlfriend in Thailand. The deadbeats and unemployables who constituted the agency staff thought they'd been rumbled, collected their expenses in and made a slow-motion scramble for the lifts, trying not to look as though they were screaming inside.

'It's time to clear our desks and go,' said Jim quietly. 'We'll never get a job as a team; we'll have to split up.'

The city was in the grip of a dire financial crisis. All around Soho, companies were crashing to their knees. We collected our final pay cheques and fled. I had no idea what to do next. Working in an ad agency had left me with a somewhat limited skill set.

Jim was offered a job later the same week, at a small production company in an alleyway off St Martin's Lane, and I was forced back into the profession, taking a position as copywriter at J. Walter Thompson in Berkeley Square.* Here I was teamed with an art director, a handsome,

---

*It all sounds so easy, doesn't it? School leaver, I'm afraid it was.

charming and slightly paranoid South African sex addict appropriately called Roger. He was oddly secretive, and kept a huge gold bar beneath a false bottom in his briefcase, in case he 'had to get out of town quickly'. He also had a lock put on our office door so that he could pick up girls in his lunch hour and bring them back for a quickie. Often he would meet a girl on the tube on his way into work, bring them into the agency and tell me to go and have coffee for half an hour. I would come back into an office reeking of perfume and post-coital cigarette smoke.

How he managed to persuade so many girls to have sex with him less than ten minutes after meeting them at eight o'clock in the morning was a complete mystery to me. I would come back to find everything swept from my work-space, and finally started complaining. 'Can you please stop having sex in here? I have to *eat* off this desk!'

Sometimes, when they were bored, Roger and a friend would go out into Berkeley Square on summer afternoons armed with a camera and persuade women to take their bras off. This being the sexist seventies, an extraordinary number of compliant females did exactly as they were asked.*

Roger was also having an affair with a female art director in the office. Sue had a pixie face, staring eyes and a rabbit-boiling temperament. She looked like someone who remembered every argument you'd ever had with her, and who'd continue calling you years after you broke up to re-evaluate, probably at two in the morning. She wasn't the kind of woman you would openly cheat on.

It seemed inevitable that she would discover he had been

---

*The *New York Times* bestseller *Body Language* had a chapter entitled 'How to Tell Girls Apart'. And there was a famous ad for trousers showing a man standing on a tiger-skin rug, but the tiger had the head of a woman. Nobody thought this remotely distasteful.

bringing girls back to the office. During an important meeting with the sherry client (very clubbable, very old-school), she stormed into the middle of our presentation and threw his underwear across the boardroom table, shouting, 'Get the hell out of my flat and stay out of my life!'

We subsequently lost the account.

Our team director was an angry little man with too many children who arrived at work with his cycle clips still on, and became angrier in direct proportion to the amount of fun Roger and I had. The tension in the department became so palpable that I dreaded going to the office, and the work (making commercials for German washing machines) was stupefyingly dull. Working in advertising, I knew now, was different from being a creative artist: it was about recycling popular misconceptions into thirty-second sales-bites. The only people who failed to cotton on to this were the 'creatives' themselves, who couldn't understand why their account executives kept complaining that there was no mention of the client's product in their commercials.

I had moved from tyres and nylon bedspreads to toothbrushes and insurance. Jumping ship at the first opportunity, I went to the venerable Masius agency in St James's Square, behind Piccadilly Circus.

In order to keep us at our desks for as long as possible, the agency had put in a hot-meal vending machine that dispensed a fully cooked carb-heavy dinner in a ring-pull can.*

My new boss was a gigantic, booming, wildly gesticulating, owl-eyed man with several chins and a deafening voice. Chris Shaper was the original jazz hands

---

*It was apparently an old invention, and must have been directly responsible for Scott failing to make the South Pole. 'Let's move on tomorrow, Oates, I'm stuffed.'

man. He looked like a huge white minstrel, and kept a grand piano in his office, frequently hosting drunken show-tunes sessions with singers like Elaine Stritch, Mel Tormé and Annie Ross. He was a committed church-going Christian with a devoted wife and loving children. He also had a strong gay streak but, through sheer willpower, transformed his wayward feelings into a source of immense enthusiasm, energy and passion for life, never acting on his private impulses. He remains the only man I've ever known who has managed to do this. I had never met anyone with so many contradictory personality traits, or who was so fun and so frightening to be with. He filled the few people who didn't love him with hatred and terror. He was whispered about behind his back. He polarized everyone, including the company's managing director. Working on his floor was like being trapped in court between Cardinal Wolsey and Henry VIII.

He became my mentor, but by a bizarre coincidence that neither of us was aware of, had also been Jim's mentor before me, employing my best pal when he had been a storyboard artist, even giving him the chance to become a television producer. He instilled in us both a high level of fearlessness, by being so fabulously embarrassing that it was an act of bravery even to go out with him in public. You never knew if you would survive the evening without glasses being smashed, punches being thrown and methuselahs of champagne that nobody could pay for being ordered.

He, in turn, had been mentored by a giant bearded yeti of a man, an advertising legend called Desmond who was so fat that he regularly broke his belts and had to knot his trousers together with his tie.

Being mentored was a fast track to a professional career, but it only worked with input from both teacher and pupil. The more questions you asked, the more responsive your mentor became. With growing confidence came the ability to challenge and question, and gradually the Socratic method of enquiry and debate developed to a discerning, sophisticated level. But by that time you were usually hammered.

This was the era of the four-hour agency lunch, of sending magnums of bubbly across bars by way of saying 'hello', of bellowing in bad Italian restaurants and falling off bar stools in grubby mid-afternoon boozers. Soho's afternoon drinking dens existed on the cusp of legality. Their owners bemoaned the fall from grace of their establishments: where Brendan Behan and Dylan Thomas once sat there were now only the acolytes of Francis Bacon, permanently plastered journalist Jeffrey Bernard and a bunch of agency ad execs arguing about vacuum cleaners or peas. Chris Shaper was a dyed-in-the-wool adman, but had an enthusiasm for all of God's gifts: charm, beauty, grace, the lyrics of Cole Porter, Gershwin harmonies, the thrill of instinct and the mysteries of intelligence. He needed to understand how and why things worked, and if he had known how to control his emotions he would have made a wonderful judge.

Charming, terrifying and increasingly wasted in a profession that was changing beneath his feet, he should have been a singer-songwriter, a showman-*flâneur*, but found himself knocking out jingle-filled commercials for fish fingers. Like so many other talented individuals he had been born out of his time, and ended up in the job of creative director because it was the nearest he could get to doing what he really wanted.

The agencies were filled with would-be scriptwriters, novelists, artists, singers, actors and composers who had novels, screenplays and paintings in their bottom drawers but who needed to pay the bills, and one day found that their dreams were irretrievably lost from view. An army of accountants was coming to replace their creativity, even in the reduced world of advertising, with data, demographics and a pile 'em high, sell 'em cheap philosophy.

In a way this was a good thing, because there were also a great many hopeless pretenders who assumed they were artists when they were simply making floor-polish commercials. The industry needed a spring clean. Agencies colluded in the belief that they were somehow improving the world with glamorous aspirations, when the reverse was true: they were filling a void with dead chatter, like badly tuned radio stations, and forcing rubbishy products on to people who didn't know that their lives were incomplete without them. If advertising had been required to advertise its own services with a strapline, it would have been: 'Providing The World With Detritus Since 1836'.* Not exactly something to be proud of.

But buried in the chatter were original voices, and Shaper's was one. Being singled out as the boss's favourite was the worst thing that could have happened to me. All the staff knew he looked kindly upon young men (in the same way that pupils always spot a gay teacher) and suspected ulterior motives where there were none. Shaper merely wanted to be surrounded by others who were fast enough to appreciate the barrage of ideas and banter that flew around him. Cleverness is not intelligence, but a curse that makes you disparage and dismiss those who can't keep up. Consequently, Shaper was in a dangerous position. Those staff members who were out of favour viewed him as a paedophile priest, but those who basked in his attention treated him as a god. He was tolerated by his superiors so long as he continued to deliver, and he worked hard to maintain his position.

*The date of the first paid advertisement, in the French newspaper *La Presse*.

With a Cheshire Cat smile plastered across his wide face he would drag me into his office, hammer out a piece of Stephen Sondheim and shout, 'You see what he's done with the internal rhyme and how it falls across the dominant chord so that it goes da-da-DA-dit-dit da? Don't you LOVE it?' before flinging me back to my desk.

He hired inappropriate performers for all kinds of commercials, simply because he wanted to work with them. At one point I found him rehearsing 'Consider Yourself' with the original Artful Dodger, Jack Wild, for yet another yoghurt commercial, simply because he admired Lionel Bart's music. Together we rewrote Cole Porter and Noël Coward to fit ads for peanuts and crisps, sausages and trains, just because we knew how to do it.

Shaper was a source of great old advertising stories, explaining to me that back in the 1950s instant cake mix had flopped because you only had to add water, which meant that housewives didn't feel as if they were contributing anything, so they changed the packaging to read 'Just add water and an egg' and it made women feel useful enough to buy it. He'd created commercials for British Rail featuring gangs of women chanting 'We travel Inter-City like the men do', which, incredibly, were seen as a feminist call-to-arms.

People with strong opinions always make enemies, and although Shaper could pull in huge accounts through the sheer force of his enthusiasm, others were sufficiently fearful of him to make sure that he would fail. His large-as-the-sun personality didn't fit the shrinking world of the recessive seventies. Oblivious to the warning bells sounding all around, he continued throwing clients out of buildings and charging opera performances to dogfood accounts. Personally I had no problem with the manufacturers of Frolic funding *Rigoletto*. Somehow it felt less fraudulent than insurance companies taking hospitality tents for the

Last Night of the Proms. These victimless crimes, in which Shaper introduced excitable clients to celebrities who got paid fortunes to be in commercials, seemed fair play.

My boss eventually overstepped his boundaries when he hired Boris Karloff to publicize English pubs. He wanted to meet the Frankenstein monster of his youthful nightmares, and he couldn't understand why the resulting commercial put punters off.

Now I realized why Jim and I had maintained our friendship; we shared the same zestful life coach. We had even picked up his catchphrases and linguistic tics. Shaper's tenure was coming to an end but we guaranteed that his deranged ideas would be carried forward.

Meanwhile, my apartment was costing too much and Jim was still living at home. 'We could rent a flat together and save a fortune,' I suggested. 'But it would have to be near a good cinema.'*

We found a ground-floor flat in north London's Belsize Park that had a rat-run through the kitchen but had a good local cinema, the Hampstead Everyman, then another on the river at Barnes that had fourteen flights of stairs and no lift (local cinema: Hammersmith Odeon). Jim had a playful side that made him everyone's naughty uncle, but he was also in some ill-defined way the father I had always wanted. He had simple sets of rules that, if followed correctly, could improve your life immeasurably. But on occasion our father–son relationship became claustrophobic; he once warned me in front of clients to put a cigar out before it made me sick, and began cutting up my steaks for me in restaurants until I finally stopped him.

Our lives seemed so intertwined and peculiarly incestuous that it felt as if we had turned into Morecambe and

---

*It's never an entirely good idea to share a flat with a co-worker. You find yourself arguing about invoices at three in the morning.

Wise. Jim hired those comedians too. I now found myself working with a lot of celebrities. One of my clients was the stationery-souk WH Smith, who hit on the idea of running interviews with celebrity authors whose books they stocked. Suddenly I was interviewing a peculiar mix of people from Irene Handl to Frankie Howerd. Morecambe and Wise turned out to be interesting, as it appeared that Ernie was essentially Eric's keeper. Upon him had fallen, it seemed to me, the unhappy task of having to keep the permanently electrified Eric under control. When we went out for lunch, Eric proved unable to sit still, sticking his spectacles on the back of his head to make the diners laugh and parodying the waiters, shouting 'Wey-Heeey!' across the restaurant until I wanted to kill him. I had grown up watching these comics, and they were heroes, but the first thing Eric Morecambe said to me was, 'You're going to be overweight. You'll probably die before you're thirty,' which I thought was a very odd opening conversational gambit.

His behaviour was funny for ten minutes, and everyone laughed indulgently, but it became relentless and finally painful. At the end of the meal, charming, patient Ernie was left to quietly clear up the chaos and smooth ruffled feathers.

The one personality who refused to publicize her book in WH Smith was Joyce Grenfell, who felt that Smith's was actively choosing to dumb down public reading taste, and stuck by her principles.

During this period, the happiest experience I had was writing six sketches for Kenneth Williams, who turned out to be quick-witted, generous and kind. I can't recognize the braying nitwit portrayed in TV biographies as being in any way the same person as the soft-spoken, thoughtful man I worked with. He sat with me explaining why certain phrases were funny and others were not, and how spoken and written humour differed. I still can't help wondering why he bothered with the *Carry On* films for so long. It couldn't have been the money. Perhaps it was like keeping a couple of awful friends and regularly meeting them for old times' sake. The early films were certainly no different from anything else coming out of the UK at that time, and a few, like *Carry On Spying* and *Carry On Up the Khyber*, were genuinely inspired, but the writing became cruder and more desperate. By the time the final film was made, the original cast had all gone and director Gerald Thomas needed to have the script's few amusing lines explained to him.

Jim and I joked about how we could see through the ruses of advertising, the commercials in which pairs of women discussed pine freshener* or frozen saveloys. Nobody wanted to sell products by examining their comparative qualities or prices. Instead, as choice proliferated and food items became indistinguishable from one another, a further intangible selling point had to be created and sold to the public, so more and more money was thrown at conceptual advertising that would eclipse the product and replace it with the idea of an espoused 'core value'.

American junk food outlets were among the first beneficiaries of this new approach. Clients no longer had to improve what they were selling to make money; they could just pay for glitzy commercial concepts and make sure that the adverts appeared with enough frequency to stick in children's minds, and so 'pester-power' was born.

---

*It tells you all you need to know about the sensitivity of people in advertising that these were commonly known in the industry as 'Two Cunts In A Kitchen' commercials. Recently a friend of mine heard the expression used in an agency presentation put together by a dozen white ad execs under thirty. They had been summoned to discuss how their client's product could espouse 'upstream values', including – ironically – diversity.

At one point I found myself in the agency kitchen (not a place where you ate, but a science lab where you invented weird new foodstuffs to flog to bored/busy consumers, a forerunner of Heston Blumenthal's goggles-and-liquid-nitrogen school of cookery) making a bright green peanut brittle/popcorn combo that tasted of peppermints.

From a writer's perspective, advertising was suddenly no longer about being clever. Instead it became a sinkhole of morally dubious, inferior products being sold on virtues that did not exist. The feeling coalesced when I watched a commercial for ready meals being created. Not enough steam was billowing from the freshly microwaved food, so a few lit cigarettes were stuck behind it. Suddenly the whole industry felt repellent. This, I imagine, is why there are so few senior executives left in advertising: there is such a thing as shame, even for a Mad Man.

Sick of selling obesity-inducing crinkle-cut crisps and lard-filled burgers, or presenting the false bonhomie of insurance sharks, we decided to set up a company that could promote something everyone liked to some degree, something that didn't make your teeth fall out or your kids hate you, something that would allow us to handle the slide into disappointment and apathy that had come to characterize the seventies, something we could mention to our friends without feeling the hot cringe of embarrassment. Ideally it would involve our passion: movies. But we simply couldn't imagine what it might be, or how it would work.

15

The History of English Film in a Single Chapter

In which the author makes a brief digression into English cinema for the purpose of illuminating his motives, featuring pullovers, pencil moustaches, drag, smut, unrelenting grimness and clockwork mice

We were all looking to get out, but we had nailed our colours to a mast without a flag. I was desperate to make a name for myself in English films, but the industry had finally expired after coughing up blood for half a dozen years. It was hardly surprising when you considered our glorious celluloid past. Thanks to our endless visits to the National Film Theatre, I always carried a potted history of English cinema around in my head. It ran something like this:

The 1920s and 1930s

With the exception of Alfred Hitchcock's native output, early movies simply transcribed old plays and music-hall acts almost as an act of preservation rather than entertainment. So while Tod Slaughter rolled his eyes and gurned in hammy melodramas like *Maria Marten – or The Murder in the Red Barn*, something he'd been performing twice nightly on stage for donkey's years, England's first film musical, *Elstree Calling*, gave audiences a variety bandbox of vaudeville acts which must have seemed wizened with age even when they premiered.

A handful of brilliant silent films, including Hitchcock's *The Lodger*, Asquith's *Underground* and Dupont's luminous *Piccadilly*, suggested we understood the new medium and had mastered it, but these films proved the exception to the rule.

Instead, Jessie Matthews attempted to become the English Ginger Rogers in a series of thick-legged, stiff-necked but relatively charming film musicals including *Evergreen* and the *Victor/Victoria* original, *First a Girl*. Comedian Will Hay was the only music-hall comedian to really emerge with a career intact, and that was more to do with the fact that his early films opened out stage routines to create a partially cinematic look. Certainly, it took a special talent to make a slapstick comedy about IRA gun-runners in *Oh, Mr Porter!*

By 1927 there were sixteen Hollywood movies showing in Britain for every English film that gained a release, so the Cinematograph Films Act required exhibitors to take a minimum percentage of English films that eventually rose to a fifth of all films shown. These 'quota quickies' had a deservedly dreadful reputation. They were generally cheap and poorly made, but often preserved music-hall acts that would otherwise have been forgotten. Hollywood's expensive polish got to us in the end. By the 1930s, most English films featured men sporting top hats and pencil moustaches, and women in silver gowns speaking in sibilant upper-class shrieks.

The 1940s

Audiences were treated to the patriotic stiff upper lip of Noël Coward, with films like *In Which We Serve* and the curiously affecting *This Happy Breed*, which chronicled the family events inside a terraced London house between the wars.* Upper-middle-class English heroes wore pullovers and ties at the same time, and always looked cold. Their women arranged flowers, seemingly for days on end.

Launder and Gilliat's *Millions Like Us* was prepared to touch on class differences during wartime, and in *Went the Day Well?* a sedate English village is shown fighting back against Nazi occupation. There were unbearable talent-vehicles for ukulele-strumming George Formby and his endless creepy penis jokes, slappable Arthur Askey, who was forever popping out of serving hatches and shouting 'Hello, playmates!' and the nails-on-a-blackboard voice of hefty Greggs-shop-assistant lookalike Gracie Fields. John Boulting made the memorably tough gangster film *Brighton Rock*, with the young Richard Attenborough turning in a cruelly amoral performance as the psychopath Pinky (Attenborough, it's worth recalling, later played the serial killer Christie in the dour *10 Rillington Place*, and, in the same year, a criminally violent policeman in *Loot*). But audiences also flocked to American westerns, weepies, thrillers and gaudy reactionary musicals which at least were more emotionally suited to the big screen than our brittle aesthetic ironies and cut-glass theatrics.

*Coward was obsessed with trying to get an overview on the passing decades, his most painful being *Cavalcade*, a pageant that covered the years 1899–1930. He was much more fun when he let his hair down and was sexually suggestive.

The 1950s

In retrospect, this turned out to be a relatively golden time for English cinema, with populist capers and heartfelt comedies, but the decade's austerity drives and changing social mores prepared the way for the previously unseen realism of single motherhood and furtive single-bed sex in films like *Room at the Top* and *A Taste of Honey*. The class-conscious dramas of the post-war years brought *The L-shaped Room*, *The Loneliness of the Long Distance Runner*, *Billy Liar* and *Saturday Night and Sunday Morning*. Writers like Alan Sillitoe and Keith Waterhouse perfectly caught the disturbing transitional mood of fifties teens. Other, lesser films were as much fun as visiting half-forgotten relatives on wet Sundays.

What's most noticeable now is how everyone seemed to be living in boarding houses after the war, and how dark and shadowy the damp, soot-stained cities were. While we were watching *Genevieve* at my parents' house, my father Bill remarked that he really enjoyed the film, even though he had gone out for a cup of tea and a smoke in the most crucial part of it. 'Oh, it wasn't the story,' he explained. 'I just liked looking at how clean the streets were back then.'

The films of Powell and Pressburger were unclassifiable, covering a range of subjects that included the power of landscape, sexual repression, the changing face of warfare, the afterlife, opera, ballet and voyeurism. *The Red Shoes* created a generation of would-be dancers, but I imagine that the rest of their output would have been an acquired taste at the time.

Best of all there were the Ealing comedies: unsentimentally written and exquisitely constructed, created by a small team of regulars who pitted quirky underdogs against bureaucratic forces, they examined the self-deprecating aspects of Englishness. *Passport to Pimlico* was made to celebrate the end of rationing. The opening scene leads us to think we're in a hot Latin country, until the samba music turns out to be a radio tuned to 'Les Norman and his Bethnal Green Bambinos', and the camera reveals that we're above a wet-fish shop on a sweltering day in London. When the borough of Pimlico is discovered to be a part of France, the sun shines and everyone is happy. As the law returns it to English soil, the temperature plunges and it starts to rain. These are films from an era slightly before my memory, and yet it feels as if they form my childhood; perhaps we all yearn to discover the secrets of the period immediately before we were born.

The 1960s

The fifties' neo-realist trend ended in the sixties after *This Sporting Life*, and thanks to the Beatles crossing over successfully into cinemas with *A Hard Day's Night* and *Help!*, English film exploded into widescreen colour. Even a comedian of such peculiarly narrow talents as Charlie Drake* could make widescreen comedies such as *The Cracksman*. When a frozen-faced Cliff Richard drove a London bus from dull, rainy, monochrome England to Technicolor France in Peter Yates's *Summer Holiday*, the moment touched a national nerve, and young audiences, lured by the strapline 'The Young Ones have gone abroad!', queued around the block to hear him sing about why he would always remain a Bachelor Boy. Tony Richardson's astonishing *The Charge of the Light Brigade* rewrote the rulebook on historical epics – although few realized it at the time – by revising the tragedy and reversing its heroics into a blackly comic exploration of military

---

*His irritating catchphrase 'Hello, my darlings!' made him a distant relation of Arthur Askey. Audiences had their patience repaid when his on-screen co-stars hit him, often very hard.

pigheadedness. Even comedies became sumptuous, as the Pink Panther films brought a steady parade of glamorous, heavily cantilevered European starlets to our screens.

A disproportionately large number of influential films in the fifties and sixties were homegrown. The raising of UK actors to iconic status often seemed accidental. In fact, the story of English film is a history of accidents. It created unlikely celebrities, and brought out the best in them. Comedic chameleons Alec Guinness and Peter Sellers were both bankable stars. Audiences loved Rex Harrison, David Niven and John Gregson, all of whom were a bit long in the tooth to be matinee idols. Dirk Bogarde stood alone as someone who could move between artistically brave films like *Victim* and *The Servant* to *Doctor at Sea*. Elderly Margaret Rutherford took the lead role in a series of energetic Miss Marple films, forever climbing up ladders and hoicking her bulk over walls. Michael Caine raised his profile to action hero by starring with Stanley Baker in the hugely popular *Zulu*, a film which schoolboys everywhere went to see because it featured bare-breasted native women jumping up and down. Even the annoyingly cheerful Tommy Steele turned in a halfway decent performance in *Where's Jack?*, a biography of the highwayman Jack Sheppard.

By the middle of the sixties, films had the confidence of style to produce *Darling*, *Tom Jones*, *The Ipcress File*, *The Italian Job*, *Performance* and many others, but the final stage, in the way of all cycles, shifted away from genteel black comedy into overblown surrealism and decadence.

Hammer endlessly recycled sets and extras, shooting films back-to-back so closely that they appeared to be in matching pairs. *Carry On Cleo* was only made because it could reuse the set from the disastrous *Cleopatra*, while *Curse of the Werewolf* found itself with a Spanish setting in order to use sets originally built for a Spanish Inquisition drama called *The Rape of Sabena*. The make-do-and-mend mentality of wartime had infiltrated English film because it was always treated as the poor cousin to the rest of the arts. Hollywood was shameless about its intention of making money but Rank and Gainsborough appeared unable to countenance the thought, because financial success wrought from popular entertainment was simply an embarrassment. As a consequence, by the time we entered the seventies there were only two types of English film left: bin-scraping comedies nobody wanted and art films nobody watched.

The 1970s

The optimism of the previous decade had rotted into an odd form of English cynicism. How could satirical, darkly surreal films like *If . . .* and *The Bed-Sitting Room* ever have made it through the funding system? Peter Medak's filmed version of Peter Barnes's play *The Ruling Class*, about madness, old money and the entropy of the upper classes, is a particularly tough one to explain. A scabrous condemnation of inherited old-school values, its delirious central image has Peter O'Toole as an earl who believes he is Jesus Christ and Jack the Ripper. It uses song and dance routines to break the fourth wall and bring vaudeville into a tragic farce. The closing image of the House of Lords presented as a mausoleum of rotting corpses was considered clichéd at the time, but was widely copied.

Meanwhile, director Lindsay Anderson's repeated efforts to bite the hand that fed him featured Malcolm McDowell as Mick Travis, an everyman stumbling through the collapsing standards of burned-out Britain, but Anderson's jaundiced state-of-the-nation reports succumbed to the curse of broadside satire. The manic, club-footed jibes at health, monarchy, labour unions, management and workers in *Britannia Hospital* made *If . . .* look positively restrained, and provided the nail in this cycle's coffin.

The only other English films on show were smutty farces like *I'm Not Feeling Myself Tonight**, low-rent horror films like *Schizo*†, bizarrely camp comedies like *Our Miss Fred*, starring 'male actress' Danny La Rue, and TV spin-offs like *Are You Being Served?* The plots of these usually involved small-screen characters going on Spanish holidays and making weirdly inappropriate sexual innuendos while in drag. Occasionally comics were so convincingly cross-dressed that it messed with the audience's sexuality. Don't even talk to me about Norman Wisdom dolled up as a nurse in *A Stitch in Time*. I was seven, okay?

The 1980s

A new decadence appeared in the eighties. Everyone suddenly had to be young and pretty and rich for ever. This new infantilization led to moments of horror, as TV's *Golden Girls* forced us to think about very old ladies cruising for sex. With the Ages of Man reset to single figures, Linda Evans wrestled Joan Collins on *Dynasty* and Jamie Lee Curtis raised her leg-warmers in *Perfect*. The bright-hued films of John Hughes and John Landis danced into our blond-wood and pastel-toned decade, leaving English films stranded on rainswept council estates and caravan sites. With an air of conscious perversity, Mike Leigh's films continued to show glum couples sitting in terraced houses asking each other, 'You all right, darlin'?' while mainstream audiences looked the other way.‡

---

*A film notable for featuring the only female member of the seminal industrial band Throbbing Gristle.
†Which had the tasteful tag-line, 'Schizophrenia . . . When the left hand doesn't know who the right hand is killing!!'
‡Yet in decades to come, Leigh may provide the only truly accurate portrait of England on film.

Worse was to come: popular films sought ever-younger audiences in the knowledge that children were less discerning, and the box-office take was always higher for a movie with a general certificate. All of which left adult audiences stranded on their chrome microscooters in three-quarter-length trousers, texting rubbish into cellphones, desperately trying to keep up with The New Yoof. Decadence is the substitution of sensation for feeling, and, for the most part, it looks like it's here to stay.

One other strand of late English film needs to be mentioned – the so-called 'Heritage cinema' films sparked by Ismail Merchant and James Ivory, usually starring Helena Bonham Carter. The critics hated them because they appeared to be shaped around conservative, traditional narratives, conforming to the American image of Ye Olde England.

This is neither fair nor true. The Merchant Ivory team's writer, Ruth Prawer Jhabvala, a German/Polish liberal living in Delhi and New York, crafted wonderfully intelligent screenplays from good source books. Likewise, director Charles Sturridge was producing his own version of 'Heritage cinema', first with *Brideshead Revisited*, then with *Where Angels Fear to Tread* and *A Handful of Dust*, Evelyn Waugh's coruscating satire about the New Philistinism, which confused and divided critics.

But why? Satire is not always easy to appreciate. Make it too broad (as in Lindsay Anderson's *Britannia Hospital*) and it displeases the cognoscenti; make it too surreal (as in Ivory's *Savages*) and it displeases general audiences. 'Heritage cinema' was a lazy catch-all that imagined ladies in big frocks emoting beneath proscenium arches. But Sturridge did something very clever. He played *A Handful of Dust* straight, turning satire into Greek tragedy. There's a good reason why James Wilby's Tony has the surname 'Last' – he'll prove to be the end of his line. Just as his wife

Brenda, always seen in fox-furs, is later confronted by the caged fox that she is doomed to become.

As was the case in *Howard's End*, *A Handful of Dust* concerns property, a country house called Hetton that has been in Tony's family's hands for centuries. He has married beautiful Brenda (Kristen Scott-Thomas) and they have a son who will inherit. Bored in the country, she starts a dalliance with pretty London wastrel Beaver (Rupert Graves) that leads to tragedy. That's the framework – except that the tragedy occurs not at the end but at the midpoint, and the fallout from it brings in Judi Dench, Angelica Huston and Alec Guinness in a comedy so black that the final chapter of the book was often repackaged in collections of horror stories.

Sturridge ameliorated the source-book, opening the film with a surreal dream that only makes sense after the film has ended. By the time Tony heads off to placate Brazilian tribes, armed with a box of yellow clockwork mice, we should have realized we were a very long way indeed from the patriotic cinema of *Chariots of Fire* – this is about the end of empire, the failure to adapt, the hypocrisy and pointlessness of moral decency.

And there you have it: a cycle that went from music hall to patriotism to naturalism, then back to low farce. English film creativity in a nutshell. In the following two decades there would be a number of excellent homegrown arthouse hits, but the age of consistently popular English cinema was gone for ever.*

---

*The heritage industry rolled on. *The King's Speech*, with its winning combination of royal intrigue and an adorable speech impediment, was touted as a hit even before its completion, and consisted of three people wittily complaining in a very drab room; proof that nothing had really changed.

16

Beautiful Women

Stopping a landslide with your knickers, acid-tongued women, heroes and flower-arranging

If English film had its tweedy, pipe-sucking heroes, it also had a surprisingly strong line-up of women who weren't merely beautiful on the outside. There has been a long line of glamorous English stars from Greer Garson to Jacqueline Bisset, Samantha Eggar and Kate Winslet, but they have tended to seek out more fully fleshed roles than their US counterparts. The curiously English pleasure taken in linguistic sarcasm and spite led to a surprising number of roles for sharp-tongued women, including Eileen Atkins, Dora Bryan, Joan Collins, Hermione Gingold and the castratingly vituperative Glenda Jackson.

Jenny Agutter must have grown tired of being remembered as the schoolgirl attempting to stop a landslide with her knickers in *The Railway Children* (especially when the film was largely stolen by her wonderfully dignified on-screen mother Dinah Sheridan), but there were hundreds of other iconic females in English films, from the ethereal Anna May Wong in *Piccadilly*, to tough-talking Honor Blackman in *Goldfinger*. I loved the moment when Julie

Christie came swinging around the street corner in *Billy Liar*: it was an image of freedom, youth and independence that did not simply rely on sex appeal. Diana Dors (née Diana Fluck), on the other hand, was promoted as the English Marilyn Monroe – some of the photographs in which she wears skin-tight silver dresses are astonishingly curvaceous – but she finally transcended her cheesecake roles to become a fine character actress.

Many of our leading ladies found film success in later life, having first established themselves on the stage. Margaret Rutherford, Dame Edith Evans and Maggie Smith all made themselves indelible presences through carefully chosen roles. A great many had the kind of earthy qualities you rarely found in Hollywood films that probably stemmed from their backgrounds. Jessie Matthews came from a huge poor family in Soho. Sheila Hancock's parents ran a pub in King's Cross. Shirley Anne Field was raised in an orphanage. Vivien Leigh, Merle Oberon and Joanna Lumley were all born in India.

There were plenty of very proper English roses, too, from Dinah Sheridan and Jean Simmons to Julie Andrews, Claire Bloom and the husky-voiced trio, Valerie Hobson, Fenella Fielding and Joan Greenwood (who subverted her image brilliantly as the amoral Sibella in *Kind Hearts and Coronets*).

Hollywood produced few drily funny women, but English films are peppered with them,* including jolly-hockey-

---

*And they very often got to make jokes about drinking, for some reason:
SISTER: It's Matron's round.
PATIENT: Mine's a pint!   (*Carry On Nurse*)

RAYMOND HUNTLEY (*working out value of treasures*): Pitchers, goblets and ewers to the value of—
BLOKE AT BAR: What's 'ewers'?
WOMAN AT BAR: Mine's a pint!   (*Passport to Pimlico*)

sticks Joyce Grenfell,* Irene Handl, June Whitfield, Thora Hird, Kathleen Harrison, Barbara Windsor, Kay Kendall, Margaret Leighton, Hattie Jacques, Glynis Johns, Peggy Mount, Beryl Reid, Joan Sims and Julie Walters.

English female roles often allowed women to be acidic, domineering, angry, tough, complex or simply unusual. Lynn and Vanessa Redgrave, Celia Johnson and Deborah Kerr made films in which women did not simply fit into standard romantic roles. With the exception of a handful of stars like Bette Davis, Joan Crawford and Jean Harlow, Hollywood preferred to use its ladies as little more than set dressing, and most of them never said anything rude. Back in the UK, secondhand clothes dealer Irene Handl was telling a customer in *Smashing Time*, 'You've got to watch these teenagers. Turn your back on 'em for a minute and a nice bit of skunk vanishes up their knickers.'

The cheekier our women were, the more we liked it. The idea of a nurse inserting a daffodil into cantankerous Wilfred Hyde-White's bottom as a practical joke tickled the national funny-bone and propelled the *Carry On* films into becoming the nation's longest-running film series. We were equally obsessed with dressing our men up as women, something that was done with such a spirit of affection that it was impossible to take offence.

Through the decades of English film-making, one type of story vanished completely: the real-life hero genre. Once we had biographies of everyone from Lawrence of Arabia to Florence Nightingale, tales of explorers, conquerors, political leaders, kings, queens and captains, but the subject became confused by a fragmenting of perspective, so that one person's hero became someone else's enemy.

*As WPC Ruby Gates she harassed her fellow St Trinian's copper with, 'Oh Sammy, you used to call me your little Blue Lamp Baby.' This is only funny if you know what she looked like.

This meant that, just as there can be few new statues to political leaders unless everyone is in agreement about their true place in history and their status as role models, the only popular hero films we feel comfortable about viewing now are ones where a man in tights lifts burning rocks.

Did English films feature strong women because our men were so passively portrayed? It certainly seems that way. Brenda De Banzie ruled the roost in *Hobson's Choice*, and you only have to look at the family in *This Happy Breed*, where it is clear that the head of the household was Celia Johnson, not her contemplative husband Robert Newton. There's another factor at work here, though: the English antipathy towards sentiment in any form prevented women from being portrayed as mere outlets for grief and sympathy. The war had scoured away the little patience we had with middle-class ladies who merely arranged flowers on our screens.

17

The Big Idea

The art of selling films, conned artists, the
Rank way of doing things, and George Hamilton
in a caff with a crusty cheese roll

'We need to invent a company of our own,' I told Jim in the smoky snug bar of The Lemon Tree in Covent Garden one evening. The pub was filled with musicians from the English National Opera, who used to slam down as many gins as possible before performances. 'All we have to do is come up with something no one's ever thought of before.'

Jim didn't say much. He didn't need to – the single raised eyebrow spoke volumes.

'What's wrong with that idea?'

'Well.' He sat back and released a jet of blue smoke into the already fuggy air. 'We're in lousy jobs, we've no money, we've no way of raising any, and we're out of ideas.'

'Yeah,' I agreed, 'but apart from that.'

'I suppose we could borrow some.' Jim was permanently in debt. He collected so many parking tickets that the kindly, despairing judge at Bow Street used to cut deals with him, just so that when they bumped into each other in the pub it wouldn't be embarrassing.

'What are you working on this week?' I asked. Jim had moved to a production company in Goodwins Court, off St Martin's Lane, where Joe Orton's agent Peggy Ramsay still had her offices. The courtyard was managed by two tiny old thespian brothers who made most of their money appearing in pantomime. Every Christmas they wandered down the ginnel wearing matching Santa Claus outfits, giving out presents.

Jim sipped his pint of Kronenberg and thought for a moment. 'I'm doing a documentary on Country and Western music and a broadcast from a North Sea oil rig. They haven't paid me since I arrived. What about you?'

'I'm thinking of writing a history of English cinema.'

'That should be a short book.'

'I can't imagine I'll sell it.'

'Then why bother to write it?'

'Perhaps English cinema will become popular again.' Even as I said those words aloud, I knew it was a doomed idea, like suggesting we would once more become a naval power to be reckoned with. We were both screwed.

Hollywood had tightened its grip on English audiences. The hits at the box office that month included *Rocky* and *The Bad News Bears*, films which were proved by test-screening results to hold little or no interest for local cinema-goers. But what people liked no longer mattered. If you sold any product hard enough people would buy it, because there was nothing else. Print five thousand copies of anything, books or films, and you'll sell a proportion of that figure.

Three weeks later we were still sitting nursing warm lagers, Jim and I, this time in The Ship, Wardour Street, still racking our brains. I was in my mid-twenties and he was hitting his mid-thirties, and neither of us was going anywhere fast. We needed to come up with something before we joined a long and illustrious line of embittered, frustrated Soho alcoholics in a slow waltz to the career grave.

One option was getting out of the business completely and joining the burgeoning ranks of property developers who were busy destroying London's homogenous high streets. The other option was to find a tiny untainted area that no one had claimed and make it ours. Jim tapped his bitten fingernails on the tabletop and racked his brains. I stared vacantly into my beer.

With hindsight I can see that Britain was gearing up for the eighties, and the ugly but partly necessary cruelties of Thatcherism. Lured by the rebellious glamour of the 1968 Paris riots and the Prague Spring, too many students had gone to art colleges. Finding a job was increasingly a game of musical chairs, and when the music stopped most found themselves without a seat to sit on.* Ideally, Jim and I wanted to find something that wouldn't make us feel humiliated when we went to work. We loved film, but his career as a producer and mine as a writer had not taken flight. What was the next best thing? How about combining an evil we knew – advertising – and something we liked – movies?

In the late 1970s, selling films was a relatively simple process: film distribution company executives saw a bunch of movies, often bought them in batches that allowed, say, one good picture and two B-movies, and, being committed to releasing them, visited three middle-aged men who sat in two rooms in Charlotte Street. One of these men, Eric Pulford, hand-drew the *Carry On* film posters. The other two, Vic Fair and John Stockle, did the same with Hammer horror film posters and everything else that came through

---

*Now, degrees in media studies and psychotherapy are largely reduced to the value of knitting or papier mâché, and technically count as hobbies.

Rank Films. All three were brilliant artists, immensely talented, underpaid and under-appreciated. Now that far fewer art directors can draw, they increasingly look like Michelangelos.

They surrendered their artwork (often finished in felt-tip pen because Rank Films were too cheap to pay for paint) and it was printed. The posters were loaded into vans along with the film cans, because the cans had to be delivered to cinemas. And that was it. No planning, hardly any research that wasn't hearsay, just instinct and ideas – and the system sort of worked. Britain needed its own film posters because of a peculiarity in our national architecture. We had 'quads', a landscape-shaped poster that fitted in the gap below the nation's shop windows. The artists did not own the rights to their own artwork, and rarely even bothered to keep copies.

But then the system collapsed. There were hardly any more English films, and the distributors lost touch with their audiences. When Rank executives saw *The Wicker Man* they were horrified, and famously chopped it to shreds. The missing sections of film supposedly ended up beneath a section of motorway, although this story is most likely apocryphal. I wish I could have seen the faces at Rank when they sat through Nic Roeg's *Performance*. The company had once produced and released the cream of English films, but had badly lost its way. Now it was run like a branch of Woolworths, and nobody knew quite what they were meant to be selling. More problematically, they had no idea what young audiences wanted any more, or what constituted a good film. What if we could reconnect the distributors and the audiences?

We decided to set up a company purely to market films. The name 'Bialystock & Bloom' was taken, so we called ourselves, with a stunning lack of originality, The Creative Partnership. After registering the name we went to see the three artists, who now had an agency in Wardour Street, and offered to handle film advertising in exchange for a couple of rent-free rooms. To our utter amazement they agreed. We moved in a day later and started work. My careers advisor had clearly missed a trick there.

In Hollywood, distribution companies worked out of glittering glass and steel offices surrounded by tall palm trees. Rank Film Distributors looked like a sub-post office in Ipswich. Decorated in olive-green and nicotine-brown paint, the Rank building had an outside toilet, filthy windows and flickering strip lights. It seemed to be entirely staffed by chain-smoking old men hanging on for their pensions.

The best position any woman could expect to achieve in the company was that of tea-maker. Wandering around offices stuffed with metal filing cabinets and faded girlie pin-ups made one lose the will to live. In the basement, the staff screening room was presided over by a lovely gentleman called Brian who was nicknamed Beryl, because he was famous for his Christmas performances as a pantomime dame.* It was an unspoken understanding that females were not welcome in the screening room. Occasionally a secretary would be allowed in as a treat,

---

*England has a peculiarly complex relationship with camp men and drag queens: they're the stars of children's pantomimes, they still feature on TV during the family hour and have regularly appeared in sketch shows from *Monty Python* through to *The League of Gentlemen*.

Camden Town's Black Cap pub still has a drag bar in the middle of a busy high street, and it is common to find locals there for a night out. Of the many former music-hall comics who appeared at the venue, Mrs Shufflewick, an elderly man who played a rather sad little old lady, is the most fondly remembered. Sample joke: 'I can't believe the price of things today. I went to the shops and bought a packet of biscuits, half a pound of butter and two bottles of gin and it came to fourteen pounds! I must switch to margarine.'

and could come down to watch something if it had been decided that it was 'a woman's picture'.

London's projectionists were a strange, closed society. Everyone's favourite was a small, precise, watery-eyed man called George who used to screen films for Princess Diana. He would never tell you if the film he was about to screen was bad, but would simply raise his eyebrows in surprise and ask, 'Are you *sure* you want to see it?' After about fifty years in the business of sitting in the dark changing reels, he retired. 'I'm off to run a smallholding in Broadstairs,' he told me, 'I need the excitement.'

We had insisted we could do the job, and now we were stuck with the promise. It was a ludicrous undertaking; cinema admissions were on the slide* and video was seen as an apocalyptic threat to the future of the industry. Surrounded by dire warnings of failure and debt, we started making radio commercials for our first film client, a charming old gentleman called Ron, who was the most ancient man still in gainful employment that I'd ever met, with the exception of the man who runs the bank in *Mary Poppins*. He wore a huge deaf aid because he suffered from tinnitus. He walked so slowly that to get him to one particular studio we had to stick him in a goods lift. Jim would ask him if he liked the sound mix of a radio spot, and he would tremulously admit, 'I don't know, Jim, it's like I'm living under a waterfall.'

I think people started working with us simply because they liked being around Jim. He always got into parties without an invitation, but had to enter first in order to sneak me in, knowing I was more likely to be turned away. In most jobs, people want to work with their peers; having fun makes the day go faster. It's why so many workers in

---

*Annual UK cinema admissions slipped from 1.64 billion in 1946 to an all-time low of 54 million in 1984.

middle age often feel left out – nobody young is going to ask them to a nightclub or a late-night movie just because they share a workspace. The English film industry is unique in that its creative staff comprise people of all ages, huddling together for warmth, united by their debilitating passion for a medium that will offer no rewards until they are already successful.*

During the ensuing years of late nights and loud fights we often found ourselves creating huge campaigns for very small films, and personally losing money on them. We revived our old agency trick of contacting stars direct to record for us. It threw up some very odd sights. I remember seeing Jim and a ridiculously immaculate George Hamilton eating sandwiches together at a tiny Formica table in Bruno's, the Italian snack bar in Wardour Street.

'Everything all right?' I asked, watching incredulously as the godlike actor who had worked with everyone from Brigitte Bardot to Mae West tried to get his teeth around a crusty cheese roll.

'Awesome,' he grinned happily. 'I've never eaten anywhere like this before.'

'Good. Have a gherkin,' said Jim.

At a party in Cannes, Jim asked a somewhat befuddled Liza Minnelli to mind my pint while I went to the toilet. She seemed happy to oblige, and was very chatty. This talent for treating the famous like everyone else turned out to be the right approach. The film industry was littered with the corpses of those who had fallen in love with the so-called

---

*The catch-22 of the English film industry is that your first film is made by scraping together pennies, and if that is successful, your second will have Hollywood millions thrown at it so long as you leave your country. Hollywood cannily gets someone else to pay for the years of research and development.

glamour of the business, so it was important not to buy into the hype.* Prior to the days of PR micromanagement and fans posting every second of their lives on mobile networks, stars were bored on publicity tours and ready to let their hair down, hanging out with whomever they pleased. This culminated with me spending an evening in a hotel suite with Jamie Lee Curtis and Melanie Griffiths, who just wanted to have a laugh and a beer with someone who wasn't going to try to sell them a script. Sadly, such occasions were replaced by a panicky siege mentality that requires the talent to be accountable day and night until their film has opened. Their managers and PR teams effectively become jailers, ready to pounce if there's any sign of behaviour that hasn't previously been discussed and signed off.

Of course, all this was in the future. For now, there was just a company consisting of two men, one room, a type-writer and an unlimited supply of secondhand printer paper. If we proved the bank manager right and went bankrupt, we would have to sell everything we owned, which I figured would come to about twenty pounds.

---

*English film companies have always paid badly; throwing a couple of preview tickets to an overworked assistant that might allow her to glimpse the back of Tom Cruise's head at a premiere is usually seen as recompense enough. It's the equivalent of paying someone who works for Cadbury's in bars of Fruit & Nut.

18

Straps

Banking, *My Fair Lady*, summing up the classics,
Sean Connery's feet, censorship, promotions
and a bit of common sense

We walked across to the bank in Wardour Street and opened our first business account at Barclays. It was very different from the Victorian edifice I'd first entered on the day I met Jim. The manager was wearing a dandruff-covered pinstriped suit. He sat us down very seriously in his poky windowless office and stared at his blotter. For a manager, he seemed to have a horrible work environment that consisted of a pale veneer desk and some cheap shelves containing *Reader's Digest* volumes, a plastic globe and an ashtray with a pewter eagle attached. 'Which one of you is going to be the majority shareholder?' he asked, carefully wiping his glasses.

We looked at each other blankly. 'What do you mean?' I asked.

'Well,' he explained with laborious effort, 'over seventy per cent of all business partnerships break up within the first eighteen months, and one of you has to take a larger responsibility than the other, so that you'll know what to do when it comes to paying off your debts. Which one of you is it to be?'

'No, you don't understand,' I said, 'we're not going to go broke.'

'Statistically, I'd say you're wrong,' replied the bank manager. 'What is this company of yours going to make?' He checked the page of information we had supplied. 'Films, you say?'

'No, we're not actually going to make them,' I started to explain.

'Then what are you going to do?'

'We're going to tell people about them.'

'You mean you're going to start a film magazine? It's a bad time for—'

'No, we're going to produce movie posters and trailers.'

'But surely somebody already does that.'

'Nobody specializes in doing it from an intellectual angle, no.'

He looked at me as if I was mad. 'But if somebody *does* already do it, why would anyone need you?' he asked doggedly. It was all a bit too intangible for him.

'Well, they don't need us yet, but they will,' I replied.

'Look,' said Jim, 'we're not asking you for a loan so don't worry about what we're going to do.'

That seemed to put the bank manager back on track. I could hear him mentally putting his pocketbook away. 'All right,' he said, 'shares – who'll have the majority?'

Jim laughed. 'Whether we go broke or not, we're always going to be best friends until the day one of us dies, so make it fifty-fifty.'

'But it's highly irregular—'

'Fifty-fifty. And never tell us we're going to go broke, or we'll take our overdraft elsewhere.' With a sigh, the manager reluctantly drew up the paperwork. Jim lit a fresh fag from the end of his last one and looked out of the window, ending the conversation. 'This is a really depressing office,' he told the manager.

The idea of not signing everything fifty-fifty had never crossed our minds. For the rest of our careers, everything – with the exception of Jim's spectacular mountain of parking fines – was split down the middle.

The company was up and running. We were being paid to see ten films a week, and I'd be lying if I said the work was hard. There was nothing I loved more than going to work on a rainy Monday morning and spending the next two hours watching a truly dreadful science-fiction movie with two or three smoking, hacking elderly men from Rank Films in a screening room that smelled of tobacco and cough sweets. After all, I did the same thing for fun in the evenings.

Individual scenes from films had always remained in my mind because of the story twists they involved: Audrey Hepburn smashing lightbulbs with a walking stick in *Wait Until Dark*, Mia Farrow piecing together an ominous Scrabble clue in *Rosemary's Baby*, Susan George provocatively chewing gum to distract Dustin Hoffman in *Straw Dogs*, Ellen Burstyn keeping her sunglasses on while she seeks out a priest incognito in *The Exorcist*, these were films I would have loved to market.

Instead I got *The Last Snows of Spring*, one of a series of maudlin Italian tearjerkers based around the plotline: boy meets girl, girl takes two hours to die. For that I had 'TAKE SOMEONE WITH YOU TO WIPE AWAY A TEAR' printed on packets of Kleenex. Movies were exempt from job boredom for the simple reason that – for better or worse – every one was different, and just about all of them had an audience somewhere. I hated every second of *The Last Snows of Spring*, but I met a woman from Lancaster who had seen it over ninety times.

My first actual movie poster job was to come up with a strapline for the reissue of *My Fair Lady* (a film I detested – all those cheery cockneys and not a case of rickets in sight). I chose a photograph of Henry Higgins coaching Eliza Doolittle, and above it wrote 'THE RAIN IN SPAIN FALLS MAINLY ON THE PLAIN – AGAIN'. The client examined it for about two days and finally said, 'Yes, I like it, I can see where you're coming from. How about a small tweak?'

'How small?'

'Just a minor alteration.'

He changed the line to 'SIXTEEN GLORIOUS SONGS IN THE FILM THAT WILL LIVE FOREVER!'

I should have sensed something was wrong right then and quit. It might not have been rocket science, but summarizing ninety minutes in a few words was tough when you knew the movie was a pig and your client thought he was releasing a golden goose.

We were soon churning out straplines, cinema trailers and posters for everything from art to exploitation. We could be life-affirmingly profound in eight words, but if the client wanted something for a cheapo *Alien*-ripoff like *Inseminoid*, we could do that too.* We identified the films that people would have fistfights to get tickets to, and the ones you couldn't drag audiences in off a rainswept street to watch. For the ludicrous horror fantasy *Phantasm* I penned 'IF THIS ONE DOESN'T SCARE YOU, YOU'RE ALREADY DEAD!' For *Evil Dead 2* I came up with 'KISS YOUR NERVES GOODBYE!' and on through the years to *Carry On Columbus* – 'UP YOUR ANCHOR FOR A WELL-CREWED VOYAGE!'

Unsurprisingly, it was easier to provide lines for trashy films (for *U.F.O.*, the Roy 'Chubby' Brown space 'epic' – 'DON'T ASK TO SEE THE CAPTAIN'S LOG!') than for a quality

---

*Decades later we were still doing it – *Bride of Chucky* got 'HERE COMES THE BRIDE – THERE GOES EVERYONE ELSE!'

product. You couldn't really sum up the classics in a few words, although it was fun to try.

'IF ONLY THEY COULD CONNECT!' – *Howard's End*

'HE WAS SUCH STUFF AS DREAMS WERE MADE ON . . .'
  – *The Tempest*

'VIEWER, SHE MARRIED HIM.' – *Jane Eyre*

'ALL HELL WILL BREAK LOOSE WHEN HE FINALLY MAKES UP
  HIS MIND!' – *Hamlet*

'FIRST SHE FELL UNDER HIS SPELL. THEN SHE FELL UNDER A
  TRAIN.' – *Anna Karenina*

'GREGOR SAMSA'S NOT FEELING HIMSELF TODAY'
  – Frank Kafka's *Metamorphosis*

Sometimes you made interesting connections of your own. Attempting to find a line for Bernardo Bertolucci's film of Paul Bowles's novel *The Sheltering Sky*, I was unable to discover the reference of the title until, digging back into Bowles's writing, I found the quote which became the strap: 'ALL THAT STANDS BETWEEN MAN AND INFINITE DARKNESS IS THE SHELTERING SKY'.

Over the last few years, the faithful strapline has all but vanished in favour of style-magazine graphics, and one of the reasons for this – apart from the sheer hokiness of much movie copy – is that before computers, typographers sat with art directors and set their text for them. Copywriters guaranteed their own spelling and grammar, but tended to keep more regular hours than art directors, who fought to meet press deadlines through the night. With the advent of computers, artists found themselves working late with no one to check text, and because they weren't always confident of their language usage, they dropped copy in favour of pictures. For the record, though, my favourite movie strapline of all was the one written for *Citizen Kane* that simply said, 'IT'S TERRIFIC!'

Nowadays hardly anyone draws posters. As Hollywood stars get rights of approval that allow them to stop artists from rendering their image in paint, we may never return to the heady days of the realistically illustrated poster. To see how wonderfully deranged these could be, take a look at the early James Bond campaigns. The poster for *You Only Live Twice* features 007 walking at a 45-degree angle upside down across the roof of a volcano in a tuxedo. The oddest part is that he has cloven hooves instead of shoes. This is because the artist was told that Bond scales a sheer wall in the script, and as he hadn't seen a single frame of the film he used his own imagination to work out how the superspy might manage such a feat.

Similarly, McGinnis's illustration for *The Mercenaries/ Dark of the Sun* featured Rod Taylor in a saucily torn shirt nonchalantly riding the roof of a runaway train across an exploding viaduct while being strafed by fighter aircraft as an adoring semi-clad Yvette Mimieux clings to his trouser leg. In a funny way this is not misrepresentative of the film, more a temporal condensation of its wilder moments rendered into something utterly daft and gravity-defying.

The artwork for *Barbarella* said more about swinging London than future space, and was bordered by joyous psychedelics, with the title amended to 'BARBARELLA-AAAAAAH!'

Artwork allowed for subtle cheats, in the same way that the cover scenes of Superman comics hardly ever found their way into the actual stories. Roger Moore's legs were usually lengthened to an absurd degree – on the posters for *Octopussy* and *A View to a Kill* he looks like a tuxedoed torso attached to a stepladder. Women were made more pneumatic, Nicholas Cage's hair was thickened, and special effects were massively exaggerated. Everyone knows that William Castle wired up the cinema seats for *The Tingler*, but the tacky spirit of showbiz lived on as journalists received pewter *Planet of the Apes* gorilla pen-holders to sit beside their *King Kong* plush monkeys.* Movie posters go through fashions that date them badly. In the nineties, Californian romcoms were signified by a couple kissing, the girl kicking up one leg while a dog in sunglasses looked on.†

Worse was to come when politically correct advertising took a grip on cinema in the eighties. One day we ran foul of London Transport's draconian team of policymakers. Despite the fact that there had been underwear ads on the tube since the 1950s, London Transport became exercised by the idea of 'the woman travelling alone' who would become frightened after seeing a bit of advertising. We had created a poster for the film *Salvador*, a brilliant piece of political film-making that used as its central figure two sexless silhouettes, one kneeling, one wielding a gun. The image was taken directly from the film and rendered into a two-colour graphic that was honestly intended to signify power and its abuse – the subject of the script.

The night before the poster was due to go up throughout the underground system, London Transport banned it. When we asked them why, they said it degraded women, which was interesting as neither character could be gender-identified. When we pointed this out, they replied that this was precisely the problem.

'If you can't identify the sexes, that means one of them could be a woman and one could be a man, and then it

---

*The most tragic giveaway I ever saw was for the film *Soapdish*. It was a soapdish. Some marketing guru really pushed the boat out with that one.
†Lately the style has been for the Receding Row of Figures, reaching an absurd nadir with the poster for *Downton Abbey*, which assembled its cast like a supremely awkward football team line-up.

would be a degrading image,' came the reply. So Jim and I sat up all night gluing patches over the non-offending non-male-or-female image that might be read as a female, in case someone fantasized an image, in the same way that you might imagine seeing an elephant in a cloud formation. This act of censorship made people all the more intrigued as they tried to scrape the patches off.

The fundamental flaw within the desire for film censorship has always been in thinking that film initiates aberrant behaviour. Censors have a long and unlovely history of shooting themselves in the foot; as soon as they seek to justify decisions that cannot have definable values attached to them, they start tying themselves in ideological knots.

England has had an ugly history of banning and cutting films for the public good, and has nearly always got it wrong.* The outrage that greeted classics like *Peeping Tom* and *Straw Dogs* seemed all the more absurd when compared with the silent acquiescence of censors to the release of prurient tat like *Circus of Horrors*, or the right-wing violence of the *Death Wish* movies. Marlon Brando's *The Wild One* was banned in the UK for a quarter of a century, and *Child's Play* was erroneously blamed for the death of Jamie Bulger, killed by two children who had supposedly watched the movie. Censors have always believed in the power of imitative violence. I loved horror films but was never too fussed about seeing trimmed seconds of gore because they were merely unpleasant, and obsessing about them felt too transpotterish. If the human condition was really influenced by popular images, we'd

---

*America had – and still has – even less of a clue what to do about English films. They subtitled, renamed, re-edited and generally mucked about with imports, killing them. Even *The Italian Job*, with all of its comedy Britishness, proved a flop after much tampering.

all be chucking ourselves off roofs on skateboards as they do in hillbilly YouTube clips.*

Meanwhile, never ones to go in for subtlety, distribution companies staged embarrassingly literal publicity stunts for their films. During the premiere of *Hair* at the Dominion Cinema, Tottenham Court Road, the unimpressed audience was pelted with flowers while the ushers were made to wear beads and long wigs that made them look like crazy old tramp-women. The distributors thought carefully about the words 'music' and 'England' and came up with a Morris-dancing display outside the cinema afterwards, thus sealing the film's fate. The premiere of the killer-rodent movie *Willard* was preceded by a giant red-eyed rat being driven about London on the roof of a window-cleaner's van, while the vomit-inducing *Mark of the Devil* had its logo printed on sick-bags.

Film premieres were the best perk of the job, though. At the opening of Peter Weir's sublime *Picnic at Hanging Rock*, as we were left pondering the fate of the film's missing schoolgirls, we rode up in a Regent Street elevator to a rooftop club for the after-party and were greeted by the girls in their film costumes, standing in a line to welcome the unnerved guests. More recently, the *Sex and the City* premiere party housed its four leads in mocked-up movie sets separated by fencing, like a kind of movie-stars petting zoo. 'Come on, we've stroked Sarah Jessica Parker, let's go and feed Carrie-Anne Moss now!'

And occasionally the job would throw up startling surprises. One summer's evening we gathered in the

*These days the pitiful old BBFC has been superseded by technology, stranded in some Victorian neverland by the internet. We live in a world where anyone can show anything to anyone else with the aid of a phone, and they still worry about susceptible teens stumbling across shocking film footage.

Blue Posts,* a strange rockabilly pub at the bottom of Tottenham Court Road that looked like a one-storey plank shack (eventually torn down and replaced with a concrete box housing a Muji store), and grabbed a few beers before stumbling off to see an SF B-movie nobody knew anything about. Arriving late, we grabbed the last few seats in the front row and watched in astonishment as an unimaginably vast spaceship passed over our heads on London's biggest screen. We were attending the cast-and-crew screening of *Star Wars* – its first showing in the world. By the end, we felt that cinema had been reinvented.

A similar thing happened with *Alien*, screened one morning at the Leicester Square Odeon for the cast and crew and the handful of marketing folk who were working on it. All we had seen before that was a specially shot photo of what appeared to be a green egg.

Asked to provide poster straplines for *Alien*, I wrote several pages, one of which was 'IN SPACE NO ONE CAN HEAR YOU SCREAM'. I assume I wasn't the only person to think of this – it's an obvious line – but coming up with such stuff was part of the job, and we were back-room boys who certainly didn't expect credit, any more than the artists who painted posters.

We became so blasé about premieres that we wouldn't go if the after-party looked even slightly cheap.† There was a story that did the rounds about Entertainment Films, the legendarily tight-fisted outfit run by the (actually very charming) Green family, one of Soho's great film dynasties. Supposedly the brothers Green got their mother to make all the sandwiches for screenings to save money.

---

*There still is another Blue Posts, in Soho, where the aged remnants of the film industry occasionally gather for a beef roll and a pint.
†Famously, the best premiere party in anyone's collective memory was for *Moulin Rouge*, a film about a massive party.

They were demanding and made a few terrible English films, but at least they honestly fulfilled their promise to continue making them, and they were bloody good fun to work with.*

Ten Things I Knew About Film Premieres

1. Allow an extra ten minutes to find the way in. The entrances to film premieres are more carefully hidden than the train to Hogwarts.

2. Forget glamour. Remember that this is England and it will be pissing down.

3. Approach the red carpet slowly. Don't race up it at a terrified gallop.

4. There's a sweet spot near the entrance to the cinema where all stars stop and slowly turn to their fans. It's where the camera that shows footage inside the auditorium is situated. Ushers will try to move you past it. Don't let them.

5. Never get bunched up at the bottleneck around the stars' photo-call. You may end up standing on the back of J-Lo's gown. And she *really* doesn't like it.

6. Watch the people behind the barriers to see if you know anyone. If necessary, plant someone there.†

7. If Tom Cruise is attending the premiere, get ready for a long wait while he wanders around

---

*Rock-bottom production: *Sex Lives of the Potato Men*, about potato-deliverers getting sex wherever they can, and probably the least aspirational film of all time. Lately being rehabilitated as a classic of the genre.
†At one premiere I was greeted by a fan of my books. My excitement at being stopped on the red carpet for an autograph was dampened by him saying, 'I'm the only one here who knows who you are.'

Leicester Square being filmed on fans' mobiles for at least an hour. No sense of urgency, that man.

8. Once inside, you will find yourself watching horrendously embarrassing interviews conducted by eleven-year-old yoof presenters for at least an hour. They will ask Bruce Willis, visibly weary from visiting seventeen countries in five days, things like 'Are you excited to be here?'

9. After the director has told everyone how excited he is to be here and has introduced his cast, none of them will be able to find their way off-stage without help. No matter how slick and big-budget the film, there will be much fumbling with the curtains. This used to happen every single time until around 2010, when they finally cracked the problem. Although it occasionally still happens.

10. At a royal premiere, you'll find the cinema filled with fresh flowers and Grenadier Guards. Presumably the Queen thinks cinemas are like this all the time.

I felt guilty being at premieres. After all, I was only in film marketing, and it was regarded as the arse-end of show-business. But it still felt a lot more respectable than advertising, and for us it was really taking off.

As we accepted new work and hired our first members of staff, Jim continued to treat me like the son he would never have. We must have confused clients, holding family conversations in front of them, but my business partner seemed to make no distinction between home and work life. We didn't have meetings so much as fights that began in the office and brawled into the pub. Jim saw no point in

hiding anything, exhibiting a disarming honesty in front
of others that would be regarded with narrowed eyes now;
his old-school bluntness was going out of style even in the
seventies. He showed an astonishing amount of nerve when
faced with officials, once attempting to join a private party
at BAFTA in a state of drunken merriment by insisting
that he had won the Oscar for best documentary. When
they asked which film he had made, he waved his cigarette
airily and said, 'Oh, you know, the one about the cripples.'

On the face of it, we had nothing in common. I was a
cautious, nervous liberal, he was an optimistic but determined Conservative. But he could do all the things that
defeated me, and vice versa, so a strange, symbiotic relationship developed between us that was akin to being a
love affair.

'How can you possibly be a Conservative?' I asked him
one evening in The Ship.

'It's simple,' he replied. 'You can't get anything done
by committee, and Labour is founded on referendum decisions. I believe in the benign dictatorship. The world
would be a better place if everyone did what I told them.'

'And what would you tell them?' I demanded to know,
nettled.

'To be decisive.'

'Even if they turn out to be wrong?'

'Yes. Better a bad decision than no decision.'

'Anything else I should know, while we're working out
how to run the world?'

'I would make people check every decision against their
basic common sense. It's the only way to get anything
done.'

'So what's your common-sense advice for our career
advancement?'

'Well,' he said finally, 'we've got a bit of money coming
in.'

'Yes.' I was already uncomfortable with what he might suggest next. 'But not very much. We need to set some cash aside to repair the leaky roof. Let's not do anything rash.'

'No, of course not. But we're not getting a reputation. Not making a splash. I think we need to do something bigger.'

'Like what?' I asked.

'We need to hit the Cannes Film Festival like a ton of bricks.' He grinned, and I groaned.

19

No Cannes Do

Disgusting hotels, slamming doors, being fleeced, the horror of the Swiss, 1968, a weekend in Monte Carlo, Shirley Bassey and losing your shirt

Every Cannes Film Festival is announced with the same pair of newspaper headlines. If it's going to be a good year, the line is 'In the Cannes'. If it's bad, it's 'No Cannes Do'. Attending the festival seemed like a fantasy idea, but six months after the company was registered Jim and I found ourselves on a plane heading for the Côte d'Azur. There were no cheap flights in the late seventies, but every seat was taken. The English film industry might have been on the ropes but its survivors still headed to the Riviera with determination on their faces, straw hats on their heads and red wine in their nose veins.

We weren't going to show, sell or buy a film, but to try to convince producers to place their precious product in the hands of total strangers. Quite why we thought we were qualified to do this was a mystery; we might equally have decided to become bakers.

Finding a hotel room proved tricky. The first one was so disgusting, and its owners so desperate to get us to stay, that Jim eventually climbed out of the hotel window and fled rather than face a barrage of vindictive questions about why he didn't want a room that smelled of dead pets.

All I knew about Cannes was what I had read: blue skies, palm trees, golden beaches, film stars, girls in bikinis. We arrived in the middle of May in a howling, freezing rainstorm and checked into a hotel that looked like an abandoned potato farm, dug into the wrong side of the dual carriageway that separated Cannes from graffiti-spattered hillside suburbs filled with angry-faced local toughs looking for something to steal.

The hotel name translated into something like 'The grand chateau of the sunny hillside', and the place had not been modernized since the First World War. The main building's strange wool-coated corridors smelled strongly of rancid sweat, as if a number of fat old men had died against the walls in a heatwave. Each room had a cracked avocado-green bath with a single hand towel that must have been beaten with rocks by the river to give it a crusty sandpaper texture. My bedroom window overlooked the motorway and an alarmingly popular public toilet. The hotel was run by an elderly couple who looked as though the place was slowly finishing them off. Incredibly, they had a grandfather who worked in the vegetable patch. Every time I saw him from the window I thought of the Godfather keeling over. I imagine by now he's buried underneath his beans. The couple told me that there had been many famous French guests, but presumably the last one to look in had been Marcel Proust in one of his blacker moods.

In the mornings, breakfast was served beside the verdigris-coated plastic swimming pool at the end of a dried-out garden filled with sunbleached children's toys, far beyond the dried-out dog turds that ringed the house.

This was not the South of France I had imagined.

When Jim asked for a boiled egg (he had simple tastes: for lunch most days in London he ate a sandwich consisting of a thin slice of beef, with salt, on bare white bread) the harassed ancient maid, who was also the chef, cleaner and laundress, asked him how many minutes he would like it cooked. Seeing that this was about all we could afford to eat, every day he ordered a four-minute egg and every day he removed the top of the shell to find a clear raw egg floating inside like a jaundiced eyeball.

'Are you sure this is a four-minute egg?' he would ask.

The reply always came back, 'Yes, sir. Exactly four minutes.'

Unconvinced, he went to the tiny kitchen to examine the ancient stove upon which it was cooked. A fierce flame burned beneath the pan, blowlamp hot. He couldn't figure out the problem and characteristically refused to stop until he had.

'So you put the egg in this pan, on this flame, and cook it for four minutes?' he asked.

'No,' said the maid, 'I only cook it for twenty seconds because it takes me over three and a half minutes to get the egg up the garden to you.'

This was typical of the miscommunication that enveloped the whole of Cannes. We had arrived carrying six giant cartons of brochures that I had written and hand-drawn in Letraset.* Our bags and clothes were stuffed with them. We stuck them on car windscreens, left them in coffee bars, doorstepped producers and schlepped along infinite gloomy hotel corridors handing them out, but were greeted with puzzlement and hostility.

Letters you painstakingly transferred one by one, trying not to lean on the plastic sheet. Almost impossible to use without years of practice: you wanted an 'L', you got a 'PJ&%&dgGT'.

Clearly, nobody understood the service we were offering.

Office doors were held open for twenty seconds, then slammed in our faces. One American producer misunderstood when we told him we made trailers, and thought we manufactured caravans. Jewish producers shut the door on us because we weren't Jewish, and Arabic producers shut the doors because we'd just been seen talking to Jews. The Americans bellowed across us to each other, ignoring us as they made their deals, and the English slumped disconsolately in their deserted offices, wondering why nobody wanted to buy the international rights to films about skinheads swearing at each other on run-down south London council estates.

We had made another mistake: the Cannes Film Festival has nothing to do with buying and selling films. That's the Cannes Film Market, and although the two events had been running concurrently for decades, they had never remotely impinged on each other. The premieres were held in a grand auditorium beyond a mile of red carpet, and the Market screenings were held in disgusting little cinemas up and down the Rue d'Antibes. The Festival had Catherine Deneuve in a Givenchy gown. The Market had rat-faced men trying to sell Michael Winner's back catalogue.

The glamour of the Cannes Film Festival was muted if not undermined entirely by the seedy surreality of the surrounding Market, a freewheeling nightmare for even the hardiest buyers and sellers, many of whom worked through the event without ever seeing natural daylight. The Market cinemas were old and cramped, the chances of finding a cinematic gem rare, and bidding frenzies transformed even the sweetest producers into rabid werewolves. Somehow, despite all efforts at quality control, you always ended up seeing the Market's very worst film in an auditorium that smelled of poor personal hygiene and snack food, while over at the Festival even directors were sometimes unable to gain admittance to their own movies. I thought LA doormen were tough until I saw French fans held in headlocks while tiny gum-snapping Tom Cruise made his entrance.*

Meanwhile, we were running out of money fast.

We could no longer afford meals for two and took to sharing starter-portion salads, but had no intention of giving up. 'If I'd known it was going to be like this,' sighed Jim, 'I'd have brought sandwiches.'

There was another problem in Cannes: the town was filled with liars, thieves, mountebanks and charlatans. French and American distributors would come up to us in cafés, promise us all their business and swear to make us rich before promptly vanishing, leaving us with their lunch bills. Restaurateurs charged us triple, stole from our bags and skimmed our credit cards. We watched money changing hands under tables, behind backs, tucked inside menus, under plates, smoothly palmed to maître d's; bribes to secure tickets, seats, drinks, reservations, hookers, drugs. Goody bags of perfumes, pens, wallets and aftershaves vanished from under guests' noses right off their tables in mid-meal, stolen by fleets of light-fingered waiters. The entire town was geared to thieving. I had never encountered corruption on such an endemic, shameless scale before.

In twenty-five years of attending the Cannes Film Festival I had my credit cards ripped off maybe ten times, usually in the most reputable, expensive establishments.

---

*The Market remains brilliantly tacky. In front of the Carlton Hotel I saw a high-tech (i.e., late eighties) set for yet another *Terminator* movie complete with shiny robots and sliding steel doors from which popped a very stretched-looking Arnold Schwarzenegger. The overall effect was like a modernist Guinness Clock.

One year, we were ripped off even before we got to Cannes. Driving down from London in Jim's beloved white 1969 Mercedes convertible saloon, an automobile that could be parked anywhere on the Riviera without getting a ticket, we stopped overnight in Geneva, a city so anodyne and devoid of interest that it played host to the Business Park Recreation Area Design Fair.* In a hotel that Hitler would have been comfortable planning the invasion of Poland in, we sat in a huge empty restaurant while the pianist dragged himself through 'High On A Hill Was A Lonely Goatherd' for the third time that night.

By the time of this story, we were taking around twelve staff members with us and had the entire company float in cash, because many Cannes establishments still refused to take credit cards. The Napoleon Route is long and astoundingly beautiful, and just as we were driving into Cannes, we realized to our horror that we had left the float in the room safe. We had no money on us at all. As soon as we could find a telephone we called the hotel in Geneva.

The manager told us he had put the money away in the hotel safe and very kindly offered to send it down to us.

We thanked him, gushing that he had saved us from an ignominious situation. A bad idea, as it turned out, because he promptly asked for twenty per cent of the take, and held out until he got it. Suddenly the entire history of Switzerland made itself clear to me.

There are good reasons why Cannes is twin-towned with Beverly Hills: both cities are sun-dazzled and indefinably sinister. Both exist more in the imagination than the real

---

*The saddest stand I saw was an English businessman trying to sell a new crazy golf challenge called 'The Channel Tunnel', which consisted of a grey plastic drainpipe with a Union Jack at one end and the French Tricolour at the other.

world. Both are filled with wealthy, paranoid stars living in the hills under cyanic skies, both host high-profile movie events, both have given birth to parasite industries like the restaurant and hotel trades,* and both have police forces that adopt uncompromising attitudes to outsiders. The Mayor of Cannes infamously bussed the homeless out of town for the duration of the film festival. Cannes is also like a film set: a façade of elegance propped up by a disgruntled, stressed-out workforce.

Everyone has horror stories about Cannes, the audacious thievery, the profligate waste, the staggering cost of a salad, the rubbernecking crowds, the rudeness of the police, the sheer blank-eyed effrontery of hotel staff. Over the years there were surreal, bleary memories: the Leningrad Cowboys playing rockabilly with the Red Army; the Python team holding four-in-the-morning sidewalk salons; Madonna and Tina Turner hitting the dance floor as excited as schoolgirls; outrageous, uncomfortable parties held at villas in the hills, where everyone watched everyone else and nobody had fun.

Everyone recalls specific events: the night the power failed and all Cannes was candlelit, the tear-gas attack on the English bar, the black-tie guests who were stranded aboard a ship full of porn stars, the year the dot.com millionaires turned up.† There was a rough, reckless edge to the late nights, a frisson of danger that counterbalanced the glitz and pricked the pomposity of the proceedings.

By creating a division between the awards ceremonies

---

*These have such grotesque seasonal pricing structures that you actually squeak and shut one eye in pain when you unfold their bills.
†Wide-boys who thought they could make movies about English geezer-gangsters because they hosted websites featuring porn, poker and dancing cats, and who wanted to date models. But the models wanted elderly men with yachts and the movie deals never materialized. They came once and never came back.

and the marketplace, the Cannes Film Festival had freed itself up to concentrate on the artistry of film, even if that meant grappling with political issues. In May 1968, while protesting students were being baton-charged along La Croisette, the directors invited to Cannes squabbled about solidarity, yanking the curtains shut during a screening of Carlos Saura's *Peppermint Frappé* as the jury members resigned. To show their solidarity, well-meaning film-makers raised the same flags all the young intellectuals in Communist countries were trying to tear down. It's interesting to note that the year's most critically lauded film, Stanley Kubrick's emotionally detached *2001: A Space Odyssey*, came from America and did not voice discontent with the ruling class.

In France, subsidization and the cultural imperative kept French-language films rolling from the production line, but halted their spread in English-speaking territories – a triumph for art over profit, perhaps, but a reduction in visibility that prevented some of the world's most enjoyable films from receiving international attention.

Like Berlin, Geneva, Venice or even Sicily's Taormina, Cannes was a trade-show town; visit it in a different month and you would find yourself surrounded by dentists or antique dealers. Despite this cosmopolitanism, Cannes managed to prove exasperating and impenetrable to the casual visitor; just ordering a coffee became an obstacle course of ritual humiliation. There were hotels that only accepted cash, menus that switched to higher figures at 1.00 p.m., arcane rules governing the availability of cabs, the entrance into bars and behaviour aboard yachts. There were film-sellers who had been attending for decades, but who could not afford to travel beyond the Bunker, the un-lovely trade-fair dungeon wherein films were hawked.

Occasionally we watched press conferences with the stars, and realized that the same level of miscommunication infected them as it did everyone else. Nations were at war, democracies were in danger of collapse and the Italian press wanted to know if Nicholas Cage was wearing a wig. Press questions were – and are now, more than ever – not just fawning, ignorant and vacuous, but offensive, deranged or hopelessly lost in translation. Starlet Bridget Fonda was asked if she'd like a shag.* Halle Berry was asked why she bothered to act at all. Sometimes the stars fought back. Helena Bonham Carter wearily admitted, 'I don't get out much. I don't watch many films. I'm not much of a cineaste.' Director-provocateur Jean-Luc Godard criticized the press and slagged off Cannes jury member Fanny Ardant for good measure. More recently, a flippant remark from Lars Von Trier was interpreted as an admission of Nazism.

On the fourth day of our first year at Cannes, we ran out of money and started borrowing on our one and only credit card. We tried to get into parties and failed. We took to sharing burgers at a filthy workmen's café behind the station where unshaven men drank cheap brandy at 8.00 a.m. We had made no sales. We still had several huge cartons of flyers to get rid of. The rain fell harder. We blagged our way into the Festival's least exclusive party, only to find that it was a paying bar with beer pegged at ten quid a bottle. Film-company runners were peeing behind the dance floor rather than queue for toilets.

The gilt had gone from the Riviera.

It took me years to realize just how much you pay for a sea view in France. Down the road from Cannes, in Monte Carlo, a principality where the average resident has seven bank accounts, things get worse. A pristine city where your

---

*She had just starred in the eponymous movie *Shag*, about a dance craze. Everyone misunderstood the title. She was a very nice girl, and taught me to do the dance on a rooftop.

every move is monitored by people in Raybans and blue uniforms, it still reminds me of Geneva.* Traditionally, it had always been a shirt-and-tie kind of place, so the tourists in Mambo shorts and sports socks who snapped the gull-wing sports cars parked in front of the casino had no chance of glimpsing what really went on. All that secret money and tainted glamour made for a highly peculiar vibe. There were the parties, for a start, mindlessly vulgar nights out where fashion models paraded in bikinis and white mink coats, Brazilian dancers (carefully clad in non-revealing body-stockings) somersaulted around champagne pyramids, and the only black people you saw were holding drinks-trays or brooms. Anyone caught spraying graffiti was presumably beaten to death with blackjacks while the offending marks were coated with Edwardian terracotta tilework.

Producers actually took weekend vacations in Monte Carlo to get away from Cannes, which made me suspect they were either masochists, Satanists or Russian. Monaco was geared to amusing thin old white rich people. At one venue, you entered through a runway of *Hello Dolly*-style waiters on a stage that silently folded flat while you were seated, before the entire atrium started glittering with starlit waterfalls, like Vegas without the fat people and token buckets. At another, an icy diamond of a bar virtually floated above the sea. It, too, was a convention town, not so much geared to generating cash – Heaven knows, Monaco has enough of that – but to ensuring that the wealthy could have fun in a scarily controlled environment

---

*Never trust a city with more pipe shops than bookstores. Geneva is a great destination for all your urgent brooch and pocket-watch needs, the creeping waiters are like *fin-de-siècle* vampires and the main monument is a very large spout of water, which must play havoc with cystitis sufferers.

that might suddenly go wrong, like 'Westworld'.

Unlike Vegas, where there's at least the hint of a suggestion that anyone can join in, an invisible wall existed between those who were invited to Monte Carlo and those who peered in from outside. At Christmas, the world's poshest funfair was held in the harbour, where stalls let you throw a dart and win a designer wristwatch, and the fast-food stands sold Serrano ham baguettes with foie gras. For decoration, giant chandeliers transformed entire streets into ballrooms.

Monaco never changes. It's a safe bet that any park which has a framed photograph of Shirley Bassey in it isn't going to have a basketball court. Baby Bentley licence plates still carry the blue and white Monaco coat of arms, the policemen look like male models, bow-ties and strapless gowns are de rigueur for evening wear, and there are no homeless people, although there is a ratty English pub.* Meanwhile, down in the bay, elderly couples watch TV on their yachts in what is effectively the world's most expensive floating caravan site. This is Old Europe at its richest and creepiest, attracting serious wealth while simultaneously fish-eyeing the tourist classes, whom the principality regards as street bums. Old Europe is infinitely crafty – after centuries of practice, it knows how to take your money while making you feel like a grateful, filthy little nonentity.

Back in Cannes, Day Six had now arrived and I was so wet that I had no more fresh clothes. As I couldn't afford to get anything pressed, I perversely decided to go mad and buy a new shirt with what remained of my month's credit. We had an important presentation – our last one

---

*I asked the barman, 'Where is your loo?' and he replied, 'In a bush outside, mate. Take your own toilet paper.' Made me feel quite homesick.

– lined up, and I wanted to at least feel good about it. We were running late, so I dived into a little French bar with my purchase and went to the bathroom to change.

I carefully removed the pins from my new white shirt and stood it on top of its upright cardboard bag, on the cistern of the world's filthiest toilet, a brown bowl that made the loo in *Trainspotting* look like one in a Swiss finishing school. I took off my old shirt, screwed it into a ball and threw it disdainfully on to the piss-soaked floor. Then I watched in horror as the shopping bag folded in half and dropped the new shirt straight down into the excrement-stained toilet.

I was forced to retrieve the old shirt and put it back on. This wasn't quite the last straw. The presentation was a disaster, and it transpired that the assistant in the shirt shop had skimmed my credit card, getting me into debt by buying two thousand pounds' worth of computer equipment in Sophia-Antipolis. I spent the next few hours in the fraud office.

You'd think it couldn't get worse after that, but over the next two decades of Cannes-going, there were trips filled with such toxic levels of humiliation that standing on the sand at sunset did not make us think of our glamorous lifestyle, it made us think of becoming nuns.* There were other festivals in other cities, of course, and I have fond memories of watching Catherine Zeta-Jones descend an opera-house staircase in full Spanish national dress to an enthralled San Sebastian crowd, and a moment over dinner with Bond's 'Q', Desmond Llewelyn, when he confided that he couldn't work a single gadget without breaking it. But Cannes, like it or not, remained the king.

The Festival was coming to an end. Our contacts had

*Victoria Wood said: 'Nuns have more fun. At least they get to play billiards.'

all gone home, our clothes were ruined, our leaflets were sodden, we had no money, I had been robbed, we were hungry in a town where hotel staff were throwing away lobsters and nobody – *not one person* – wanted to talk to us, unless it was to give us a bill in the most disdainful manner possible. And it got even worse when I ended up trapped in a very small lift for hours with five fat Russian producers and no cellphone reception.

'Well, that was fun, wasn't it?' smiled Jim, lighting a fag and happily staring out at the rain from the peeling, wretched hotel room. 'I like it here.'

'Why on earth would you like it?' I asked, screwing up my face at him in impatience.

'You can smoke anywhere you want,' he said, cheerfully filling the room with choking blue clouds.

20

Let's Dance!

A Soho sideline, including bent coppers, the death
of disco and Steve Guttenberg in tiny shorts

We had developed the English ability to work ridiculously long hours without ever quite breaking even. The
Americans would have figured out how to turn a profit;
not us. If a movie failed at the box office (and in the early
days of VHS, most did) we were blamed and our invoices
were reduced. In an effort to save money I moved to a
rented ground-floor flat in Brixton that had achieved the
notoriety of having been burgled more than a dozen times
in three years. One end of the sloping living room was
damp, then very damp, then under water, so while I waited
for a response from the absent landlord I shifted the furniture further and further up the flat until it looked like the
Titanic in the final stages of inundation.

'Blimey,' said Jim, looking around at the mildew-stained
walls. 'Are you sure it's a good idea for someone who's had
childhood pneumonia to be living here? Who rented this
before, Captain Nemo?' We repainted, but the stains came
through. The carpets made squishy noises as you walked
across the room. The landlord remained invisible. Getting

mugged on the doorstep one night was the last straw.

Meanwhile, London was in the grip of disco. Legendary disco the Fridge had opened in Brixton.* Donna Summer, the Village People, Linda Clifford, the Boystown Gang, Cerrone, Earth, Wind and Fire, the Ritchie Family and all the stars of the Casablanca label filled the clubs with shiny happy people up to their eyeballs in coke and Quaaludes.† Newly invented red and green lasers shone into the wide, wide pupils of dancers, giving them free eye operations. Giant video screens were deployed for the first time, allowing everyone to enjoy the horror that was Tavares lock-stepping before cameras in white spangly loons. For the first time, DJs became famous for their ability to play records in sequential order. Some of them were even under thirty. Without today's draconian Health and Safety regulations, nightclub owners built raised steel platforms for dancers, who promptly fell off their stacked heels and landed on their heads ten feet below.

As we worked late and watched the clubbers roller-skating past our office window, I could tell Jim was trying to think of a way to prise their hard-earned cash away from them. Cannes had left us broke and humiliated. He would only be happy when he had figured out a way to even the balance.

The question I asked him at least twice a day was 'What are you thinking?' Eventually, it got so I knew without having to ask, but even then he threw the odd curveball.

'There's a basement available in the Chinese restaurant

---

*Nearby was a bar called the Oven, and another called the Freezer, so posters read: 'Come to the Freezer, it's above the Fridge next to the Oven.'
†Quaaludes had been invented to provide hysteria-riddled sixties housewives with a Quiet Interlude' – they numbed you so completely you spent the evening stumbling into coffee tables and woke up the next morning with leopardskin legs.

over the road,' he said, taking a long, slow hit on his Rothmans.

'No,' I said, 'absolutely not. We've enough to do here.'

'A nightclub. We could run it in the evenings, charge for membership, get friends to help us, easy.'

'Oh no, not this time.' Back then I was a naysayer, a worst-case-scenario-fearing pessimist who tried to pour cold water on all his ideas but always failed.

He arranged for us to view the basement. The old Chinese owner used it to store beer and beanshoots, and was happy to be rid of the damp space. The walls were covered in huge paintings of Chinese warriors bending their knees and sticking their tongues out. 'We'll keep those, they're quite nice,' said Jim admiringly. We called the club Gypsy after his favourite film, in the sense of 'dancer', not Romany nomadic traveller. We printed membership cards and opening-night invitations, paid two months' rent in advance, ordered in booze, some coloured bulbs, a DJ, and some ancient sofas for a chillout area that looked remarkably like my nan's lounge, then carpet-bombed the whole of Soho with leaflets. Finally we recruited a girl Jim had once worked with to run the cloakroom, and hired my mate Roger to be the barman.

'There, that's done,' said Jim proudly, looking around at the transformed Frith Street basement. It looked like a Chinese restaurant full of traffic lights. I was unnerved: we were now deep in debt, and had no assurance that anyone would turn up.

Then the gangsters arrived, in the form of a weaselly little man in a raincoat, like a character actor from a bad fifties English comedy, who pulled up a bar stool, helped himself to a large whisky and insinuated that he would be happy with a few hundred quid a week, depending on how well we did. But it turned out he wasn't a gangster, he was a genuine Soho copper on the take. We agreed to pay him his money, anything to get rid of him, and prepared to open our doors.

Thanks to the ubiquity of disco on the London club scene, our opening night was insanely oversubscribed. Punters would have attended the opening of a biscuit tin if it was accompanied by a Sylvester song. We had lines going down the street. Our barman became so excited that he got more paralytically pissed than the chef in *Fawlty Towers*. When someone asked him for a gin he handed them the bottle and said, 'Help yourself, darling.' Eventually he fell asleep under the counter. A flock of spectacularly attired drag queens – de rigueur to ensure any successful opening – arrived and swept about the place in feathered headdresses, with the startled attitude of flamingos that had been deposed from an African lagoon and deposited in a damp Soho basement.

The music got louder. The temperature rose. We had no air vents. I wondered how soon it would be before somebody passed out or fell over in a slick of their own sweat. I tapped my watch and nervously looked for Jim, who was drifting about with his hands in the pockets of a double-breasted white jacket, like Rick in *Casablanca*. I indicated it was closing time and he shrugged – how could we clear out so many people when they were obviously having a great time at our expense?

For the next month we shot past our closing times and kept the party going around the clock. We raised our entry prices to try to keep people away, but nothing would stop them from forming lines outside. It was all about sex, of course. England had been slow to catch up with the US club scene. While the so-called beautiful people on Santa Monica Boulevard were shovelling coke and burning out in the end of days, English clubbers were passing around a brand of cough syrup that was supposed to be a bit speedy.

Because we had no insurance, I stayed up late, night

after night, to make sure the place didn't get burned to the ground, and crept into work shattered the next morning. The ridiculous hours soon took their toll on everyone except Jim, who seemed to be thoroughly enjoying himself. We couldn't lose money even with the barman nightly giving away the stock.

I suppose the mistake we made was staying open right through Easter, which was apparently illegal. The weaselly policeman decided that we weren't paying him enough. 'Right,' he said, wandering around on Sunday morning and waving at the flamingo-people wrapping themselves in the decorations, 'The Queen's on her way to church at Balmoral. Have some respect. Close this lot down.'

'Do you want a gin and tonic?' asked Jim.

'No I bloody don't!' shouted the weasel. 'Turn the music off, shut the bloody bar and stop those people dancing!'

'Well,' Jim said cheerfully, lighting a Rothmans as the cops confiscated the last of the booze, 'I thought that was fun.'

With a yell of frustration, I went back to my flat and slept for two days. Jim had lately developed a persistent and annoying double-cough. If he had been a character in a film, it would have signified his death by the fifth reel. He had a terrible lifestyle: late nights, grabbed snacks, a diet of booze, laughter and cigarettes without vegetables, exercise or self-control.

The music was about to stop everywhere. Back at the office, we were working on a film called *Discoland*, but by the time it went into production, disco was as dead as Donna Summer's reputation,* so the title was changed

---

*Having secured her success through the spending power of gay men, the diva went on record with some ill-advised remarks about her biggest fans. They turned their whistles and gold appliqué fans elsewhere, and her career collapsed.

to *Discoland: Where the Music Never Stops*, and finally, with an air of desperation, to *Can't Stop the Music*.

When we saw the finished cut our jaws dropped. The film had dated badly even before it had opened. It was impossible to imagine who director Nancy Walker thought she was making her magnum opus for. Walker was an old hoofer/chorus girl from films like *On the Town*, and had filled the film with gay men and old broads. Steve Guttenberg* ran around in tiny shorts and a tank top squeaking and shrieking, the Village People attempted some butch posturing that made them look like lesbians at a fancy-dress ball, and, in one spectacularly misjudged scene, posed with some eight-year-old boys, dressed in chaps and cockrings. Meanwhile, the love interest, Valerie Perrine, thrust out her bust and laughed at nothing in a game attempt to stay cheerful, as if she'd just been told she was dying. For the film's doomed Z-list premiere, the distributors decided that we, the marketeers, should surrender the last shreds of our dignity and show up in tiny shorts and roller skates. Unfortunately the cinema had a steeply raked floor, so that when the ridicule began we found ourselves unable to move without shooting down to the front of the theatre and vanishing into the organ pit. The audience laughed with the desperation of cancer-stricken children at their last panto.

Was this the free-spirited final flowering of freedom before the grim AIDS pandemic of the eighties? For Londoners, yes, it was a time of naive joy and brotherhood. You felt connected to everyone else because people were deciding their own futures. Bound to political beliefs,

---

*Never proven gay. You know, like Cliff Richard. Please don't sue me. Guttenberg was later filmed jogging in Central Park without any pants on at all, something he says he does daily. I guess making *Can't Stop the Music* left its mark.

sexual freedom had not yet been usurped by the corporate world. It felt as if you were in control.

Now it all seems very long ago. In fact, now that I live in a world where my moisturizer sends me more emails than my family, it seems like another planet.

21

Flesh and Blood

Old horrors, repertory glories,
a weird relationship, sex and violence,
Michael Powell, Mary Whitehouse
and girls in chains

Once again Jim and I were at the pictures, watching a retro triple bill of crime and horror. The shabby second-run cinema stood on Charing Cross Road, and was frequented by tramps and junkies looking for a place to dump the wallets and handbags they had stolen. It was very possible to get mugged in the auditorium, but it was the only place to see such fare, and I always felt strangely relaxed there. Jim toddled along on these ugly outings with nary a complaint. Hauled off to see a Danish drama at the NFT, all he said afterwards was, 'They make good bacon.'

London's largest repertory house, the Scala Cinema, had the same effect; it was filled with social outcasts, autistic film nuts and, well, 'loners' is possibly too kind a word for the swivel-eyed, skinny-jeaned burnouts it attracted. The Scala Cinema began on Scala Street just off Tottenham Court Road. It had a stained screen and a café with red and blue plastic tablecloths, and sold strange brands of booze no one had ever heard of, and showed double bills like *Thundercrack* and *Eraserhead*. It moved to a huge old building in King's Cross that had lately been named The London Primatarium – a monkey house. Typically, the new Scala showed *King Kong* there, just so you could enjoy the primate smell as well. A lot of creepy ancient grindhouse legends introduced their scratchy old film shows, glad to finally be recognized as geniuses, and even more were found drunk or making out with groupies in the all-night bar. One time, one of the cinema's cats got stuck in the middle of the screen during an Ingmar Bergman movie. I virtually lived in the place.

The Scala was always in trouble. It never made money, but Londoners loved its weird mix of erudition and schlock. I kept a diary that covered their more esoteric foreign films, especially ones with really bad subtitles.*

Fassbinder, Herzog, Mario Bava, John Waters and Russ Meyer were always favoured over Godard or Resnais. The emphasis was on the bad boys of cinema, directors who revelled in a collective loss of innocence. Steven Spielberg and Stephen King brilliantly depicted American childhoods – so brilliantly, in fact, that they tended to stumble when they left the subject behind. Cult-film fans, myself included, were allergic to warm cinematic life-lessons. The less real a film was, the more real it seemed. We found the early kitchen-sink dramas of Ken Loach and Mike Leigh profoundly depressing and rather arrogant; we didn't want to watch film directors holding mirrors up to working-class life as if attempting to dissect it for its betters.

---

*I appear to have made a note of one in which a police chief handed over his report and said: 'Read this among your calves.' The trailer for an Asian action film featured an on-screen caption that read: 'Contains Many Modern Scientific Instruments!'

The Scala had a special place in its dark heart for American noir thrillers.

A Short Detour into Film Noir

The great noir thrillers of the forties and fifties often clocked in at around sixty-five minutes, but boy, they packed in wit, ingenuity, bad attitude and style. In most horror or crime films the criminals know they're guilty, but in noir B-thrillers they're dumb enough to think they're innocent. The noirs place us firmly on the side of the deluded sleazeballs. *Kiss Me Deadly*, with its cynical PI, hot mystery blonde and radioactive suitcase (borrowed for everything from *Repo Man* to *Pulp Fiction*), is generally accepted as the best noir ever, but I'd plump for the poverty row *Detour*, with Tom Neal's mean-mouthed nightclub pianist complaining, 'When this drunk gave me a ten spot, I couldn't get excited. What was it? A piece of paper crawling with germs.'

Detour also contains another staple of the noir film: a jaw-dropping murder, in this case a telephone-cord strangling accidentally performed through a closed motel door. Death, it seems, is always just around the corner in noir movies, and can come from anywhere, delivered via crop-sprayer or helicopter blades, sheets of falling glass, coffee pots, chainsaws, time travel, identical twins, H-bombs, circus geeks, or simply very bad women.

The noirs have always inhabited a macho world where good girls are generally sidelined into a handful of thankless roles: hand-wringing girlfriend, nightclub singer, homebody, mother. The bad girls had all the amoral, sarcastic fun, and they got the good lines. 'You're not too smart, are you?' Kathleen Turner pointed out in *Body Heat*. 'I like that in a man.' The line was flipped by barfly Bruce Campbell in *Crimewave*. 'I haven't seen you in here before,' he smarmed. 'I like that in a woman.'

Still, cult cinema seemed to attract a special kind of crazy. My pal Bal used to run a shop called Psychotronic Video in the damp basement of a Camden warehouse, and a sweating, goggle-spectacled man used to come in every week and ask, 'Do you have any videos in which men kill their mothers?' We had to hope he wasn't after tips.

The great days of repertory are over, and we've lost the chance to re-evaluate movies in a relaxed shared space. Some favourite late-nighters would seem impossible to fathom now: why did we sit through Frank Zappa's *200 Motels* or the Australian navel-gazing surf documentary *Crystal Voyager*? What was the attraction of *The Valley Obscured by Clouds*? Well, drugs must have had a lot to do with it, but the Scala gave you the chance to check out old mainstream films, too.

Looking at the opening title sequence of *Bullitt*, from English director Peter Yates, I was surprised to find that it still appeared fresh. Perhaps there's something about non-digitized graphics on film that never dates. Viewing the film today, you realize that its cynical attitude to endemic corruption is still current, although acceptability of tough language has grown. Probably the thing that stands out most in such films, apart from the immensity of cars the size of carnival floats, is the men's hats, lots of them, trilbies and skinny-brimmed things with feathers in their bands. If the societal mindset remains, only the fashions date.

This was also true of the unsettling horror films we saw that night in Charing Cross Road. Before this pair, horror movies were aimed at teenagers, but both *Rosemary's Baby* and *The Exorcist* presented situations that were impossible for the young to fully grasp: the alienation of childbirth and parental loss of control. *The Exorcist* was almost a sequel to *Rosemary's Baby*: a mother's worst fears are confirmed when she realizes that the child she carries is tainted with evil, and years later, the child becomes an enemy of everything the mother stands for. Both films could have been presented as straight psychological dramas, but for the almost superficial element of the supernatural. That was their trick, to work independently in the arena of adult emotions.

After these films, there had been a division of the genres into distinctly separate supernatural and psychological dramas, but it was to the benefit of neither. It's intriguing to search for a mystical reason behind aberrant human behaviour: we look for patterns in our lives and try to make sense of sudden change. To lock those patterns into purely psychological or supernatural roots is to provide explanations that are too pat and tidy. Real life is more complex. It seems to me that the most memorable horror films have an element that remains unfathomable.

By this time, Jim had developed an extreme aversion to Larry Cohen's film *It's Alive!* Its central image of a demonic baby creeping through the suburban undergrowth haunted his dreams, but the film often turned up on the lower half of double bills I wanted to see, so he was obliged to sit through the closing minutes again and again.

And yet he still came to the movies with me at least three times a week. Men who go to the pictures together with that level of frequency aren't just working companions, they're partly in love with each other. Our relationship was unconventional by any standards, but neither of us could quite explain our need to be together all day, every day. Kenneth Tynan once wrote, 'You don't need to know why two people are in love, you just need to know that they are.' I couldn't accept that this was what it was, but I really had no other explanation.* If either of us went out with other people, it usually felt like a bit of a wasted evening. Worse still, we dragged other friends into the relationship, so that going out for dinner with an old pal involved booking a table for three. Film was work and play and the whole world, and discussing anything else felt wrong.

Such relationships are not uncommon, but they're painful for anyone else involved because the laws of mental attraction simply don't make sense, and therefore can't be adequately explained to a third party. It was something we resigned ourselves to living with. Jim was, in some sense, the father I wished I'd had, and yet my own father adored him, holding him up as the man he also wished he had been. It was too complicated to think about in any depth, but I clearly couldn't function without him. He was controlling, single-minded and often impossible, but emotionally becalmed. Nothing ever seemed to worry him, and as a consequence he attracted those who were less able to make decisions. In turn, he enjoyed deciding for them, and so encouraged a weird symbiosis that locked people into his orbit as tightly as satellites.

'We're going to have to choose our projects more carefully from now on,' said Jim the next morning, lighting a Marlboro in the kipper-smoking yard he laughingly called his office. 'We can't have people making fun of us.'

'What do you mean?' I asked. We had gone on to a late-late bar after the movies, and had argued about film-making for half the night. Jim never seemed to have hangovers. He was in bright and early, waving about a crude piece of artwork for a film poster that showed a

* Now we have the word 'bromance', which still doesn't quite cover it.

semi-naked woman bound and chained to a chair. 'Do you really want to work on this?' he asked.

A problem had arisen. The seventies were awash with sex films, from the tawdry tat of English comedies like *No Sex Please, We're British* to soft-core, fuzzy-focus romps like *Emmanuelle** and *Bilitis*. Although we needed the money, we also needed to ask ourselves if we should be handling them. It would be easy to take the company down the path that Rank Films had chosen, putting all their energy into the promotion of barrel-scraping trash.

The gong man† had lost his class. Rank and Hammer took a long, slow swan-dive from producing intelligent films like the Venice-set chiller *Don't Look Now* and *Taste the Blood of Dracula* (which used its eponymous villain to expose Victorian hypocrisy) to junk like *Nearest and Dearest – The Movie*, which was something to do with Blackpool and pickled onions.

Famously, Rank chased a mythical youth market and reached a point where they had no idea what they were seeing any more. Horrified by *Performance*, mystified by *The Man Who Fell to Earth*, they either shelved or chopped up features for double bills, removing nuance, wit, subtlety and genius. Finally they made a fortune from film versions of bad television sitcoms, and when that well ran dry they were flogged to a television company who promised to go back to making serious features before

---

*As a curious side effect of the film's success, *Emmanuelle* single-handedly created the fashion for wide-backed wicker chairs after Sylvia Kristel sat on one wearing only a pearl necklace. I mean a necklace made of pearls.
†The gong man introduced every Rank film. My father often told me the gong was made from a huge piece of glass. I was never entirely sure how to react to this piece of information. I found out years later that, like so much else he had told me, it wasn't true.

asset-stripping Rank's catalogue and firing everyone.*

We had to start thinking about the kind of films we were prepared to take on. Producers were creeping out of the woodwork with horrendous movies under their arms, and we didn't want to soil our hands with their tacky, demeaning exploitation flicks. I didn't personally enjoy sex scenes in films – they were always the same, and got in the way of the plot.

The first avowedly 'serious' film dealing with sex that many English kids of my era saw in the cinema had been the erotic, tender Swedish drama *Seventeen*, which played the circuit with drive-in sleazefest *Lady in a Cage*, the latter pairing an ageing Olivia de Havilland with a psychotic youth played by gum-snapping James Caan. The idea of teaming a horror film with a sex film (no matter that one was art and the other exploitation) is clearly ludicrous, as they occupied entirely separate genres. However, sex, still largely regarded by the English as shameful, probably seemed at the time the perfect stablemate to horror. Colour always overrode black and white in double bills, so the monochrome *Lady in a Cage* ran first. This meant that before schoolboys got to see a girl massage her breasts and reveal that she had (gasp!) pubic hair, they had to watch James Caan and his henchman getting their eyes stabbed out and their heads run over.

The linking of sex and violence was the biggest issue bothering the film censors of Soho Square, but they could do nothing about the juxtaposition of subjects in double bills. Sex and violence were inextricably bound together by wily film-makers out to entice impressionable youngsters. In English film the precedent for prurience had been set

---

*The Rank Organization had been the central pillar of the English film industry, and was killed off just a few months short of its fiftieth anniversary.

by Michael Powell's entertaining but misjudged *Peeping Tom** and gratuitously sleazy B-movies like *Horrors of the Black Museum*. These films rode the surrounding tide of new permissiveness to introduce more explicit links between sexual sensation and murder. Still, there's a sense of perverse artifice about them that broke all connection with the prevailing taste in kitchen-sink dramas.

The newly bared link between girls of easy virtue and sadistic killers set English films off on a path that caused the critics to pen violently reactionary editorials. Powell's career was all but destroyed, as the critics dismissed the rest of his startlingly original oeuvre by focusing on *Peeping Tom*'s uncomfortable link between sex and voyeurism. When it failed, it was as much because the bitter screenplay provided no one with whom the audience could identify; the outcome felt claustrophobically narrow and predictable.

Peter Brook's *Lord of the Flies* approached the same problem from a more visceral angle. His film version of William Golding's school-syllabus novel exposed the innate savagery lurking within the breast of every well-educated English pupil and reminded audiences that civilization was acquired, and not an inherited trait. Brook, like Peter Watkins, Tony Richardson and Alan Clarke, had little time for the heroic approach to English film-making; all took an anti-establishment stance and directed some of the most disturbing films seen in the UK (Watkins made *The War Game*, Richardson made *The Loneliness of the Long Distance Runner*, Clarke made *Scum* and Brook made *Marat/Sade*). Only Alexander Mackendrick's film version of *A High Wind in Jamaica* failed to entirely capture the innate cruelty of children made so explicit in the novel.

*The ladies of the night were filmed above the Newman Arms pub in Newman Street, London, in such vivid boudoir colours that the process should have had a brand-name, like CorsetScope or BrassiereVision.

Carefully wrought explorations of psychology such as these were dumped in the seventies, as lurid sensationalism swept in. Against this a rising tide of feminism fought to prevent the objectification of women. Mrs Mary Whitehouse didn't care about feminism; she was obsessed with smut. This apoplectic old harridan was never off our screens, sitting on sofas in her winged glasses, cardigan and huge false teeth, ranting about decency and morals and good taste, although, like Sarah Palin, she barred any questions from the public that she didn't feel like debating. Without realizing it, she kept the public attention firmly focused on sex for years.

There were a few exploitation directors who knew exactly what they were doing, and one of them was Peter Walker. The maverick cult director clearly had an agenda beyond merely making money (despite what he has since said to the contrary), and in this he followed a through-line that extended from W. S. Gilbert, whose satirical attacks on Church and state delayed his knighthood. Walker's films explicitly condemned the judicial system, the Church and the government while filling the screen with flesh and blood. In *House of Mortal Sin*, a priest strangles a parishioner with a rosary, clubs another to death with an incense burner and delivers poisoned communion wafers.

His films haunted me for another reason. Walker rooted his horrors in specific areas of London in order to save money, but incidentally caught the strangeness of its urban landscape. In *Frightmare*, Andrew Sachs walked across a deserted Battersea Fairground on the way to his death, other characters arranged sinister meetings on Shepherd's Bush Green, and a gradual accretion of co-ordinates located the film's murderous activities in specific run-down parts of south London. Walker's independent films broke with Hammer's traditional sense of fair play. In his world the wrongs weren't righted, the innocents suffered and the guilty were allowed to escape. His endings were unjust as well as being unhappy.

Walker had an avatar through his film cycle: the Scottish actress Sheila Keith, who regularly appeared as a children's TV presenter, but who also starred in his films as a deranged psychopath. She usually started out normal and slowly went bananas, sometimes with a power drill or a whip. In *Frightmare* she joyously licks the spray of blood from her lips as she drills through someone's skull, loving every minute of it. The image stayed with me for years. I saw her across a room at a party once and wanted to run away yelling.

As the producers of Wardour Street started bringing us its tawdriest product, Jim and I held a meeting. We left a dodgy-looking producer smoking a roll-up in our board-room while we nipped outside to discuss what to do.

'If we turn him down, we'll lose his business,' said Jim. 'It's his first film.'

'If we take it there may be many more, and they could all be worse,' I pointed out. 'Have you seen the poster?' I unrolled a painting of a naked, whipped girl hanging in chains. 'We can't have anything to do with this.'

'You really have a problem with it?'

I studied the blood-spattered breasts. 'Well, it's not very nice, is it?'

'All right, we turn it down.'

We went back into the room. 'I'm sorry,' said Jim, 'we can't take on your film because Chris here thinks it's offensive to women.' He tapped out a cigarette and turned the meeting over to me.

Thanks a bunch, I thought.

The client sighed. 'You're right, I know it is.' He sent me a look of abject apology. 'Of course I agree with you, it's horribly offensive, but it's the only film I could afford to buy. Things are bad. Tell you what, I'll come back next time when I've got something that's a bit less crap. How would that be?'

Jim and I looked at each other in amazement. The client got up and humbly backed out of the building.

He was as good as his word, though. A year later he returned with a halfway decent film, and a better one after that.

Was it really this easy to change people's behaviour? Surely it was a truism that moral emancipation would always lead to economic destruction? We plotted out an ethical mission statement. We would only work on films that had no racism, no sexism, no homophobia. It felt like signing a death warrant.

To our surprise, word quickly got out about what we were doing, and soon we were fielding calls from potential clients who asked: 'Are you the guys who won't work on offensive exploitation movies? Can you work on my film? I hope it will meet your standards.'

They wanted their low-budget movies to look big while paying small. Business was suddenly booming, and took a qualitative leap. Eventually we worked on films by Peter Greenaway (whose scripts were incomprehensibly intellectual but whose films often turned out wonderfully), Mike Leigh, Terence Davies, Ken Loach, Neil Jordan and a host of other directors whose work spearheaded a revived English boom in quality cinema.

We employed a secretary – companies still had such things then, and besides, Bialystock & Bloom had hired one in *The Producers*,* so we had to have one. She was useless, but drank and smoked heavily, and often fell asleep with her head on her desk, so Jim thought she was cool.

We were working incredibly hard, staying late every

*Ulla (Lee Meredith) was Swedish and couldn't speak a word of English, but she could really dance.

night. Jim's smoking rate climbed, to the point where he admitted that his body kicked him awake at 3.00 a.m. to make him have a cigarette. I started to worry about my sanity and his health. We made a bet: I would give up sugar if he gave up snouts.

I still don't take sugar.

22

A Bit of Fresh Air

Locations, Michael Powell, favourite places, dwarves,
Blow Up, ***Witchfinder General***, **Mike Leigh**
and using films as photo albums

'What are we doing in a field?' asked Jim, coughing as though he was about to drop dead.

'It's not a field, it's a park,' I explained, leading the way. 'I thought we needed a bit of fresh air.'

The concept was clearly a new one. 'What do you mean?'

'It makes a change to breathe something we can't actually see.'

'What's being here got to do with films?' He knew something was up. By this time, I never did anything that wasn't tangentially connected with cinema.

'I'll show you,' I said, slipping my arm through his. 'You'll be fine. Think of the place as a giant ashtray.'

We had become strangers to the great outdoors. It bothered me, but not Jim. After all, he had told me that his favourite dream was one in which he was locked inside his mother's handbag. Sigmund Freud would have had a field-day with that one.

As a boy I would visit places I had seen on the screen,

so long as they were reachable by bus. All films are partly about recognition, so it matters where they are set. Being able to identify a local area when it appears on the big screen adds resonance to a story, and all films have an element of geography.* Before the invention of computer-generated backgrounds, American movies often had a wonderful sense of location. Theirs was a lateral society, an open, sprawling, outdoor canvas upon which to paint colourful visuals. English films, by comparison, reflected an indoor sensibility. Where Americans rode and drove and waved and shouted and fired guns at the sky, we sat and discussed and declaimed and apologized and cupped our cigarettes inside our hands so as not to annoy the person next to us. This private indoor distinction, our careful attention to space and dialogue, was one of the most noticeable traits in our films.

Displays of emotion were considered a sign of innate vulgarity by the English middle classes. The front rooms of our terraced and semi-detached houses were the ones you could see from the street, so they were always saved for best, and often still are. We didn't 'do' loud and emotional, which disqualified us from making popular movies. You could count the number of successful action films which were truly English on one hand. For a while in the sixties, films like *Zulu*, *The Italian Job* and *The Ipcress File* managed to compete with American product in terms of thrills, but as soon as the boom started it was over, and the directors decamped to California.

This move was hardly surprising. After the war, Hollywood was sending John Wayne across the Nevada horizon while we were busy transcribing the delicate slights of *The*

---

*You can always spot a US film shot in Canada – it looks generic and slightly too cold, the cinematic equivalent of a supermarket own-brand white sliced loaf.

Importance of Being Earnest to celluloid. Only a handful of our films had any sense of landscape, and those that did had but a fragmentary connection with our past, which, in a country with a two-thousand-year-old social structure, struck me as a little odd.

Cop films made us all overfamiliar with the streets of Los Angeles, but we saw little of our home ground – perhaps it was all too small and uncinematic, but England still carried the traces of its venerable history.

Probably no film had a greater sense of English geography than Powell and Pressburger's *A Canterbury Tale*, which avoided conventional categorization so easily that you ended up wondering why more tales hadn't been told in this manner. The plot is deceptive and very odd: in wartime England, a land-girl and two soldiers set out to discover the identity of 'The Glue Man', a bizarre night attacker who pours gum into the hair of girls seen with soldiers. The mystery is obliquely solved and the villain, a likeable decent man, goes unpunished, because this is not what the film is really about. It's a meditation on the land, its people, the loss of old ways and the birth of the new, set on the Pilgrims' Way and in the area around Canterbury Cathedral. It suggests continuity with a Chaucerian past, but also shows how the present time is coming to an end.

For a film so opaquely constructed, there are scenes of astonishing power, of clouds and fields and pastoral lives, and finally a lengthy sequence in the cathedral, where Bach's Toccata and Fugue and Sullivan's 'Onward Christian Soldiers' reveal a country uneasily at war but at peace with itself. There are shades of novelist Alan Garner's style in a scene where a girl hears pilgrims' horse bells sounding in the present. God knows what the poor befuddled Rank executives made of it.

Powell's *Black Narcissus* achieved a miraculous sense

of place – the Himalayas – considering it was entirely filmed on English sets with painted glass mattes. Powell used an extraordinary colour palette to capture the sense of mountain light, and the sound of the ever-present wind never allowed the audience to forget the film's locale. This aural trick became strongly associated with Fellini, who frequently used wind to suggest uncontrolled sensuality.

In my head, I had a list of films whose locations meant something to me:

No Place for Jennifer (1949): This featured a little girl walking beneath the immense Euston Arch before it was torn down and replaced with retail chain outlets.

I Believe in You (1952) and *Entertaining Mr Sloane* (1970): Both films featured central London's only open-air swimming pool, the Oasis. The former had Joan Collins leering at Harry Fowler, the latter had virtually the same scene with Harry Andrews and Peter McEnery.

The Ladykillers (1955): Mrs Wilberforce's house was constructed in a dead-end street in King's Cross. The same area, showing iconic gas-holders, was used for *Chaplin* and *Richard III*.

A Clockwork Orange (1971): The Droogs gathered in tunnels under the new south-east London town of Thamesmead, which looked more appealing later in *Beautiful Thing*.

Seven Days to Noon (1950) and *28 Days Later* (2002): Both showed a London devoid of human beings, the former because of a bomb scare, the latter because of a virus.

I could think of dozens more examples, from Hitchcock's Covent Garden in *Frenzy* to Gary Oldman's brilliant rendition of south London life in *Nil by Mouth*. The chill wind of the future finally came when I saw some green-screen test footage for an upcoming action movie, with the location to be decided after the actors had finished performing. After that it was only a small step further to films created mainly on computers, ones that showed robot figures diving in hyper slow motion through train windows and across hotel lobbies, firing guns and throwing bombs, entirely freed from the restrictions of gravity.

This meant that a century of film-making had finally been reversed. In the early days of CGI, the artists had rotoscoped* the movements of the actors to make lifelike animation. Later, actors were entirely replaced for their stunts. With films costing so much, the executives wanted all elements of chance to be removed from the performances so that everything could be predicted. This guaranteed that the finished feature would contain none of the disturbing surprises proper acting might throw up.

Cinema is now about turning actors into penguins, chipmunks or cats, which can then be sold. Ideally they should be holding, riding or wearing other objects which are also for sale. By preplanning highs into their films, companies eliminate the kind of spaces that let you think, keeping you reactive and receptive. The more relentless a film is the duller it becomes, until it is so action-packed that it achieves a state of inertness, becoming a meaning-less flypast of colour and noise that you can tune in or out of at will. Try watching *Resident Evil* or *Underworld*

---

*A technique in which animators trace over live action footage frame by frame. It turned up in all kinds of unlikely places, such as when a bandaged Norman Wisdom gets thrown from the roof of a careening ambulance in *A Stitch in Time*.

or *Transformers 3** without periodically zoning into an alpha state that involves thinking about the weather, your laundry, or, in my case, nailing some corporate drone's living flesh to a post.

Locations were thus rendered pointless. Why set a film in Paris when you could set it in Shanghai or on the moon for no extra cost? Especially if it would help you get distribution there?

Mainly, though, the history of English film was one of elaborate sets, not location work. There were some practical reasons for this: our notoriously unreliable weather, of course, and for many years it was impossible to get permission to film in certain locations. But the city remained under-used, or spectacularly misrepresented.

In the 1990s the Rolls-Royce aircraft-engine factory at Leavesden in Hertfordshire was found to be perfect for conversion into a film studio, because the curvature of its horizons (former runways criss-cross the site) prevented distant buildings from spoiling shots. *Goldeneye* was the first really big film to be lensed there, and when St Petersburg location shooting had to be cancelled after it was discovered that the weight of an army tank cracked the elderly sewers under the roads, it was a simple matter to reconstruct the city streets on its backlot. Thus *Onegin* was able to utilize trick perspectives by creating reduced horizons and populating the back of the set with dwarves.

As a result of my obsession with tracking down film locations, Jim and I were now standing in Charlton's Maryon-Wilson Park, an odd, hilly landscape chosen for its sightlines by Michelangelo Antonioni. *Blow Up* was

---

*If the *Transformers* series, the film equivalent of staring into your cutlery drawer and rattling it for several hours, is ever looked back on with affection, I'm walking into the nearest river with my pockets full of stones.

partly filmed here, and the perspectives were exaggerated with specially constructed buildings. The effect is one of dislocation, alienation and a powerful sense of unease, if not narrative cohesion.

'Shall we go now?' said Jim, looking around for somewhere to stick his dog-end. 'It's below zero.' The nice thing was that he never complained about where we were going. Actually, he never complained about anything. It was such a disconcerting habit that people often tried to annoy him, only to become infuriated when they failed. Through the long, miserable English winter I dragged Jim from one freezing location to another. He'd stand there, take a look around, say 'Had enough?', and then we'd head for the nearest pub.

From this process I learned a great many useless facts, including that John Schlesinger used Greenwich Park for *Sunday Bloody Sunday*, an area also employed by Ken Russell to stand in for Imperial Russia in *The Music Lovers*. Russell deserved some kind of award for the sheer perversity of his location decisions, choosing the Regent's Canal for Tchaikovsky's attempt at drowning himself. The thought of Richard Chamberlain contracting Weil's Disease in a sludgy channel full of shopping trolleys while dressed as a Russian composer just made me love Russell all the more.

Jim allowed me to burn out my obsessions by pandering to them. In the same way, my mother had told me, new workers in a chocolate factory were allowed to eat all the sweets they could manage on the first day, so that they would make themselves sick and never want to touch another one. Actually, I think she got this idea from watching *I'm All Right Jack*, in which new worker Ian Carmichael throws up into a chocolate machine after seeing how sweets are made.

All good friendships are founded on a level of symbiosis. It was said that Fred Astaire gave Ginger Rogers class and she gave him sex appeal. Jim gave me confidence and I gave him a degree of erudition. Beyond this, it was difficult to see what we had in common.

'Why is Tower Bridge on your list of locations?' he asked as we shivered beneath the park's dripping plane trees.

'John Wayne runs across it in the movie *Brannigan*,' I replied, as if the answer should be obvious. It wasn't an English film but it had been shot in London, which was enough.

English films inadvertently revealed truths about times past. When the BBC started wiping videotapes to save money, they elected to keep Shakespearean productions, which told us nothing, and obliterated the inconsequential dramas and sitcoms that would eventually provide cultural markers to the passing decades. *Trainspotting* captured a certain kind of Scottish sensibility at a very specific period in its history, just as *East Is East* caught Salford in a time of awkward growing pains. In both, location was virtually a cast member.

For me, one of the films with the most surprisingly powerful sense of place remained *Witchfinder General*, set in Lavenham, and various other Suffolk and Norfolk towns. It was filled with the kind of country soundscape one could no longer hear. Many scenes took place at dawn or dusk. Meadows rustled beneath darkening skies, where people, to quote Tony Selby's character in the film, 'may not be who they appear to be'. One sensed the unnerving uncertainty of the period and the lack of trust sweeping a country in the throes of civil war. Behind the standard revenge plot was a film that allowed for silences, for wind, for space and twilight, containing scenes that left room for the land to quietly reveal itself.

For David Lean, location was often an integral part of each film, whether the surroundings were the Hogarthian slums of the city or the tea-drinking London suburbs of Noël Coward, and one can't imagine *Brief Encounter* without its Lancashire railway station. Even lowly *Carry On* films often gave you a sense of being in real London areas (usually Middlesex), because Rank could rarely afford decent sets, and I imagine they probably stuck the entire cast on a homegoing bus from the studio, with Hattie Jacques hopping off at Earl's Court and Kenneth Williams going on to the Euston Road.

Polanski's *Repulsion* dug under the surface elegance of Knightsbridge to expose the corruption lurking below – and of course even if you hated the film it was always fascinating to see the London of the 1960s, in this case one which boasted a cohesive, integrated attitude to street design. Many films from this period, such as *Darling*, *Help!*, *Alfie*, *Robbery*, *Smashing Time*, *Bedazzled* and *Morgan – A Suitable Case for Treatment*, provide virtual style-guides to swinging English fashion and architecture.

Mike Leigh often chose to look behind the landmarks at the city we fail to notice: the ugly backstreets, the dead spaces next to main roads, the unintentional comedy of suburban juxtapositions. In his hilarious short film about an asthmatic hairdresser, *Short and Curlies*, there's a shot of a chemist's shop wedged under a flyover that's so dismally funny no one else would ever have thought of using it as a location. In this dry-witted approach, Leigh is diametrically opposed to the view of England proposed by Walt Disney. To be fair, Disney's artists went to the trouble of carefully photographing Primrose Hill for sequences in the original animated *One Hundred and One Dalmatians*, but for the live-action remake the studio produced another of those warped geographies of London that linked Big Ben to Trafalgar Square via Tower Bridge, Brighton, Burlington Arcade and Wimbledon.*

Americans have always been presented with an absurdly anachronistic view of London involving cheeky coster-mongers, beefeaters and cockerney knees-ups, but when we photograph our own landscape we're drawn to darker corners.

One day, Jim and I were heading to work and passed a firetruck spraying dirty water over the windows of a semi-derelict council block. 'Look out,' said Jim, 'Mike Leigh's making another film.' When we arrived at work and did some checking, we found this to be the case.

Leigh used the dingy alleyways of King's Cross for his comedy *High Hopes*, while Sheffield was home to *The Full Monty*; Liverpool housed *Letter to Brezhnev*, the strangeness of Fen Country was captured in *Waterland*, and Michael Winterbottom brought out the alienating beauty of the capital's night streets in *Wonderland*. But the real London has always remained an under-used loca-tion, and we still rarely see its most interesting areas on film. Cornwall shares a remarkable visual affinity with the West Coast of America, but few films have been shot there apart from *Blue Juice* and *Straw Dogs*. This may be because the elements that shape each area are changing, or have gone for ever.

As the hoplands and windmills of Kent disappeared, so did the reason for using Kent as a specific location. Accents became ironed-out and the arrival of superstores ensured that homogeneity replaced local eccentricity, so there seemed little point in locating films within particular

---

*English film-makers are just as bad at this sort of thing. There's a trip made in *About a Boy* that feels like the most roundabout route across London ever devised.

areas. Communities exist as much in the mind now as they do in specific places.

'Ready?' asked Jim, holding out his hand to see if it had stopped raining. We were standing by the courts where David Hemmings witnessed the imaginary tennis match in *Blow Up*.

'Yeah, I've had enough,' I agreed, looking for further filmic angles around the park and finding none. 'Let's go to the pub.'

'I know a good one near here,' Jim replied. He always did. He also had a favourite London location of his own. A film starring Peter Sellers called *The Optimists of Nine Elms* had been shot all around the railway bridges of Battersea and the Elephant & Castle. Watching the film he would say, 'That's where my dad used to park his lorry', or 'That's the pub we used to go to', as if leafing through an old family photo album rather than being at the pictures, cinema providing the accurate background details of a subjectively remembered past.

23

Old School Dies

The heyday of Wardour Street, working in pubs,
handshake deals, month-old sausages, really dreadful
films and treating Hollywood stars badly

The atmosphere in the film pubs of Wardour Street was
joyously argumentative, the beer was flat, the jokes as old
as the sausages, and The Ship in particular became our
second home. A two-hour visit there would require you
to wash the fag-smoke out of your clothes before donning
them again.

This was the year in which videotape recorders really
started to gain a foothold, but films were only available to
rent. The only place you could buy pre-recorded videotapes
was in dodgy shops on the Charing Cross Road which
had formerly sold surgical trusses and under-the-counter
naturist magazines. The tapes cost around fifty pounds
each, and were often designed to look like books so that
you could hide them in a bookcase and nobody would
think you were vulgar.

Up until then, many films had worked on a seven-year
cycle of theatrical re-release. Disney was especially good
at getting new audiences into old films. They figured that

animation would live for ever, and endlessly relaunched films like *Bambi*, which had first made its appearance in 1942.* The same cycle continued in 'limited edition' releases of DVDs, which were then withdrawn after a specific period of time, just as films are now made available for streaming for a limited period only.

The arrival of video was treated as if it were an outbreak of bubonic plague. Its first purveyors weren't real dyed-in-the-wool cineastes, Rank employees told each other, but Johnny-Come-Latelys, opportunists who had probably been used-car dealers or pornographers. A number of films appeared in that first burst of video which have since disappeared from view. They were transferred to tape because the rights were available, but sometimes nobody had even bothered to check.

There was something about videos that was seen as being common, from the people who sold them to the people who wanted to buy them. Jim and I had decided from the outset that we would have nothing to do with home entertainment. Now, it makes more money than theatrical releases – and games make more still.

The mistake I made was thinking that writing film copy would be like writing a film – I'd thought it would give me a licence to be clever. Clients didn't want clever wordplay, but a message that instantly communicated without frills. Film advertising was the opposite to regular advertising. Instead of creating a concept between the product and the consumer, you removed it to present the product by itself. The result was rarely pretty, but it did the job.

With virtually the whole of the English film industry

*In the nineties it was re-released on screens yet again, and I recorded the comments of modern audiences. I asked one modern mother and daughter what they thought of it and the mother replied, 'Fucking boring.'

concentrated in one small Soho pub, it was easy to pick up work. Jim would start chatting to someone at the bar and I would chip in with a few witty ideas. There was no paperwork of any kind; everything was agreed over a pint. Hands were shaken. Beers were bought. Sausages were consumed. Deals were done on a wink and a back-pat. Soon we were working on an ever-widening array of ghastly films. Jim was in his element, smoking and drinking and listening, a Soho Prospero watching his elementals clashing and colluding.

Jim had a key weapon in his business arsenal: he made sure we consistently under-promised and over-delivered. By now, English films had boiled away to almost nothing, their currency with audiences tarnished by so many reeking flops that they could no longer be trusted to provide entertainment. The films we got to work on through those pub handshakes were truly appalling.

> *Inseminoid*: On a faraway planet (Chislehurst Caves) a pink rubber alien chews off Judy Geeson's foot. If you want to convince an audience that your astronauts are really in functioning spacesuits, it's best not to let their visors steam up.
>
> *Let's Get Laid*: A comedy about a man called Gordon Laid, starring Robin Askwith, from *Confessions of a Window Cleaner*. A caper, apparently.
>
> *Escape to Athena*: Right-wing action! Roger Moore and Telly Savalas acting together, sometimes in the same room.
>
> *Richard's Things*: Liv Ullman and Amanda Redman realize they share the same man, Richard. The key dialogue moment comes from Ullman, as she carries a box of Richard's things with Redman.

Ullman *(looking down at box, meaningfully)*: You. Me. Richard's *things*.

North Sea Hijack: Right-wing action! Roger Moore and James Mason acting together on an oil rig. But not in the same room. Or league.

That Sinking Feeling: A muddy-looking Scottish film about a boy who steals some sinks. Brought desperate new meaning to term 'kitchen-sink drama', although it did have a funny bit with a cat in a coma.

The Sea Wolves: Right-wing action! Roger Moore acting in the same room with a visibly tired Gregory Peck and a bewildered, Riviera-wizened David Niven.

Excalibur: John Boorman buries the Arthurian legend for good while Merlin (Nicol Williamson) parades around in a silly silver hat.

An Unsuitable Job for a Woman: Staggeringly bad art film that became known around the office as 'An Unsuitable Film for an Audience'. It was described by one critic as 'not so much a film noir as chronically underlit'.

Who Dares Wins: Right-wing action! Richard Widmark and Lewis Collins compare square jaws while firing gigantic guns.

Where Is Parsifal?: Very possibly the worst comedy of all time, starring Orson Welles, obviously.*

---

*This was a vanity project that required us to trick the director into thinking the film was on national release by papering posters on her chosen route to the 'premiere'. Not such a rare occurrence as you'd think.

In the desperate days that followed, Rank and the few other film companies that still remained scrabbled around for some magic formula that would reconnect them with the youth of the late 1970s. The absolute nadir eventually arrived with a film called *Car Trouble*, in which Julie Walters* and air traffic controller Ian Charleson become locked by a vaginal spasm in a Jaguar, and Charleson drops planes out of the sky in a fit of pique. Unlikely to be screened post 9/11.

It was simply too late for the English film industry's big companies by now: most of their staffers were old before their time and hopelessly institutionalized. They had not been able to understand why *Easy Rider* had proved such a huge hit back in 1968, and were no nearer discovering what interested the cinema-going core in the 1980s. Their biggest audiences, they knew, tailed off after twenty-one, when couples started making babies and could no longer afford to go out. This was the fear – that they would stay in and watch videos for a fraction of the cost and effort.

Up until this moment, the industry maxim that cinema was recession-proof had always proved true. Video would surely destroy that belief. As box-office takings dropped, cinemas were carved up into T-shirt shops and super-markets. Some of the most astonishing and beautiful buildings vanished overnight in order to beat being listed. The great neon fountain that rose outside Studios Six and Seven near Oxford Circus was torn down. Further along the same street, the black marble pantheon of the Academy Cinemas had offered the finest in world arthouse, in

---

*Julie, a national treasure, has probably kept another film off her CV. *She'll be Wearing Pink Pyjamas* featured a group of moaning, sour-tempered women on a dank hiking holiday, and could have been sold as a contraceptive.

London's only non-smoking zone. It was turned into a Marks & Spencer store. Beside Tottenham Court Road tube station, two cinemas on the south side of Oxford Street were turned into the London Dolphinarium, a disastrous and wrong-headed enterprise, while another three opposite became a Virgin Megastore. This, in a single London street.*

A few desultory attempts were made to interest the shrinking hard core of English cinema-goers, and the turning decade did produce some terrific English films like *Quadrophenia*, *Scum*, *Midnight Express*, *The Elephant Man*, *The Long Good Friday* and *Monty Python's Life of Brian*, but nearly all of these initially had trouble finding finance.

Back in Wardour Street, the last of the old cigar-smoking producers ventured out of their poky brown offices to scrape together cash for a few more smutty English comedies and shoestring horror films. But the writing was on the wall. Brent Walker, a company known more for gambling dens and pubs, had been founded by George Walker, brother of Billy Walker, the boxing champion, and released brain-shrinking tat like *The Stud* and *The Bitch*, both starring a topless Joan Collins in her slutty-vamp mode. Producer Stanley Long, directors Peter Walker and Norman J. Warren, and writers David McGillivray and Michael Armstrong struggled on with a few low-grade gore films and soft-core farces that might be relied upon to fill the last of the old Jacey Tatler cinemas dotted around the West End. The grand cravat-wearing Tudor Gates, who could only ever have become a horror writer with a name like that, ventured down from his Covent Garden flat, situated above the actors' club Macready's, to try to

*There were fifty-one cinemas in the borough of Camden. Now there's one.

sell the kind of lovely gothic scripts he had once pitched to Hammer, but it was all too little, too late.

If an English film was any good, it was usually regarded as an anomaly. The producers who had survived the golden decade of the sixties were now smoking roll-ups, cadging halves of Watneys in The Ship and boring for Britain about the good old days. But they needed someone to sell their films, and continued to come to us.

Soon we had outgrown our tiny office and decided to rent premises in Soho's Greek Street. The building housed an art deco screening room, but before that it had been a pyjama factory: every time we shifted furniture across the floor, hundreds of mother-of-pearl buttons shook themselves loose and cascaded from the ceiling. Because the building had a cinema, it had also been soundproofed with sand between the floors, which tended to sift down on to clients' heads when people walked overhead.

Paradoxically, just as the English film industry curled up and died, our business had started booming. American films needed publicity, and word had got out that a tiny new London company could handle the work cheaply. We opened an art studio, hiring an array of talented if slightly ethereal artists who could draw and paint film posters. Jim would raise an eyebrow slightly every time I interviewed someone too strange, but luckily for me his tolerance of the artistic temperament was surprisingly high.

We found a girl who wrote beautifully and hired her. I was surprised that the male bastions in Wardour Street were prepared to accept the work of a woman until I realized that, with a name like Leo, they had assumed she was a man. After they discovered her gender, they kept asking her to make the tea, thinking she'd find it funny. She didn't, and left.

Meanwhile, our receptionist was placed behind a desk on the ground floor, and soon discovered the disadvantage of being a lone girl displayed behind glass in what had formerly been a street full of strippers, brothels and porn cinemas. One such cinema* was still next door, and the receptionist found herself unable to use the loo because it backed on to the club's projection room, so that she was forced to listen to yelping orgasms as she was trying to pee. Retired majors would elbow their way into reception and try to buy tickets, having muddled the venue's door number.

One street further over, myopic elderly gentlemen queued outside the Sunset Strip with Tupperware sandwich boxes, waiting for the doors to open at noon so that they could get front-row seats. The girls opposite, in their pink nighties (probably purchased from Brentford Nylons), called down to punters and the hatchet-faced old madam would let them in.†

On the other side of the building a tiny kiosk exploited a loophole in the smoking laws by flogging fags wholesale to anyone who wanted them. Jim was in seventh heaven.

Many of the films we worked on had young directors who were just starting their careers. One of these, *Phantom of the Paradise*, was a Faustian rock musical by a talented young director called Brian De Palma, and we were asked to attend the premiere, presumably to make up numbers, as many English film distributors would rather tear off an arm than give away a ticket. An old-school client had picked up the film and, this being a satire aimed at the young, was completely mystified by it. I always loved the look on these executives' faces when they were faced with a film that didn't star David Niven. They were hopelessly

---

*'For the more mature bachelor gentleman', the old broad who worked the ticket office explained.
†We put a stopwatch on her callers – the average visit lasted seven minutes.

lost. But we loved the movie's outrageous styling, and virtually every dialogue line from it became a catchphrase around the office, always a benchmark of popularity.

Such was our client's faith in *Phantom of the Paradise*, he opened it at a tiny fleapit in Chelsea on a rainswept Sunday night. I arrived to find the leading lady, the exquisite Jessica Harper from *Suspiria*, standing in the foyer alone and confused. She had been flown in for a publicity tour and had gamely turned up in full premiere regalia, clearly thinking *What the hell am I doing in this dump?*

A junior executive dressed in a ratty cardigan and jeans came over and stuck a melting Wall's choc-ice in her hand. Horrified, Jim and I apologized to her for the dreadful state of the entire English film industry, and bought her a glass of champagne.

In the months that followed, we found ourselves doing this a lot. In 1986 Rank asked Melanie Griffiths* to publicize her film *Something Wild* by sprawling herself across the bonnet of a pink Cadillac and being driven around Leicester Square in the rain. She told them to fuck off. I liked her for that.

Rank had a long history of taking their stars out to dinner, but as the stars got younger and the executives grew ever older, dinner became a grim trial for both sides. I remember later spotting Ms Griffiths in a hotel restaurant filled with hunchbacked waiters delivering Windsor soup, seated opposite a pair of septuagenarian executives, wondering what on earth to say to them.

It didn't take long for us to master the art of selling films, because there were no courses on the subject. You simply acted on instinct. There was no internet, no YouTube, no

---

*Daughter of Tippi Hedren, the Hitchcock star who later appeared in a film made from a short story of mine, *Through the Eyes of a Killer*. I didn't get to meet Ms Hedren as I was just the writer.

texting, nothing except TV and radio and the odd poster, and we worked around school holidays, Christmas and summer holiday releases. Digital editing was still a long way off, so everything closed down when Technicolor shut at night. All we had to do was lead punters to films they might like. And if the public was happy enough to watch Roger Moore pretending to be a secret agent in a sky-blue nylon blazer with patch-pockets, who were we to argue?

Nothing could stop us now, so Jim and I decided to take the next big step in our plan for world domination.

24

Starry-Eyed

Locking actors up, personality management, the toxicity of celebrities, the *News of the World* and other bottom-feeders, pectoral muscles and what not to say to a screen star

'I saw you on the television!' said my mother excitedly. 'I thought you were wonderful. It was the interviewer's fault that you came over like you didn't know what you were talking about.'

I had certainly not been wonderful. I had been nervous, embarrassed and uncomfortable, and it definitely showed, but I was her son and therefore Kath cut me a little slack. Not too much, though; she was the queen of the accidentally insulting compliment. I had been representing the company for a profile on BBC1's *Film Night* because even though we didn't actually make films, we had become noticed and therefore vaguely fashionable in a sort of pointless 'Do they actually employ people to do that job?' way.

Lately we had become familiar faces to the producers and directors who dined in the area's French and Italian restaurants. Everyone recognized the classic Mercedes

Jim drove, and stopped to chat, although, generally speaking, he wasn't interested in talking to them. The secret of succeeding in media is to not look like you're desperately trying to succeed, and we were the company best known for turning away work. The thrill of arriving in Wardour Street every morning as the industry geared up in the buildings all around us, ready for another day of stretching the truth in the service of celluloid, was strangely intoxicating.

We were now handling photo shoots,* shooting interviews and generally glamorizing our films' stars. And we were working with an astonishing number of them, most of whom arrived at our offices without PR agents or minders. Mickey Rourke hung out at the office with us, and we became so blasé about the famous that we once accidentally locked the Warhol cult-film star Udo Kier in our basement when we went home. My confidence had grown so much that I could now cheerfully admit to Peter Greenaway that even though I liked his films I had no idea at all what he was on about.

Mickey Rourke proved to be intelligent, self-deprecating and charming, but I had started to learn the rules governing certain other celebrities whose PR flacks warned us would require 'personality management'.

1. A great many celebrities were like vampires, only instead of wanting your blood they demanded your attention. All of it, all the time.
2. They were charming until you disagreed with them, after which it was like stamping on the tail of a mad

---

*We had to shoot stars on set while they were still in the mindset (and make-up) of the film they were making. If you left it until the film came out there was always the possibility that they might have shaved their heads, got fat or gone mad by then.

dog every time you asked them something, or they discreetly had you fired.

3. They weren't used to hearing the word no and had never been told off by anyone. Bette Davis said until people think you're a monster, you're not a star.

4. They drove their agents to alcoholism and their families to suicide, and still didn't understand that they were doing anything wrong.

5. Watching a star prepare to meet the public was an exercise in fabrication, like having your house repainted before you sold it.

6. A star could, if he so chose, look right through you so hard that you'd turn around to see if he'd left a spot on the wall. He would never initiate a conversation. He didn't have to; he was a star. We were required to provide the basic motor skills that kept the shark moving through the water.

7. Stars were not interested in us. They had that indefinable quality the public called magic and we called rudeness. The best we could ever do was make them feel warm and protected, like a dog next to a radiator.

8. The real secret to managing fame was to make the public think they knew everything. But they only saw what we let them see, which is true today more than ever.

As we grew less starry-eyed we started holding our own against stroppy celebrities. One female star stayed in her trailer and refused to be interviewed for a documentary we had been asked to direct, telling us to come back in a few hours. She did this a few times, until we politely told her we'd leave her out of the film, at which point she miraculously made herself available in a new outfit and full make-up.*

These conversations were conducted through PR people, and the ones who looked after really big stars had a much tougher time than anyone realized. I asked Suzy Tullett, who has handled most of the major stars of the last three decades, what you needed to get on in the job, and she replied, 'Strong arms, for a start. You try carrying Cameron Diaz's luggage up four flights of stairs in a hotel with a broken lift at two in the morning.'

Some of the stars I interviewed were merely imperious. The grandest of these was Dame Joan Plowright, who warned me that she would not answer any of my interview questions but would only talk about subjects that interested her. As the camera started rolling she spat a boiled sweet across the set and adopted a smiling, grandmotherly pose that she dropped the instant the lights were shut off. What a professional.

One day we received a mysterious telephone call via a press agent. Her client, she said, was a world-famous celebrity who had set up a production company to make family films. She needed someone to fly out and meet him, then design some movie posters that could go to the Cannes Film Festival. We chose to send a young art director who had never been abroad, so first we had to get him a passport. He arrived in the US and was shown into a room where a man in red flannel long-johns and a bowler hat greeted him.

Michael Jackson wanted to make a series of classic

---

*Over the years we ended up with a shortlist of stars we loved working with, including Leslie Neilsen, Nick Nolte and Jude Law, and a few who were so deranged that we would cross the street to avoid them or their agents.

family movies that would appeal to all ages. He gave the art director a detailed brief, and the art director flew home. We worked on the posters and were paid handsomely, and apart from the detail of the bowler hat (donned, I suppose, in naive respect for his English visitor) we forgot about the job.

Shortly after, accusations of paedophilia were levelled at Jackson, and while we were clearing out the storeroom we found the old poster artwork for one of the films. It was for a proposed remake of *The Pied Piper of Hamelin*, and depicted a musician leading dozens of naked children out of town. At the time, the poster had seemed innocent enough, but in the light of the press furore it looked toxic.*

Through a private comment made in passing to a friend at *Time Out*, the *News of the World* found out about the poster and started going through our bins at night. They doorstepped employees, made fake phonecalls pretending to be friends, and tried every trick in the book to get hold of the artwork. In deference to the client, we burned the so-called incriminating evidence precisely because it was no such thing. The press had thrown itself behind a witch-hunt to sell papers, nothing more.

After establishing ourselves in film we made a move into TV production, but I didn't enjoy the experience of working with television executives. It seemed they were the opposite of the nicotine-fingered kerb-crawlers of Wardour Street: they didn't have an opportunistic bone in their bodies, to the point where they completely overlooked or failed to understand good ideas. What most of them

---

*I never believed the stories about him and don't to this day, knowing how easy it was for the press to vindictively turn a childlike man into a man who liked children. When readers don't understand what motivates a celebrity – and how could they? – it's very easy to twist their opinions.

wanted to do was 'democratize' television by making it all fit one low, low demographic.

Jim appeared unfazed through all of this. 'You think it's bad now?' he said. 'Wait until a few years' time, they'll have shows that'll just be like spying on your neighbours. We're going to find ourselves watching stupid people with no talents of any kind sitting around at home talking rubbish.'

Every profession has its bottom-feeders, and fired incompetents do not give up and leave the business; they just move on to a slightly lower rung. By now I could name a dozen of these irresponsible creativity killers who drifted from film quango to indie production to sales team, leaving trails of destruction in their wake, like poisonous snails. We went out of our way to be nice to them, just in case we met them again on the way down, but when I presented work I often felt like quoting John Cleese in his *Monty Python* architect sketch, in which he indignantly cries, 'Well, that's the kind of blinkered philistine pig-ignorance I expect from you non-creative garbage.'

Many executives were well educated, well spoken and over-confident, bright enough to make the phonecalls that raised money but lacking any instinctive creative intelligence. Following the narrow line of their personal taste, most were more interested in getting an office with a nice window or easy access to a tube station than they were in commissioning good art or writing, or doing anything original and innovative. I used to keep a cartoon on my wall that showed a TV programme commissioner disconsolately standing at a bar with an empty pint.

COMMISSIONER: Same again please, Harry.

Of course, as in any profession, there are some terrific commissioners, but the job seemed to lend itself to megalomania. Famously the film censor John Trevelyan loved meeting stars and regarded himself as part of their community, a paradoxical notion when one considered that, although apparently a benign man, he was the very antithesis of creativity. There he was arguing about the censoring of a throat-slitting or a gush of blood from a vampire-staking in the Hammer films, yet he had no real data on what effect he was producing, nothing real or practical to work with except gut instinct and fear of a public backlash.*

By this time, I had started writing short stories – mainly for my own amusement, but I circulated a few to friends. Eventually, though, a small collection was published. One day I was contacted by a television production company. They said they had heard about the stories and wanted me to come in and see them. In their dazzling Wardour Street office two incredibly young girls told me they wanted to film my entire output.

This was exciting. Back in 1927, Edgar Wallace had signed a deal with British Lion that had allowed the film company to option all his books, and he had become a household name. Perhaps, I thought, the same would happen to me.

The girls loved my work. They hadn't read any of it, but they'd been told it was good. They wanted to film everything I'd written, whatever it was. I was amazed. There was, one of them said, just one snag.

It wouldn't actually be my series. They had hired a writer/director whose name would be on the project instead. They were convinced he was a genius. They were sure I wouldn't mind working for him as a televisual ghost

---

*The censors actually suggested that Hammer should stop making horror films altogether, forcing them to make the kind of lightweight thrillers that contributed to the company's demise.

writer. He had written some stories of his own, and these would be interspersed with mine. The hour-long meeting consisted of them telling me how incredibly brilliant he was.

I read some of the genius's stories. They were unbelievably awful – embarrassing, dumb, clichéd, beyond boring. At our next meeting, the girls brought the genius in. When the meeting-room door opened, I found myself faced with a ridiculously handsome, six-foot three-inch bronzed bodybuilding surfer.

I was staggered. Perhaps it was payback for all those horrible old men in the English film industry who used to feel up starlets in the 1960s. My stories were never filmed. The series was ridiculed by critics and cancelled after the airing of its second show. I began to realize that the producers weren't entirely conversant with the adaptation of literature into another medium, but they knew a lot about pectoral muscles.

A lesson had been learned. Jim said very little when I told him what had happened. 'Most people's jobs are boring,' he patiently explained. 'They want to have a bit of fun, and those two saw that their surfer would be a lot more fun than being stuck with you. Don't let people overawe you.' He suggested that I should be equally undaunted in my dealings with stars.

Having endured a crippling lack of confidence for most of my life, a disability I'd inherited from a father who could not bring himself to enter a hotel for fear of embarrassment, I was aware that something had to change, and now an opportunity presented itself.

Knowing that Jim loved Hal Ashby's dark romantic satire *Harold and Maude*, I rang the Atheneum Hotel, where the film industry used to put all its celebrities, asked to speak to the film's star, Bud Cort, who was shooting in London* and gave him an invitation to Jim's birthday party. Cort happily turned up and presented Jim with a copy of the film. As a result, they remained friends for years. Cort had learned his comic timing from his extraordinary friendship with Groucho Marx, in the same way that George Cole had been mentored by Alistair Sim.

Emboldened by my success, I got in the habit of ringing famous people and asking if they fancied a drink, and was staggered by the number who unreservedly agreed. In the 1980s the issue of stalking arose for the first time[†] and after this stars were slowly incarcerated in hotels and guarded by wolf-like PR flacks.

This casual (if never quite relaxed) proximity to celebrities prevented us from ever really becoming star-struck. I had learned my lesson after finding myself seated at that dinner next to Hilary Dwyer, the luminous leading lady of *Witchfinder General*. When a situation like this occurs, you have three choices. Do you:

a. Pretend you don't know her and casually shake hands?

b. Acknowledge her fame lightly, and treat her as you would anyone else you found sitting next to you?

c. Go 'Oh my God, you used to be my favourite actress!' before quoting all of her dialogue lines back to her, then filling the uncomfortable silence at the end by

---

*It was ridiculously easy to get famous people to come to the phone until about the mid-eighties. 'Hello, is Tony Curtis there? No, I don't know him, I just wondered if he fancied a beer. Okay, I'll be there in half an hour.'

†John Lennon was shot dead in New York by a stalker on 8 December 1980, and it almost seemed as if this opened a gateway to a new psychopathology.

saying 'Still, you're probably glad you got out of the business'?

The main rule of thumb I used when finding myself stuck alone with celebrities was this: Never say anything earnest or serious. But banter is just as taxing – as I found out after being caught in a very slow lift with Christopher Lee and hearing myself ramble on about the lift buttons when I really wanted to talk about *Dracula AD 1972*.

25

La La Land

Leaving England, living with hookers, *Xanadu*, honest
English, bad attitude and a Hot Fucking Superstar

1981 was the year of *The French Lieutenant's Woman*,
Gregory's Girl, *Chariots of Fire* and *An American
Werewolf in London*, technically all English films. It was
also the year we decided to open an office in Los Angeles.

'We should go to the source,' said Jim one morning. 'We
could set ourselves up in an affiliate company in Hollywood.
You can go around the studios selling our services.'

'Hang on,' I replied, 'what happened to "we"?'

Remembering the horror of our first Cannes, I argued
weakly against the idea. As in every argument I ever had
with Jim, I lost. 'How would we actually do it?' I asked.
I knew nothing about America except what I had seen
in films. Oh, and I'd once had a holiday in San Diego,
when I'd written off a friend's car within thirty seconds
of driving off his property. I'd been to the zoo and the
beach, and to the Hotel Coronado because it was where
they had filmed *Some Like It Hot*. Clearly, this was all
the experience I needed to breeze into the studio lots of
Universal and Paramount.

'I can't go out there by myself!' I complained. 'I'm Mr Cellophane, nobody will take any notice of me and we'll get no work and we'll go bankrupt, and in America they throw you in jail for things like that and make you share your cell with murderers and rapists.'

'I thought of that,' said Jim, cheerfully relighting his knocker.* 'I've got someone I want you to meet.'

Bryn Lloyd was a solidly built six-foot-one Australian whose open face and permanent smile charmed everyone he met. He was also a flamboyant casting agent well known for swooping around the West End armed with a constellation of rainbow-coloured helium-filled balloons. He knew the name of every secretary, everyone's baby, everyone's favourite place to be wined and dined, every birthday, and he looked after his clients like treasured old friends. He kept a permanent table open at Joe Allen, the legendary Covent Garden showbiz restaurant, and always seemed to have a magnum of champagne within arm's reach. This generosity of spirit meant that he lived well beyond his means, and he was getting into the kind of debt you can only resolve by selling something really big. But all he had to sell was his flat in Shepherd's Bush.

He'd been talking to Jim about returning to Australia, but felt it would be interpreted as a sign of failure, and that was one thing he would never do. Jim suggested an alternative: go out to Los Angeles with me, open up an office there and break into Hollywood. Bryn sold his flat and got ready to make the move.

Typically, Jim only explained all this to me after the deal was done, but he had accurately gauged my own mood. I was frustrated with London, exhausted by our claustrophobic relationship and anxious to do something

---

*A cigarette you've been required to put out, but have decided to save for later.

different, so heading to Hollywood seemed like the perfect make-or-break idea. I met Bryn and instantly liked him.

I sold my flat within a month, and on a miserable Saturday morning in spring 1980 I packed a single suitcase and met Bryn at Heathrow Airport. I'd been quite unsentimental about leaving London until that point, but when I opened the package my friends had given me for the flight out, I got a lump in my throat. Inside were framed photographs of them all waving goodbye, as if they were expecting never to see me again. It was like boarding the *Titanic*.

I knew that new arrivals in Hollywood had a spectacular drop-out rate.* I'd been warned that creativity counted for little against accountancy. It was about how much you could undercut your rivals. Luckily, we would have no overheads. Repeating the trick we'd performed in London, we rented office space in Beverly Hills from a company that operated at the very heart of the Hollywood industry. Its owner was a charming, savvy businessman who bore a startling resemblance to Clark Kent, and was intimately connected with all the major studios. His office was next door to the famous homegrown Hollywood talent agent, Irving 'Swifty' Lazar. Lazar's clients included Bogie and Bacall, Cole Porter, Gene Kelly, Ernest Hemingway, Noël Coward, Diana Ross, Richard Nixon and Tennessee Williams. It was said that his power was so great, he could negotiate a deal for someone who wasn't even his client and then collect a fee from their agent.

Faced with these neighbours, I was a know-nothing chancer. At least Bryn was a networker. The first rule towards getting what you want, Bryn told me, was to surround yourself with what you *would* want. I wasn't so ambitious, and neither was Jim, but Bryn's attitude was

---

*Gore Vidal's maxim was: 'It is not enough to succeed in Hollywood. Your best friend must also fail.'

refreshing, if a little too unnervingly focused.

We arrived and checked into a suspiciously cheap motel on the upper edge of Hollywood. It had a murky central swimming pool and rows of doors around it like changing cubicles, and blue and green striped metal lounge umbrellas. It was the kind of hotel cops had shootouts with pimps in, although no officer would need to kick in my door, as it opened by itself: the wood was so warped that it repeatedly popped and swung inwards. I looked under the broken-springed bed and glimpsed a phalanx of shiny brown cockroaches scuttling off into the darkness. I felt like a down-at-heel lounge pianist in a forties noir B-movie, wanted for murder and hiding out in a hick town, waiting to be betrayed by Barbara Stanwyck.

As the sun set on Sunset, I came to the dawning realization that we were staying in one of Hollywood's last surviving hooker motels. The corridors had filled up with gum-snapping women in cheap nylon wet-look bikinis and cork-heeled sandals, dragging fat little punters into the rooms. My door was knocked on so many times in the night that I had to wedge a chair under the handle.

Hollywood in 1980 was at a crossroads. Mostly, it was still a sleazy run-down rat-hole filled with swingers' saunas and the kind of single-storey hotels where failed salesmen were found dead on the toilet. There were rent-boys in cowboy hats and hefty go-go girls in hot pants and ridiculous Cadillacs and vacant surfers and ancient Jewish ladies and so many intellectual pot-smoking old hippies that it looked as if they were casting a Charles Manson movie up the block.*

---

*There was one thrillingly gloomy relic of old Hollywood: a damp-reeking shop that sold original movie props, scripts and memorabilia for knock-down prices. The last time I looked, it was a frozen yoghurt joint.

But the new Hollywood was also arriving: the coke-snorting Armani suits and their power-dressed girlfriends had come in to clean up. They belonged to a group we termed the New Selfish, which quickly became known as the Me Generation. They judged each other by appearances and were proudly, defiantly philistine. The car, the suit, the real estate, the movie deal, these were the only things that mattered. They were seen at the good tables in the right restaurants, and would soon start carting around the gigantic plastic bricks they called cellphones.

The 1980 Hollywood film that epitomized this dichotomy was *Xanadu*, a desperate roller-disco musical starring Olivia Newton-John and Gene Kelly. At one point the clash was perfectly summed up in a single visual metaphor, as two stage sets, one containing a 1940s-style swing orchestra, the other holding a cheesy thigh-booted leotard-wearing rock band, literally collided and combined. In the film, the old and new schools found they could work together, but in real life they wanted to kill each other.

The old building that was used for the exterior of the Xanadu nightclub was the astonishing green and silver art deco Pan Pacific Auditorium on Beverly Boulevard. It had been built in 1935 and appeared to have been created by the designers of the emerald city of Oz, with four soaring spires like gondola fins. I went to look at it just after its battle for preservation had been lost. Even with the windows boarded over, anyone could see that it was a masterpiece of art deco design, but the sharks were circling this prime piece of real estate, and the mostly wooden structure was conveniently destroyed by a fire. *Xanadu* dropped dead at the box office, yet remains a peculiarly charming encapsulation of the times, not least because of Newton-John's bizarre turn as a roller-skating Aussie-accented muse from Mount

Olympus, complete with peasant dresses and blonde highlights.

As it was our first weekend, Bryn and I drew up our contacts list beside the viscous swimming pool that looked as if corpses were regularly fished out of it, and decided to start cold-calling first thing on Monday morning.

On Sunday it was eerily hot and quiet, and I sat in the sun with my notebooks. Having been kept away from anything resembling sunshine for most of my adult life in London, I naturally got so badly burned that I looked as though I'd been in a kiln explosion. I covered my glowing, stinging crimson face with moisturizer, but still looked as if I worked with plutonium rods. So much for fitting in with the locals. I might as well have had 'Hillbilly' stencilled across my forehead.

Meanwhile, Jim had arranged for me to collect a used car from an old friend of his. I had passed my driving test three weeks before the big move,* and knew I would need a little second-hand runabout to negotiate Los Angeles. Never let a classic-car freak choose your vehicle: I found myself driving back from San Diego in a 1950s monstrosity with a dashboard-mounted chrome push-button gear-change. Both front tyres blew out in the middle of the San Diego freeway, but the cops weren't like the cool ones on the TV show *CHIPs*. They wouldn't help me because they didn't want to get run over.

Our first Monday morning appointment was with a low-rung executive at the Dino de Laurentis studio, where I got an inkling that our shared language might actually separate us. Forced to park in the extreme rear of the

---

*My instructor at the British School of Motoring Trafalgar Square was a great teacher and a chronic functioning alcoholic. I still get my bearings in London by watching out for the pubs and off-licences he used to nip into for miniatures during lessons.

backlot and schlep through the heat with my radioactive face, I entered a giant freezer-cabinet of a building and showed a bronzed, side-parted executive our company brochure, watching as he flicked through it in growing puzzlement. 'I thought you made previews,' he said finally, 'but it says here you sell trailers?'

It dawned on me that, like the guy in Cannes, he also thought we manufactured caravans. As he looked down the list of the films we had worked on, it was also clear that he didn't believe a word of it. 'How do I know you guys didn't just come up with these fancy film titles?'

'Because we would never do such a thing,' I said, shocked. 'We wouldn't lie to you. We're English.'

'Oh, is that what the accent is?' he replied. 'I just thought you were fags.'

I didn't bother to enlighten him on that score; I thought things might get too confusing. As I ran down the carefully rehearsed tick-list of our services, I could see there was another question on his lips.

'Tell me something,' he said finally. 'Why do you have such weird hair?' I was sporting the once-fashionable London buzzcut much favoured by bands like Bros.

'Er . . .'

'Why don't you have a side-parting?' The question threw me. It was a peculiarity of American corporate life that all the executives had side-partings.*

'Because I'm an individual,' I answered finally, feeling the room's temperature drop further.

'Listen, even if you did work on all this shit, why the fuck would I give work to guys from "Engerland"' – he put air-quotes around the country, as if it didn't exist – 'when they have no fucking idea what plays in Peoria?' He sounded like a character from a bad Oliver Stone movie.

*They still do. Hollywood remains the Bad Hair capital of the world.

'Because we have quality and class,' I replied, ruffled, digging my pit deeper.

'And we'll undercut your competitors' prices,' Bryn added. This, it turned out, was the key to getting work in Hollywood.

'Okay, now you're talking, and I'll level with you. We have this fucking problem,' the exec explained, suddenly our new best friend. 'We're making a movie called *Flash Gordon*. Know what that is?'

'Of course,' I said. I had seen all of the original serials at our little arthouse cinema in Scala Street, London.

'It's a fucking great big deal, stars Sam Jones, who's gonna be the hottest fucking superstar of the eighties.* But there's another *Flash Gordon*, a shitty little animated feature we had to finance to get out of some copyright issues. We've got to produce previews for it. Could you do it?'

'Yes, of course!' we replied.

'By Wednesday?'

'Easy!' I said, thinking *Where the hell are we going to find someone to cut this?* But you can't kick a rock in Los Angeles without hitting an out-of-work editor. We found one a few blocks away. Bee was a sweet-natured midwestern girl who worked freelance, and offered to turn the job around fast. While she did so, she gave us a crash course in understanding the West Coast mentality. We learned about breakfast meetings, ordering Mexican food, checking box-office figures every morning and quoting the right parts of *Variety*, along with a smattering of useful

---

*He didn't become the Hottest Fucking Superstar of the eighties. Some unflattering nude pictures of him surfaced and he promptly vanished into Direct-to-Video Hell, with movies like *TNT*, *Psychotic* and *Fists of Iron*.

Yiddish and the most helpful communications tool of all: a horrifying level of thick-skinned bluntness.

'Most Californians don't know how to hold real conversations,' Bee explained. 'They've never had any. They just talk at you until they run out of breath. You've had more practice with words. You're English. You can make them look classy.'

When we had cut the previews and delivered them in record time, we realized that the studio had no intention of releasing the movie, but had been legally committed to providing A&P* for a film no one would ever see. It was a first glimpse of the darkly labyrinthine workings of Hollywood. Bee was a find, though. Suddenly Creative Partnership (overseas branch) had another staffer.

Breaking into what turned out to be a very closed shop proved nightmarish. Bryn attempted to charm secretaries in the manner that had always worked in London, but in Hollywood the technique fell flat. 'Do you have any children?' he solicitously asked one scarily overtanned PA.

'What the fuck do you care?' she replied without looking up.

The locals were so obsessed with themselves that, to anyone from outside, they came over as breathtakingly thoughtless and arrogant. It was the start of Reagan's America, when greed was good and foreigners were to be sneered at. Suddenly it was okay for a comic like Andrew Dice-Clay[†] to stand up on national television and make jokes about the poor and 'the urine-coloured people'.

I didn't understand. This wasn't the expansive, accepting America I had fallen in love with as a child – and to many Americans, of course, Los Angeles didn't count as

---

*Advertising and publicity.
[†]His big movie break arrived with *The Adventures of Ford Fairlane*. One sensible critic described it as 'As vulgar and obnoxious as its star'.

part of their country at all. 'Reaganomics' saw a cancerous personality change that was reflected at home in a similar hardline regime, and it wasn't a good time to be an outsider. Thankfully, the poisonous arrogance that had descended on the city wasn't long-lived, although it returned with a vengeance in the Bush years.

What shocked me was how easily a city filled with essentially rootless people from all over the country had adopted such a collective 'screw you' attitude instead of learning how to work together. The town was incredibly territorial and judgemental. If you went to a smart restaurant in casual clothes, the waiters shunned you. If you went near the surfers' beach they threw rocks at you. If you went into Beverly Hills the police stopped you. Gay, Jewish, black, Mexican, elderly, everyone had their own part of town and damn well stayed in it on pain of being robbed or arrested. A film executive proudly told me that the only time he saw black people was when he took his children to amusement parks.

If there was one great benefit that came from mass economic migration, it was the shaking out of Los Angeles, and the town became all the better for it.

It's still pretty horrible, though.

26

Hollywoodized

Welcome to the eighties, the new social order, casual racism, Julie Andrews topless and the aspirations of staff

Los Angelinos were not our kind of people. They were ill-mannered and vulgar and talked only about movies and money. They openly discussed each other's salary over lunch. Worse, most of what they said was hilariously awful, ignorant rubbish. They had never seen a play, read a book or visited an art gallery, and knew nothing of the world's great philosophers, writers, artists, thinkers. They could quote old Chuck Heston movies verbatim but struggled to remember who Shakespeare was. And they hated the English. We were fine to make fun of when we came over to visit Disneyland, but when we arrived to take work away from them, we were treated with the kind of unthinking racism that they were used to inflicting on their Mexican gardeners and maids.* We were mocked whenever we opened our mouths by people who cut

---

*I remember seeing a book on sale in a local store called *How to Speak to Your Maid*, which listed words like 'toilet cleaner' in Spanish.

capers and mimicked Dick Van Dyke in *Mary Poppins*. I wondered if they might don blackface and perform cakewalks if they met Africans.

The movie executives weren't interested in whether or not we could produce admirable work. They wanted to know two things: 'Are you going to fuck this job up if I give it to you?' and 'Who else have you spoken to?' When we guilelessly told them who else was thinking of hiring us, they said, 'Don't go to them, they're losers.'

Not being invited to the important screenings, we had curiously short days. I found myself with time on my hands. In London, my idea of fun was mooching around old bookshops in the rain, but in Los Angeles it took me ages to even find a bookstore. When I finally ran across a place on Santa Monica Boulevard, I discovered sections labelled Self-Help, New Age, Home Management, Self-Diagnosis, Religion, Astrology, Altered States, but couldn't see any novels.

'Where is your fiction section?' I asked the counter girl.

'Over there by the toilet.' She pointed to a single shelf containing a couple of Mark Twains and an F. Scott Fitzgerald.*

Being literate in a town where everyone was working on their tan and their Arnie screenplay was a liability. Film executives made us park miles across the studio lot (the higher you were in the pecking order, the closer you were allowed to park to the studio – we were always right at the back) and restaurant valets shoved our bashed-up Rent-A-Wreck far off their forecourts, where it couldn't offend the eyes of diners. In London we had been popular and successful. Here we had been dumped into an invisible

---

*The few large bookshops I found all played Vivaldi's *Four Seasons* very loudly, as if to remind people that they were doing something incredibly cultural.

underclass along with Korean gardeners and Mexican maids.

One day I finally managed to get a key executive from Technicolor out to lunch, and arrived early at her favourite restaurant, Wolfgang Puck's Spago, the restaurant that became the West Coast's defining symbol of conspicuous wealth. I was eventually seated at a minuscule table next door to the toilet.

At the front of the restaurant, a morbidly obese Orson Welles was holding court at the biggest table, surrounded by guffawing sycophants. My guest arrived and nodded to Welles, who nodded back, and the waiter suddenly realized she was important. He swept over to me clicking his fingers. 'Well, don't just sit there, bring your glass, come on, let's go!' He made me jump up and follow him to a better table.*

This exaggerated esteem for the social order was entirely commonplace. One client pointed to our car and said, 'You'll never get any work in this town driving a shitheap like that!' as if our mode of transport actually affected our talent.

Deciding that if we couldn't beat them we would join them, we started to tone down our act. We suited up and got side-partings. I stopped being ironic and smart, and began working out. Bryn no longer bothered to be charming, and reeled off financial statistics instead. I reduced the linguistic complexity that came naturally to my conversation. We Hollywoodized our act so that people had no reason to hate us. But after London, it was a lonely, ghettoized existence. Nothing was spontaneous. Because of the distances we were required to travel, every meeting,

*Mark Cousins tells a story that shows nothing has changed. He was ignored in a restaurant until the waiters saw he was sitting with Buck Henry, after which the compliments began.

every meal, every casual contact was carefully planned in advance. Nothing ever happened by chance. Back home, I could wander out into Soho without a plan and bump into interesting people all night. Here, there was the gym, dinner or a movie. The restaurants filled at 6.00 p.m. and the town was dead four hours later.

I missed Jim. I missed the arguments in shabby pubs, the nights spent in run-down soon-to-close cinemas. I even missed the rainy traffic jams spent coughing in his smoke-filled Mercedes. Every evening I called or telexed him – a painful process that involved punching tiny holes into miles of tickertape without making mistakes. I told him all the news, not that there was ever much to tell. We had a couple of earthquakes. The windows fell out of some people's offices, but nobody seemed that interested. What did it take to excite these people?

If Los Angeles had one saving grace, it was the women.

Not only were they required to constantly justify their jobs to unbelievably sexist men, they had to look damned good while doing it or face insulting assessment from their bosses. They had to talk hard and drink hard, and many became alcoholics. The women of the Los Angeles film industry were tougher, smarter, braver, ballsier and more honest than any of the males I worked with there. They rarely found stable relationships because their chosen career path appeared to require a virtual vow of celibacy. They worked insanely long hours to prove themselves, and had their work cut out to stop the industry from backsliding into a kind of 1950s time-warp where they would once again become secretaries. There were angels in the city after all.

Back in London, Jim had been sent his first Hollywood client. It was raining hard, and a glamorous female MGM executive arrived at our Soho office in a pale blue twin-set with bobbed California-blonde hair, looking like a Barbie doll that had been dropped in a filthy pond. She had got caught in the downpour and had become hopelessly lost on the journey from Knightsbridge, where it seemed all Americans stayed.

At that time we were in the middle of moving our film edit suites from the second floor of a two-hundred-year-old terraced house in Greek Street. The building was half-emptied and in semi-darkness as Jim showed the Hollywood executive upstairs. Somewhere above her, rainwater was piddling through the ceiling. The only hall light had fizzed and burned out half an hour earlier.

Our Californian executive was reserved but game, and soldiered on in her pink patent-leather high heels until she fell up the stairs in the dark, laddering her tights, her hair falling down over one eye. She had brushed against a sooty banister and blackened her jacket. Jim looked at her bravely struggling on in the dark on all fours without a word of complaint, and welcomed her to the London way of doing things.

Back in LA, we were working on some of the worst films to come out of the eighties, none of which is now remembered with any fondness: *Cattle Annie and Little Britches*, *Take This Job and Shove It*, *Happy Birthday to Me*, *S.O.B.*,* *Comin' At Ya!*† or *Honky Tonk Freeway*, anyone? We worked long hours and late nights, because there was nothing else to do.

The city's strange intellectual vacuum was both a symptom and a result of its residents' loneliness. Nobody got together with anyone else unless it was to discuss

---

*Famous for featuring Julie Andrews topless, it was called 'as uncomfortable as watching your mother get undressed'.
†This third-rate spaghetti western was a big success because it heralded the start of a 3D craze that quickly burned itself out. A lesson not heeded, I feel.

making money. LA life was phenomenally static. Nobody seemed to achieve anything.*

Everyone talked incessantly about their dreams, but these were usually hopelessly unrealistic, and remained permanently stuck on the horizon. Waiters said they were models, but hadn't actually done any legal modelling work. Shop assistants spoke of becoming famous actors, but had no interest in the theatre. The girl in my carwash told me she longed to be a famous writer, but said she never had the time to read books. Of course the key word was 'famous', an aspiration in itself, and the actual category of fame was added as a random afterthought.

Two films, both by the excellent Michael Tolkin, came to epitomize the LA lifestyle. *The Player* told the story of an executive who not only gets away with murder but parlays it into further success, and *The New Age* follows the downward spiral of a film executive who ends up selling personalized pencils by phone to his old colleagues. It seemed like either option might come true for us.

There's a great moment at the beginning of Martin Scorsese's *After Hours* when Griffin Dunne is explaining a computer system to job applicant Bronson Pinchot, who snaps at him, 'I won't be doing this for long.' Even before his training has finished, he feels the need to show people that the job is beneath him. In 1980s Los Angeles the only people you saw who actually appeared to be doing something to earn their money were waiters and sales staff – the very ones who were desperate to tell you that they soon planned to be doing something else.

*I tried on a pair of trousers in Fred Siegel, but they didn't have my size. I looked in just over a year later and the counter girl smiled vacantly and said, 'Your pants are in.'

27

Burnout

Dubious tenants, lawsuits, blame, guilt, drugs,
paradoxes and the Four Horsemen of the Apocalypse

It seemed to me that the older, poorer Los Angelinos had
the better end of the deal. The residents of Echo Park and
Silverlake inhabited traditional West Coast wooden shacks,
built out between spurs and ridges of land pierced with
spindly palms that were nightly silhouetted by the sinking
sun. These areas to the east and south of Hollywood felt
like the real LA, where a main street still had grocery stores
and an old neon cinema. West Hollywood and Beverly
Hills were nondescript upmarket suburbs virtually devoid
of street activity. It was hardly surprising that we weren't
making friends – there was no one around.

But Bryn was determined to charm at least some studio
executives into friendship. He decided to throw a sushi
party.

'Okay,' I said, 'but first we have to find somewhere
decent to live. I don't think I can keep the punters out of
my room much longer. I may just give in, buy a push-up
bra and start charging them.'

Decent rented accommodation at an affordable price

proved hard to find. I saw one apartment currently rented by a new friend, David. It was the most terrifying flat I ever stepped into. Situated on the third floor at the apex of a triangular building, it was exactly level with a freeway that ran head-on at the front of the building with the lanes dividing on either side of the lounge, so that you lived in fear of a truck smashing through the picture window. The air was petrol-drenched and you couldn't hear yourself for revving engines. The only other tenants were deaf old ladies.

'Why did you rent this place?' I shouted incredulously.

'It was really cheap,' he replied. 'It had frightened the last owner to death.'

We finally found a rental apartment in West Hollywood that had puce shagpile carpeting, stippled yellow walls and a communal sunbathing area populated by predatory alligator-skinned residents who shamelessly costed us out as we walked past with the shopping. Our neighbours decided that walking to the shops was the sort of bizarre behaviour you might expect from Englishmen in LA, as it was already assumed we wore bowler hats and called umbrellas 'bumbershoots'.

During our first week in the building, the next-door neighbours tried to fence a stolen watch on me before vanishing overnight. There was a get-rich-quick Wild West vibe at work in the apartment block. Tenants appeared and evaporated at an incredible rate, often followed by police officers. On their day of arrival they would turn up with a nail-gun and several bolts of cloth, and would redecorate an entire apartment in a few hours, renting all their furniture, including vases and picture-frames, from Bekins on Highland Avenue. This meant that they could always make a quick getaway. In a town where so many people were working a scam, I now understood why studio execs didn't believe our credentials. Any-one else would have simply made them up. The spirit of

P. T. Barnum was alive and living in Hollywood.

Bryn became excited about his upcoming sushi party. 'It'll be a great leveller in every sense,' he explained. 'I'm going to take all the furniture out of the room. They'll all have to sit on tatami mats and that will force them into holding conversations.' I wasn't convinced by his logic, but I agreed to go along with it.

Bryn and I found a great Japanese restaurant that would deliver sushi (nobody would dream of cooking in LA). Everyone arrived at an insanely early time and obediently sat on the floor, trying not to look horrified at the sight of so much rented furniture, or walls that were painted the colour of French's mustard. As long as we talked only about the movie industry everyone could join in, but the evening was essentially an agonizing series of eulogies. If one person spoke, everyone else fell reverently silent until they had finished. The dinner conversation ended with awkward prepared compliments, and everyone vanished on the stroke of ten.

Within a few months of our arrival, we were hit with a half-million-dollar lawsuit. Studios didn't like using union talent because it was too expensive, and encouraged us to work outside the system. We had booked an actor in our usual manner, guaranteeing him a royalty every time his film piece aired rather than arranging a buyout, but the studio decided to use the piece across the nation, and realized what it would cost. 'Don't take this personally,' said the lawyer who was arranging to sue us. 'Everything's fine, it's just insurance to make sure that you sort the problem out quickly. It's the way we do business. Afterwards, we'll go to a great wetback* restaurant I know.'

---

*Ah, the eighties: the mullets, the leg warmers, the casual racist terminology that nobody thought was wrong. Mexicans were known as 'wetbacks' because they swam rivers to try to get into the US.

Jim seemed to find my anguished phonecall highly amusing. 'Don't worry about it,' he advised. 'Act like nothing has happened. Show them it hasn't rattled you. Take them out to dinner. Get them pissed.'

'Nobody here drinks,' I said miserably.

It didn't take a genius to work out why everyone in LA was so health-conscious. The city encouraged bad habits. Nobody had learned the European art of casual light drinking. Everyone was from somewhere else so they were free to reinvent themselves, and the new sense of freedom led to excesses that quickly killed most of them. For every gym-freak executive there was a drug-fried burnout, for every model a hooker, for every actress a titty-bar dancer, for every actor a rent-boy. There were more small-time drug dealers and porn stars with two-year career spans than there were studio employees.

For all our efforts to integrate it was clear that Los Angelinos would continue to do Dick Van Dyke impersonations every time we spoke. I had never met a people so willing to revel in their own ignorance. I'd foolishly assumed that the smartest workers would occupy the top jobs, but this quickly proved not to be the case. The brightest people I met were much further down the food chain, having been frozen out by their intelligence and their willingness to be different.

Although I made several great friends, hardly any of them held down a regular job. They had found themselves placed outside a system that operated in rigid compartments, and did whatever was necessary to get by. I rarely attempted to watch US TV because the few decent shows were carved into attention-deficit slivers by commercials that used patriotism as a sales tool, but one evening I saw a local news interview with a white Los Angelino who said that he would never work with the English because of the Boston Tea Party, and the fact that the English had allowed black people to freely enter their country.

Our efforts to keep the same eclectic mix of friends that we had in London failed. Blacks lived in south LA, gays lived in West Hollywood, Jews still lived on Fairfax and the rich were well hidden in the hills.

I went to dinner theatre* with my sole black friend, and we were turned away by the doorman, ostensibly for having the wrong kind of shoes. He took the snub with resigned equanimity, but I felt like buying a gun and shooting the doorman dead. Suddenly I saw how US ethnic groups must have felt all the time.

Back in the office, endlessly pitching below break-even for film projects, I had a glimpse of the pressure placed on executives when I worked on a terrible SF movie. *Yor – Hunter from the Future* was an unfinished low-budget B-movie that the producer had taken to Cannes. Recognizing that if it could be cheaply finished it would be in a fit state for US release, a studio executive from Columbia was rumoured to have slipped a cheque for one million dollars under the producer's hotel-room door, although, typically, no one could verify the story.

The finished film was unwatchable. I can think of only one worse SF film, *The Shape of Things to Come*, which bore no resemblance to anything H. G. Wells had ever touched.† A fortune was spent on publicity. The film opened on Friday and lay dead in the gutter before Monday. We were summoned to the studio lot on Monday morning, and found ourselves in a room with a dozen other hapless idiots who had worked on the film.

---

*A gruesome invention rather like a *Reader's Digest* version of real theatre, whereby you eat a huge dry meal while watching a musical with the book filleted out, leaving behind a set of blandly reorchestrated songs.
†Memorable for an apocalyptic scene in which a plastic drainpipe bounces off the head of a visibly puzzled Jack Palance.

'We're here today,' said the executive in charge of the meeting, 'to ascertain which one of you was responsible for the failure of our film.'

We were each asked in turn whose fault it was. Nobody dared to say that the film was ordure, because that would have suggested that the collective taste of the executive committee was suspect. Instead, a great medicine-ball of blame was passed around the room, until it stopped at the feet of one poor sod who couldn't think as fast as the others and was duly fired in front of them. After an hour of adrenalin-drenched, butt-clutching cruelty, I fell out of the meeting room soaked in sweat. This was what the studio executives faced every day of their working lives. No wonder they were so well paid. No wonder they were such horrible people.

Meanwhile, my love life had collapsed. I had left a relationship behind in London, and there seemed to be minimal chance of creating a new one in LA that would survive beyond the first encounter, when I opened my mouth and they discovered I was English. I occasionally went clubbing with my pal Kim, but in order to be accepted by one of the new über-cool clubs like Probe you had to be interviewed before a committee of total wankers.* Once you were accepted (no fat people, no ugly people allowed) they gave you a brushed-steel membership card and a bumper sticker that read: 'Don't worry boys, I'll be back.' Probe was an extravagantly themed nightclub that served no alcohol, but offered stacks of fresh fruit instead, knowing that the clientele would be off their faces on drugs.

Since I am the kind of person who naturally succumbs to peer pressure, LA was largely responsible for my first and last experiences with chemicals. Mercifully I don't

*The males bore a startling resemblance to Jeff Goldblum's smarmy club-owner in *Thank God It's Friday*.

have an addictive nature, so this brief era of experimentation ended as soon as I discovered that most of these things weren't very nice.

My Cause-and-Effect Chart of Chemical Experimentation

Alcohol: Budweiser in bottles. Horrifically violent headaches. Like drinking formaldehyde.

Pot: One puff made me fall face down into a bonfire. Jacket caught alight.

Coke: Turned me into an irrational, grindingly tense, staring-eyed monster. Ideal for film executives.

Quaaludes: One experience. Went completely numb, woke up covered in bruises.

MDMA: Lost all self-control, became slurring protoplasmic mess, spent next day on phone apologizing to people I didn't recall meeting.

LSD: Ingested by accident on New Year's Eve, laced into cookies mailed by a lunatic Hollywood film director who took our first business meeting in the nude. Tried to climb inside a glass coffee table. Had to be locked in a cupboard and guarded for hours.

Tea: Acceptable, except that in LA they brought you a glass of lukewarm water with a dangling paper-wrapped teabag hanging from the handle on a string, like a tampon.

Being English, I had always laboured under the misapprehension that sunshine was a cure for all ills. But for a city that basked in year-round dazzling light, LA seemed to be filled with frightened, drugged-up and depressed people who constantly talked about getting the hell out before it was too late.

As the months passed, LA offered a surreal mix of the paradoxes you might expect in a town whose only monument was emblazoned in immense white characters on a hillside.* I climbed up to the Hollywood sign late one afternoon and heard what I thought were gunshots, but it was just the metal banging as it cooled down. 'Hollywood' made a lot of noise and there was nothing behind it: an almost perfect analogy.

My smart and attractive female friends only met men who were borderline psychopaths. They spent their evenings over at my place stir-frying vegetables and sobbing into cheap wine.

One of our nicest and most loyal clients was Jerry Gross,† a Hollywood pariah who had produced the much-banned *I Spit on Your Grave*, starring Camille Keaton, Buster's granddaughter. Once again, we attracted outsiders.

The city was obsessed with fitness and health, yet an average restaurant food portion was enough for four people, and there was nowhere to walk it off. If you did so, there was a strong likelihood that the police would question you.

The only subject that got more attention than movie-making was serial killing. The Hillside Strangler and the Freeway Killer competed against Disney films for headline space.

---

*In 1932 a failed actress called Peg Entwhistle climbed to the top of the letter H of the Hollywood sign and threw herself to her death. While she lay dying in the cactuses at its base, a letter was on its way to her offering her the lead role in a play about a woman driven to suicide. Another suspect Hollywood story.

†Gross followed a line of brilliant showmen from William Castle onwards, hawking cheap movies state by state, retitling them according to what particular audiences liked. One of his films was sequentially billed as a comedy, an action adventure, a romance and a slasher flick, depending on which state showed it.

The sandy bay at Venice Beach looked beautiful but was never washed by the tide, and was infested with mites that left tiny white spots all over my skin, so I never went sunbathing.

My local bar, Barney's Beanery, was in the heart of gay West Hollywood and had 'Faggots Stay Out' printed on its matchbooks.

In a city filled with unemployed actors there was almost no serious theatre.

At the edge of Beverly Hills (right beneath its noisy sign) were the elderly homeless, their only belongings gathered in shopping trolleys.

The English accent that lost me so many jobs by day waved me into clubs by night.

It was easier to get scammed by con-artists in the elegant and expensive restaurants of Melrose than at the bus station.

Bryn and I regularly switchbacked between attending glamorous Hollywood parties and not being able to pay our rent.

Meanwhile, Barbara, our shared receptionist, married Cary Grant.*

Variety ran spectacularly myopic headlines – as well they should, because film was their only concern. A typical *Variety* headline of the time would have been: 'Chinese Earthquake: Box Office Not Affected'.

Steve Martin summed up the paradox in *LA Story* in the film's opening speech: 'I have a favourite quote about LA by William Shakespeare.'

Thankfully, the company found itself championed by a handful of genuinely brave auteurs: they were the distributors of European movies who possessed a global

---

*She introduced me to him on the street. Despite the huge difference in their ages, I could see why she married him. He had the charisma of a sun-god.

mindset and were as disgusted by the current fashion for racism as we were. Unfortunately, racism in Hollywood movies never went away; it just switched targets from Arabs to Russians to the Chinese. And through it all, one particularly vituperative strand of racism survived: that of the slimy English villain. English Hollywood actors are still largely relegated to the kind of roles that black actors had to make do with for decades, the untrustworthy drunks and comic sidekicks.

One day I went to see a studio executive at Paramount, and realized, to my horror, that he thought I was a writer coming to pitch him a film treatment. Having gone too far to be able to point out the mistake, I made up a screenplay outline on the spot about a Hollywood executive who discovers that he is, in fact, one of the Four Horsemen of the Apocalypse. An hour later I got a call from my agent, who told me that he loved it, and could I write a full treatment by Friday?

There was just one snag, the agent added. 'He thinks you invented the Four Horsemen. We have to keep him away from a bible for a week.'

I had hired an agent because I had started writing short stories in the dead time of the LA afternoons. My career as a writer didn't take off until I finally left this city of azure pools and doughnut shops. The maxim was that you arrived in Hollywood at twenty-five, fell asleep by a pool and woke up without a job when you were forty. Looking at the history of Hollywood's émigré writers, it did seem that their talents were burned away by the sun. The town ate up and spat out everyone from Edgar Wallace to Tony Hancock. Nobody survived the experience intact.

By this time, a pernicious and grotesque paranoia had seized the entire state of California as the spectre of AIDS began to tear its way through the creative community. The most frightening aspect of the disease was its sheer incomprehensibility. It did not strike the most promiscuous; often it took those who had only just become sexually active, or those with very little experience. Eventually many of my best friends died and their families were torn apart, riven by suspicion and recrimination. Another friend, Ben, had happily lived with the same lover for twenty years, the two of them building a successful business and life together. When Ben's partner grew sick from the mysterious virus that had lain dormant in his system, his estranged parents drove to LA and seized the couple's property, kicking Ben into the street. Nobody had thought about making wills.

The disease was no respecter of dignity, and without any legal rights, huge numbers of gay men were thrown out of their jobs and their homes. Companies began discreetly closing their doors. Colleagues withdrew and stopped returning calls. Insurance companies quietly cancelled policies. The Reagan era's mean-spirited attitude to society escalated fast. Grab what you can and trample everyone else to do it, that was the message behind the feeding frenzy of the eighties.

At the end of my third Christmas in LA, I returned home to Camden Town, walking into a huge surprise party filled with all my friends and family, and felt sick with gratitude. It was like being welcomed back into the world after spending time on Mars or some other hostile atmosphere-free environment, in a maximum-security jail.

I guiltily said goodbye to Bryn, who was determined to stay on and make a go of it. As an Australian abroad he was used to being treated as an alien, and he loved the incessant sunshine.

Two years later he died, another statistic added to the number of talented people lost to LA's most invasive and pernicious epidemic.

28

The Potency of Cheap Music

A digression into film music, Bernard Herrmann,
Carry On films, John Barry, waterchimes
and an usherette with a bucket

I was sitting in an almost deserted cinema in Charing
Cross Road listening to the sound of rain dropping from
the auditorium ceiling into a metal bucket. Outside it was
cold and wet, and Soho looked as if it had been lightly
sprayed in mud, but I had never been happier. I was home.

Jim and I were watching a double bill of *Razorback*
(the Australian killer-pig movie) and *A Nightmare on
Elm Street*, and all was once more right with the world.
And now I had discovered something new to drag him to:
concerts of cinema music.

Slumped in the great auditoria of pre-eighties England,
I'd always found music to be an essential ingredient of
film-going. One of the first films in which I paid attention
to the score was *The Mercenaries*, a gratuitously violent
thriller set in the Belgian Congo starring Rod Taylor and
Kenneth More, lifted to something sublime by one of the
few soundtracks from jazz composer Jacques Loussier.

For many years, Hollywood's dramatic music was

dominated by émigré Europeans: Erich Korngold, a Moravian (Czech), wrote the music for *The Private Lives of Elizabeth and Essex* and *The Adventures of Robin Hood*; Franz Waxman, a Silesian (German Pole), clocked up an impressive 272 movies with scores for everything from *A Nun's Story* to *Strange Cargo*; Miklos Rozsa, a Hungarian, scored *Ben Hur* and around 116 others, including *Adam's Rib*; Bernard Herrmann, of Russian origin, was Alfred Hitchcock's preferred composer until they fell out over the music for the murder sequence in *Torn Curtain*. Herrmann's fall from Hollywood was England's gain, and the notoriously moody composer graced a number of unworthy English films with hauntingly beautiful themes.

In older films, scores were through-written: that is to say, with virtually no break for dialogue. They included title music, dramatic stings, suspense passages, lyric themes, marches, waltzes, ballets, mazurkas and even concertos. Although musical numbers appeared independently in many films they remained separate from the score and were usually thematically linked, or were sometimes scored by the soundtrack composer as well.

The 1950s produced some memorably overheated jazz scores for films like *Cat on a Hot Tin Roof*, *Sweet Smell of Success* and *A Walk on the Wild Side*, but these were still, in effect, traditional scores for large orchestras. The sixties brought heightened realism by shooting on location, and music became something to use more sparingly. Some of the bleak endings associated with this period were played out in silence.

Lalo Schiffrin provided sensational jazzy tracks for *Bullitt*. Hugo Montenegro's score for *Lady in Cement* was the best thing about the film, and still turns up sampled on chillout tracks, and spaghetti westerns were immortalized by Ennio Morricone.

Orchestral scores were soon being dropped in favour of

more appropriately authentic sounds. *Deliverance* brought the hillbilly anthem 'Duelling Banjos'. *Bonnie and Clyde* sported similarly atmospheric tracks from the disillusioned dustbowl. But it was *Easy Rider*, a film virtually disowned by its uncomprehending studio, that wrought the greatest change, with a score composed of pre-existing rock and pop songs.

At the other end of the spectrum, the music from many *Carry On* films turned out to be wittier and subtler than the scripts, because the composer Bruce Montgomery also happened to be the brilliant crime novelist Edmund Crispin, who created one of fiction's greatest detectives, Gervase Fen. He and Eric Rogers quoted everything from Giuseppe Verdi to Percy Grainger in their slapstick soundtrack scores. The theme to *Carry On Matron* echoed part of *The Beggars' Opera* because one of the film's subtitles was 'The Preggers Opera'.

John Barry, the most evocative composer ever to work in England, disagreed with the idea that a soundtrack should be carved into two separate parts in order to showcase a title song by any band currently owned by a studio subsidiary. He argued that a soundtrack should create a single united atmosphere for its film. The James Bond scores show a marked deterioration of style once forgettable songs shared space with carefully constructed themes. There's a good chance that you can recall the title track of *Goldfinger*, but not the theme to *Casino Royale*. Barry's spare, brass-heavy orchestrations were clean, simple and impossible to forget.*

Barry hit upon a smart musical mnemonic for audiences to remember his theme songs. *Goldfinger*, *The Liquidator*,

---

*Larry Adler had taken this spareness to a higher level with his harmonica-led score for *Genevieve*. Apparently you must never call it a mouth-organ.

Born Free and *You Only Live Twice* all use memorable note sequences to match the syllables of their film titles. James Bernard also used this technique for his Hammer version of *Dracula*. His three-note sting (*Draaac*-u-la) over the name embeds so strongly into the mind that the two become synonymous. Bernard later returned from retirement to score Murnau's silent vampire classic *Nosferatu*, and utilized the same trick with four notes, this time with emphasis on the third syllable (Nos-fer-*aaah*-tu).

Occasionally, composers were able to ring startling changes by switching to unexpected sounds. Ron Grainer (of the BBC Radiophonic Workshop and *Dr Who* theme) composed an astonishing score utilizing timpani, marimba, xylophone, tabla and African drums over electric bass and strings for the SF epic *The Omega Man*. He also struck a set of different-sized discs from an old grandfather clock and immersed them in water to change their pitch. The resulting sound, from an instrument now known as waterchimes, is extremely eerie and sad, and became a staple of SF film scoring.

Paul Ferris (who sometimes worked under the pun-name Morris Jar) confounded audience expectations with his lush, lyrical score for *Witchfinder General*, probably because director Michael Reeves confided that he was making an English western. One of the most consistently surprising scores of all exists on the full-length version of *The Wicker Man*. The director's cut is sown with ancient dances and folk motifs that almost twist the horror-thriller into a rural musical, but there are repeated notes and phrases that subtly undermine the wholesome back-to-nature themes with something ungodly and disturbing. Sadly, this was one of only two scores by the talented Paul Giovanni, who, like so many members of the creative community, was lost to AIDS in the early nineties.

Ron Goodwin's music graced over sixty films, including

Alfred Hitchcock's *Frenzy* and *Those Magnificent Men in Their Flying Machines*, but he's probably best remembered for the sterling martial music he created for a string of sixties war films, including *The Battle of Britain*, *Where Eagles Dare* and *633 Squadron*, following the lead set by Eric Coates, whose *Dam Busters' March* was a regular children's favourite.

Many film composers are a combination of chameleon and magpie, adopting and adapting traditional motifs, temp tracks and pop influences. Others, like Michel Legrand, Ennio Morricone, Carter Burwell and Thomas Newman, are instantly recognizable. In the UK, David Arnold made a decent fist of mimicking John Barry, to the point where his romantic theme for *Die Another Day* seemed to stem from Barry's own hand, but for the most part, our composers took their work assignments from North America.

Many present-day film composers delight in reworking phrases from classical masters: the influences of Khachaturian, Vivaldi, Mozart and, especially, Nino Rota crop up time and again on mainstream soundtracks. Indeed, some composers, like Michael Kamen, produced their finest work when building on an existing sound. Kamen's score for *Brazil* reworked the song of the title into every conceivable style.

We had continued to work on the films of Peter Greenaway, which lost the galvanizing part of their unique flavour after he parted company with Michael Nyman. Nyman had written Greenaway's scores from *The Draughtsman's Contract* to *Prospero's Books* – in scoring the Masque sequence from *The Tempest* he was following a distinguished line of English composers that included Henry Purcell and William Walton. Nyman's rolling, mechanistic sound added a surprisingly human spirit to what could be seen as a coldly cerebral, not to mention misanthropic, film canon. One could appreciate the Hollywood executives' problem with him: his film music was so original that it became overwhelmingly a thing of its own when, traditionally, film music has been subordinate to visuals. John Barry encountered the same difficulty; his stunning score for *The Golden Child* was stripped off and replaced with the forgettable noodlings of Michel Colombier, which now sound painfully dated.

Every generation of music pays homage to past styles. For some peculiar reason, many light-hearted English films of the sixties replicated the flappers' Charleston-and-kazoo music of the 1920s. Thanks to digitization, many modern films have returned to the ponderous over-orchestrated syrup of the 1930s. There's little to separate the bland harmonies larded over *Titanic* or *Avatar* from any number of forgotten pre-war movies.

It's often noted that books are never finished, but are merely taken away from their writers. Computers have allowed for endless musical tinkering, and it's a rule of thumb that the more you work on something after it's finished, the worse it gets.

Jim particularly liked the arrangement of notes associated with the haunted screen, a density of bass, woodwind and percussion stretching an ominous line of tension that could match visuals of gloom and shadow. In large auditoria such scores could entirely alter the mood of the audience. He would lie on his sofa smoking and obsessively listening to tracks or even just musical phrases over and over again, marvelling at their power to evoke emotions, periodically demanding that I should play a tiny segment one more time, pointing out why it worked.

I was interested in the ambient sound of cinema, the relationship between screen silence and the viewer. When haunted houses were beset by deafening ghostly crashes, characters timidly asked if anyone had heard a noise, but surely in such cases the aural purpose of the film was not to describe reality or portray a psychological state, but simply to make us jump, thereby ending all attempts at plausibility. Films could disturb more cleverly with the sound of silence: listen to the eerie longueurs in *The Innocents* or *The Birds*. Brian De Palma's *Blow Out* was a film about the very essence of sound, and Tobe Hooper's *Poltergeist* virtually redefined aural effects in the eighties.

The scores Bernard Herrmann created while he was exiled in England were especially drenched in dread. His ominous moods proved even more pervasive than his shock-tactic stabbing strings, and allowed visual suspense to be inordinately lengthened. It seems remarkable now that he was prepared to work on tacky slashers like *Twisted Nerve*, but by doing so he raised their quality.

To realize the extraordinary impact that composition has on the screen you only need to turn off the sound for the opening minutes of *On Her Majesty's Secret Service*. The visuals drag on endlessly with all the allure of someone else's ancient holiday snaps, and the film all but rolls to a standstill.

When directors attached temp tracks culled from other sources to their rough cuts, they sometimes fell in love with them and decided to use the temporary music in the finished film. Stanley Kubrick commissioned Alex North to write a score for *2001*, but the composer of jazzy scores for films like *A Streetcar Named Desire* and *The Misfits* couldn't supplant Strauss's *Also sprach Zarathustra* in the director's mind, and Kubrick ran with his classical choice. Ultimately, the director's musical vision can transform his film into something haunting and memorable – another reason why song selection by committee so often fails to do justice to motion pictures. Editors hear internal beats to their cuts, and good composers match this sensibility in their music.

With the arrival of long-tail economics, soundtracks have now become big business, and there have been some astonishing appearances on the 'lost movie score' scene. One of the oddest is *The 5,000 Fingers of Dr T*, the film that inspired Tim Burton and Matt Groening (to the point where Sideshow Bob is named after one of the main characters). It represented the only time Dr Seuss worked on his own material, and it attempted to introduce fantasy-surrealism to the masses in the 1950s. Of course, it failed. But once you've seen those roller-skating twins connected by their beards and heard the dungeon symphony played with arrows, a shot-putter and men with tubas for noses there's no going back to the ordinary world . . .

'Remind me why we're watching this again?' asked Jim as one of the usherettes struggled past lugging a full bucket of dirty rainwater.

'This is the last performance here,' I explained. 'They're tearing the cinema down next week.' Earlier I had seen an enormous rat in the lavatory, and had begun to feel that, for some of London's older cinemas at least, it really was time to let go. These neglected churches of film had been living on borrowed time since the 1950s, and like real churches were in danger of collapse. The grand art deco palaces that remained would find new life as real churches, filled with largely black congregations celebrating religion in the American style.

'You know an album I'd really like?' said Jim. 'The soundtrack to *Harold and Maude*.'

'Forget it,' I told him. 'It doesn't exist.'

'If it did, would you buy it for me?'

'You know I would.'

'I could ask Bud Cort to keep an eye out for it.'

'If it existed. Which it doesn't.'

'I have a feeling it does.'*

'You could get the individual tracks from old Cat Stevens albums.'

'It wouldn't be the same. It wouldn't all be on one album and it wouldn't have the incidental music.'

'It's good to be back,' I said.

'I know,' said Jim.

One of the elderly usherettes kicked a bucket over. 'I bleedin' hate this place,' she told us. 'There's a rat in the lav. I'll be glad when it's gone. This is gonna be turned into ten screens.'

The rise of the multiplex had begun.

*He was right. It does exist. You can buy it online for around $600.

29

Outsiders

Clubbers, a writer's career, Mahatma Gandhi,
film freaks, 'Jabberwocky', black comedy, *St Trinian's*,
Tony Hancock, *Nachtkultur* and luxurious panic

London had changed since I'd abandoned it for Los
Angeles. While I was away there had been a war in the
Falklands, an event of such laughable insignificance in the
Californian psyche that it usually formed the final item on
American news programmes after pieces about cats that
could play the piano.

London had suddenly become a lawless party town,
quietest on Sunday mornings when everyone was hung-
over, except in Clerkenwell, where several hundred
clubbers who had been held captive in the Austrian cellar
that was the nightclub Trade wove their unblinking way
across Farringdon Road, staggering in front of cars like
giant babies. I've always thought of gay clubbers as being
rather reactionary at heart, but then I suppose a steady
diet of Kylie, cock and ketamine would have brainwashed
Che Guevara.

It wasn't my world. I tended to think that partying like
a madman was a product of stress that could otherwise be

relieved by curling up with a P. G. Wodehouse and a nice strong cup of tea. The latest generation of party people had been fried on MDMA for so long that they were now physically recognizable as a type.

The New Eighties London Clubber (sometimes a trendy dad) always wore a T-shirt bearing an obscure reference to a festival or band I'd never heard of, three-quarter-length camouflage trousers, low white sports socks and Adidas trainers. He had a shaved head, heavy silver rings and some kind of leather/bead surf-chain arrangement. In short, a dad looking like a gay man from a decade earlier. He'd wander up and talk to you in a pub for a while, then go off and talk to a tree or a tramp with the same level of fascinated intensity.

I couldn't be doing with it, and settled down in a new home to try to write a movie.

'So, what do you think?' I asked Jim eagerly when I had finished.

'I think it needs work,' said Jim. 'A script about a couple of idiots who open a film marketing company not knowing anything about film except what they've seen in their local cinema? It's not believable.'

Damn. I had given it my best shot. I hadn't been able to sell a film script in LA and I certainly wasn't about to sell one in London, so maybe it was time to switch tracks and try books. I knew that the pattern of writers' careers throughout the century had invariably been the same.

The Writer's Career
1. Early success (thanks to controversial subject matter).
2. The Big Hit Novel.
3. A rubbish Hollywood version that eviscerates the original.

4. An attempt to follow the big hit that flops.
5. Another smaller hit.
6. Collection of short stories (diminishing returns).
7. Disastrous move to Hollywood, divorce and mental breakdown.
8. Return to UK as a TV writer.
9. Successful adaptation of *Poldark*-like series.
10. More failed attempts to recapture early success as novelist.
11. The wilderness years.
12. Drinking/Penury/Possible arrest for brawling.
13. Meltdown after fan says s/he loved first book.
14. Last attempt at novel that critics sneeringly call 'dated'.
15. Lonely tragic death.
16. Forgotten for five years.
17. Rediscovery of backlist.
18. Out of copyright. Hailed as a genius.

'Call me fussy, but I kind of want to be successful while I'm alive,' I told Jim. I wanted to vindicate my mother's faith in me and show my father that not going into insurance hadn't been a terrible mistake.

'Why don't you do something silly and fun while you're figuring out your novel, something that will get you some publicity?' he suggested.

I had returned from LA homeless and had bought a half-share in Jim's house in north London's Kentish Town. Love and trust him as much as I did, he proved impossible to live with. He left the front door open and every TV, radio and lightbulb in the house on. The heat was turned up high all the time, and all the windows were wide open. I'm surprised Camden Council didn't declare us an ecological disaster zone. I imagined the dials at the local electricity substation whizzing around like Catherine wheels. There were usually strangers making coffee in the kitchen, vague friends of whichever spectacularly inappropriate person he was currently hanging out with. Some nights, people forgot to shut the front door. We were burgled with farcical frequency.

'This is Wolfgang,' Jim would announce as a shifty young man with good cheekbones shuffled into the room. 'He'll be staying with us for a while.' My first instinct was to lock everything up until Wolfgang had gone, not the reaction you really want from a flatmate. Having passed the first thirty years of his life in a state of complete naivety about relationships, Jim was attempting to make up for lost time. The various glittery-eyed kleptomaniacs he admitted to the house were always passing through, never stopping, and usually left with as much as they could carry.

I just wanted to be somewhere peaceful and calm where I could write. Finally I moved out, but only around the corner, so that at least I could keep an eye on my best friend. The truth was that for all his bizarre habits, Jim was still the most sensible person I knew. His suggestion to do something 'silly and fun' resulted in my first book, called *How to Impersonate Famous People.*

Here's a thought: If you're going to write a book with this title, make sure you can impersonate famous people yourself, because the first thing that happened was that I was invited on to something called the *Six O'Clock Show* on the BBC to perform live.

I didn't do impressions, but I knew someone who might accompany me and have a go. I took our old PA and former bunny girl Maggie, who was happy to get up on live national television and make a fool of herself. At Television Centre we were kept in a minuscule green room for several hours, where my fear of performing in public had a chance to fester. Then we were released into the studio. Maggie's off-colour impersonation of Mahatma Gandhi, involving a bedsheet, a bathing cap and a walking stick, broke the studio coffee table and caused the presenter to have some kind of nervous attack on camera. We weren't invited back.

I told my agent that I would not do shows where I was required to perform. Two days later, I went on to a live ITV show and found that the set consisted of a stage. 'And now,' said the compère, 'we've a surprise for you. Christopher is going to get up and show us his impersonations of famous people, which I hear are incredible.'

They were certainly incredible, but not in the way he'd meant it. I imagined people watching at home, looking like the stunned audience in *The Producers* just after the 'Springtime For Hitler' number.

Soon after this I set out to sell my first book of short stories, and was amazed to get a deal. 'I loved that show you were on,' said my new publisher. 'All that terrible mugging, very clever, very postmodern.' It hadn't been, of course. I'd just been trying my best. If I had followed one of those worthy books about how to become a successful writer, I'm fairly sure it wouldn't have recommended pretending to be Groucho Marx or the Elephant Man on national television.

By now our cast at Creative Partnership had swollen to include a humourless receptionist known alternatively by the runners as the Greek Street Gonk or the Werewolf of Wardour Street, a terrific producer called Sarah and a knockout new writer called Mike, whom we found by placing an ad that read simply: 'Wanted – Film Freak.'*

---

*Try doing that now.

One of the other people I interviewed was an immensely overweight man who turned up with four plastic carrier bags filled with photograph albums. These turned out to contain Polaroids of everyone who had attended the 1958 premiere of *Ben Hur*.

Mike and Sarah quickly started dating, but everyone pretended to be fooled by their elaborate efforts to stagger their arrival times and come into work from different directions, so as not to look unprofessional. The company expanded and took new offices, with Jim at the top of the building in a room reminiscent of a cabin; like the captain on the prow of a ship, he made sure it was the one office where the crew were allowed to smoke. Soon his office filled up with people from the rest of the building, smouldering like chimneys. The ceiling turned yellow and the windows filmed over. Meanwhile, Jim stood at the terrace railing with his hands folded behind his back, puffing away and surveying his vessel below.

The staff spent virtually every evening together discussing all aspects of film. Our arguments would range from Lubitsch and Capra comedies to hidden semiotics in the *Dirty Harry* films. These kinds of conversations were taking place all over Soho, as film freaks endlessly analysed the making of film but never got any closer to making anything of their own. Over the years I kept bumping into one earnest young man who told me he was just about to start his long-gestating horror movie. The last time I saw him, about a year ago, his hair had turned grey. He told me he was just about to start shooting his movie.

We had bought a building in Soho's Bateman Street from the owners of Illustra Films, a UK production company whose directors had graduated from commercials to features. They had made the appalling musical *Les*

Bicyclettes de Belsize,* a wafty soft-focus knock-off of *Les Parapluies de Cherbourg* which was released in probably the most inappropriate double bill of all time, as a curtain-raiser to the psycho-slasher flick *Twisted Nerve*.

Our private cinema housed two ancient carbon arc lamp projectors. The technology was primitive and pretty scary. A pair of carbon rod electrodes were connected to a current-limited source of power. They were mounted on a well-insulated, fireproof structure that allowed the distance between the rods to be controlled. The projectionist would then wind them slowly forward as they burned down, to keep the screen at a consistent level of brightness. If he overwound them, it burned the film – the blistering effect you used to get on the screen sometimes.

Above the cinema on every floor were things that looked like ship's speaking tubes. These allowed you to hear what was going on in the auditorium. The cinema floor was made of glass, because it had once been a dance floor. When we dug out editors' suites under the road we found an underground tunnel for a tributary from the River Fleet, filled with clay pipes and animal bones which had been washed down from a Victorian slaughterhouse. The company couldn't have been any quirkier if the staff had come to work dressed as their favourite film characters. Which, periodically, they did.

In the little spare time I had, I'd started writing a blackly satirical novel. I had a list of favourite black comedies in my head:

Harold and Maude (January/December cult rom-com with satirical anti-Vietnam angle)

---

*The bouffanted leading man wore a trailing yellow chiffon scarf and loons – a look that has, frankly, struggled to make a comeback.

Joe (Redneck Peter Boyle kills hippies and liberals)

Homebodies (Old ladies turn homicidal)

Where's Poppa? (George Segal tries to kill his mother while his brother-in-law is raped by a gorilla)

First Family (Grotesquely dysfunctional family win US presidency, scripted by Buck Henry)

Fire Sale (Bankrupt businessman hires psycho to torch his building)

To this list I would happily add *Fight Club*, *Death Becomes Her* and *American Psycho*. Just as Paris once thrilled to the theatre of cruelty, Grand Guignol stagings of sex and sadism, black comedy existed at the heart of much twentieth-century national literature. Evelyn Waugh, a veritable fountainhead of dark laughter, remains under-realized on celluloid.

English films have often been darkly imagined, from David Lean's gothic Dickens adaptations using Gustave Doré's shadowy engravings as a template, to the early Greenaway films with their artistic and musicological self-references, their human cruelty, their love of games and lists.

But it was the children's films you had to watch out for. Typically, George Melly wrote this little trivia gem into his swinging London family romp *Smashing Time*: if you put together all the surnames of the cast, you get most of the first verse of Lewis Carroll's 'Jabberwocky'. The English love of pantomime resulted in films that played on two tiers of appreciation, one family, one strictly adult.

In *A High Wind in Jamaica*, children prove more amoral than the pirates who kidnap them.* Even *Lord*

---

*How appropriate that one of the children was played by the young Martin Amis.

of the Flies works on one level as the blackest of black comedies.

Nowhere was this strange duality more evident than in the *St Trinian's* films. Artist Ronald Searle enlisted a surprisingly highbrow group of people to help him bring his sexy schoolgirls to the screen, including the author D. B. Wyndham-Lewis, the composer Sir Malcolm Arnold, Johnny Dankworth, the Poet Laureate Cecil Day-Lewis, Bertolt Brecht, Flanders and Swann, Sidney Gilliat and Frank Launder.

The school in question was financed by stolen money and immoral earnings, but was seen as a more decent institution than the inert, corrupt government because at least it was honest about how it earned its money. 'The school goes back to 1630,' said Headmistress Alistair Sim, 'but according to the bank it goes back to them.'

It seemed that a willingness to admit a blinkered worldview was the mark of an English leading man. In Tony Hancock's vehicle *The Rebel*, the lugubrious comic sculpts a grotesque two-ton statue in his flat.

'That is women as I see them,' he tells landlady Mrs Cravatte (Irene Handl).

'You poor man,' she sneers. And even if Hancock, the doomed seaside entertainer of *The Punch and Judy Man*, Charlie Drake, the hapless consul of *Sands of the Desert*, Peter Sellers, the emasculated unionist in *I'm All Right Jack* and Michael Palin, the ineffectual chiropodist of *A Private Function*, were the heroes in their dark comedies, they also played men for whom you could see no happy endings. In *A Private Function* (itself a cloacal pun) Palin is witheringly described as a 'jaunty, toenail-clipping little sod' and a 'festering bunion-scraping pillock' when he and wife Maggie Smith attempt to slaughter a pig in their house. You wanted him to win, but knew that his weak nature would only allow the smallest triumphs.*

It took Peter Nichols decades to find appreciative new audiences for his black comedies *A Day in the Death of Joe Egg, The National Health* and *Privates on Parade* despite the fact that all three had been filmed.

Privates concerns the members of SADUSEA ('Song And Dance Unit South East Asia) as they set out to entertain the troops and dodge communist bullets, with Dennis Quilley turning in an Oscar-worthy performance (not that Hollywood would have touched it with a bargepole) as the outrageously queeny but ultimately heroic Terri Dennis, warning his troops, 'You speak to an officer like that and I'll scream the place down.' Senior officer John Cleese even got to do a spectacularly silly walk during the end credits.

Nichols proved he hadn't mellowed by presenting the Opium Wars reimagined as a Christmas pantomime in the play *Poppy*, while fellow writer Peter Barnes treated bemused audiences to slapstick Black Death in *Red Noses*.

But this was nothing new. Our image of Weimar Republic decadence stemmed primarily from Christopher Isherwood and the various reincarnations of *Cabaret*. For years the subjectivity of his view of pre-war Berlin was unsubstantiated but accepted. The thinking ran that because Isherwood was gay, he must have been decadent enough to create a hermetic garter-belt-and-swastika world of his own. That theory held until relatively recently, when evidence hoarded in private collections of a city more decadent than we can imagine began to be reassembled. Flyers from transsexual clubs, *Nachtkultur* societies and fascistic S&M organizations (one featuring a toilet seat covered in tall spikes and its effects on bare

---

*The film became a West End musical. Surprisingly, a show filled with songs about ingrown toenails proved a less than stellar hit.

female flesh) began to turn up. The real Berlin society made Sally Bowles look bowdlerized (that very term, Bowdler, deriving from the gentleman who expurgated Shakespeare into a sanitized family edition).

As an outsider looking to get a handle on English cinema, it seemed to me that the problem remained the same as it had always been. Most writers, producers and directors were afraid of commercialization, having not yet hit on the idea of alternating personal projects with popular product. In some ways I was no more connected to the film industry than someone who said he was in fashion because he occasionally liked to go shopping for trousers.

Writing a black comedy was one thing, but selling it was another. Jim and I nightly sat in Soho pubs reading the pages aloud to each other, refining and tuning the dialogue, but we had no way of financing so much as a single scene. If we'd thought that English cinema was moribund in the late seventies, it was beneath ground level by 1984. The few films that were being financed in the UK sold England as a kind of theme park to Americans, who liked to imagine us all in top hats and crinolines, talking about croquet and teapots.*

'Can I tell you what you're doing wrong?' Jim offered one evening, as I pored over yet another set of beer-stained, dog-eared pages. I couldn't wait to hear this. 'You're trying to give people something they don't want. You should never have tried to launch your career with a comedy unless you wanted to be a comedian.'

'But I like comedy,' I countered.

'Then write something you think you won't like,' he said, finishing his pint. 'You might grow into it.'

Throughout my childhood I had been offered advice

---

*Thanks to Russell Brand, this cultural stereotype has been replaced with the image of a wasted rock-singer in eyeliner.

on writing by my mother, covertly and out of my father's hearing. Displaying imagination had always felt like a subversive activity. As a result, I was drawn – as a great number of would-be English scriptwriters were – towards the dark, strange and unpopular areas the British film industry was not strong enough to support.

There were, I had learned from sifting through hundreds of writers' CVs over years at the company, two main types of writer: those who tried very, very hard and were never more than pedestrian, and those who soared effortlessly, but largely chose outsider subjects. It seemed to me that I'd have more luck with novels – writing scripts in England had become more pointless than learning how to make wicker baskets.

Meanwhile there was work for us to do at the office; we were starting on Bond.

30

007th Heaven

Gadgets, stunts, Oscar Wilde, Bond girls, Nicholas Cage, and a thousand wasted slivers of fish

'You know the thing I hate most about the Bond scripts?' Barbara Broccoli told me. 'Passageways. In every Bond script 007 and the villains walk or run up and down tunnels and corridors, so we have to design and build them, tile them, then put in the flooring and the lighting, and they're always the first thing the director cuts out.'

Barbara was feisty and smart and took no prisoners. We needed to win her over a little. 'Here,' said Jim, 'I noticed you're a smoker.' He handed her a gift, a portable ashtray that folded into her pocket. She loved it.

On shoots you can't smoke or call out on your mobile, especially if there are electronically detonated explosives on the set. An 007 film has the reverse problem to most films – the producers need to prevent publicity, not encourage it, because so many hacks are fighting to get information that you have to keep it under control. Everything was done to keep the plot under wraps, from coding the scripts and never letting them out of head office to banning all outside communication during shoots, and yet information sometimes leaked out from unscrupulous employees bribed by the press.

We had worked in different capacities on several Bond films, and were now producing one-hour documentaries that usually aired on Boxing Day. Jim and I were fascinated by the size of the production, an army on the march headed by the producers at Cubby Broccoli's old company, Eon, who negotiated deals at government levels. Want to borrow a Stealth Battleship? Ask the French Navy. Want to film at a satellite station? Get in touch with NASA. Locations were scouted and stunts planned before scripts were finalized, so that if one location was not available in time for shooting, it could be offlaid into the next film.

In the basement of Eon's HQ was a treasure trove worthy of Bond himself: a huge set of electronically operated shelves that opened to reveal everything about Bond, from gadgets and toys to scripts and scores. Sorting through the material was like being a child again.

The Bond films were famous for shooting their stunts on camera and not just relying on computer graphics. Effects and model sequences from Derek Meddings and Chris Corbould were among the best in the film world. One of the stuntmen, Wayne Michaels, pitched an idea: he said he could bungee-jump from a helicopter and release his cord close enough to the ground to step on to it, but this seemed a step too far even for Bond, and the plan was reluctantly put on ice. However, the stuntman made a record-breaking jump from a dam in the opening sequence of *Goldeneye*, with the help of a small CGI cheat – a crane that allowed him to be suspended away from the sloping dam wall was digitally erased.

The stuntman Vic Armstrong had become the go-to stunt co-ordinator and second unit director for block-busters. He was the kind of guy dads admired, talking you through the physics of stuntmanship, then jumping from bridges, riding runaway trains and motorbikes, crashing through walls and getting blown up. I remember watching him climb into a helicopter camera-rig after a night of rabble-rousing, getting ready to film cars careening around hairpin bends from above. One of the crew told him his eyes were bloodshot. 'You want to see them from my side,' he said, taking off. Who wouldn't want a dad like that?

The Bond films sold themselves, although the idea of a gambling, drinking, smoking superspy seemed to me increasingly anachronistic in the present day. Mind you, Timothy Dalton really did look as if he had trouble running, and might collapse with his hands on his knees for a good cough and a spit the second the camera had stopped turning. At least you knew exactly what you were getting in a Bond film: they were dad-movies that promised an escape from the mundane.*

A film is a hard sell if you can't understand why it was produced. If the director doesn't know what he wants, how will the public?

When producer Marc Samuelson was planning a new film biography of Oscar Wilde, he knew that Stephen Fry would be perfect for the role, because the past should act as a refraction of the present. Casting Fry was smart because it brought a modern sensibility to the story. Samuelson had become aware of a new interest in Wilde among the young. We ran a search for websites and found hundreds; the time was right to look at the story with fresh eyes. Posters described Wilde's life as 'THE STORY OF THE FIRST

---

*In his excellent analysis of the James Bond films, *The Man Who Saved Britain*, Simon Winder points out that the loving, lingering shots of a Miami hotel in *Goldfinger* must have come as a profound shock to the English, who were used to interrupting bouts of sex with arguments about whose turn it was to nip out and feed the electricity meter for the bar-heater.

MODERN MAN', so that the public carried the idea into the cinema with them.

Sometimes we would come on board when a feature had already opened and flatlined in the US. Then our job was to interest English viewers. *Reservoir Dogs* was a bigger hit in the UK than it was in the US, because over there the characters were just another bunch of crooks. Here we were able to build iconographic American images from the striding men in black. They became cool, and seeing the film was soon a matter of peer-pressure. 'Let's go to work' became a catchphrase, and the look was considered glamorous. Unfortunately its success sparked a wave of Brit-gangster films that had none of the style and wit of Tarantino's breakout film.

With so many in-house cinematic tastes, our company meetings tended to become spirited. We all had different theories about what made pure cinema. Small films like *Distant Voices, Still Lives* and *Drowning by Numbers* have stayed with me for ever, but will mean nothing to others. Working on the campaign for the beautiful Mike Leigh film about Gilbert and Sullivan, *Topsy Turvy*, was a labour of love, but often it was easier to do a good job on a film you didn't enjoy because you remained distanced from it, and therefore more objective.

English films had their work cut out for them because audiences were instinctively drawn to US fare. American directors tackled their films with an energy rarely found over here. English films promised offbeat delights, but often lacked the strong plot-beats needed to create tension or hold interest. They seemed tentative and unsure of their effects. Audiences sensed self-doubt, and preferred to opt for a sure thing. As ticket prices rose, cinema-goers wanted to be guaranteed a good night out.

It was important to keep a sense of history when working on a new movie. Film-goers have short memories, and will cite the last film they saw as their all-time favourite. Mainstream subject matter is cyclical. Black comedies, science fiction and even musicals, possibly the most moribund genre after the western, actually do return if they've been away for a generation. Trends always resurface once someone has declared them dead.

The best cinema has the courage to venture where its audience is nervous of going, but that bravery automatically limits its popularity. What writers want to explore isn't always what audiences want to see, and in the war between art and commerce the audience gets caught in the crossfire.

Film is a contradictory medium. More people saw the *Avatar* trailer on the internet than they did at the cinema. Stars now have approval over the computerized photographs used to promote their films, so the days of great poster art are gone.* The modern studio look usually features just heads, corrected so that they're in proportion to the billing, with perhaps a smattering of imagery around the edges. The images are conservative and rather dull compared with the days of strong idea-driven design, when you could actually put names to film poster styles from artists like Saul Bass and Bob Peake.

Film advertising now carries an element of social responsibility. In the more recent 007 posters, girls don't cling adoringly to their man, although before *Skyfall* it was de rigueur for every new Bond girl to forlornly point out how independent her character was before getting into a tight bikini. Bond girls famously laboured under a curse that dictated career-death following an appearance in an

---

*A new industry has sprung up online: movie posters redesigned by graphic artists who create new iconic imagery as an alternative to a film's original committee-designed campaigns. Thus we can see films represented as we would like to imagine them.

007 film. As for ethnic referencing, inclusion is preferable to ghettoization, although America still produces ethnic-specific images for certain films it pumps around the bible belt.

But right through the 1980s and 1990s the English still had trouble getting it right. The UK-made *Captain Corelli's Mandolin* should have been a smash hit, but was notable for its perverse determination to undermine its source material. The historical nuances went, along with the sub-plots, and the characters barely aged. In came a lot of bad dancing and Penelope Cruz trudging up and down hills with baskets of olives. Nicholas Cage's performance became a thing of eerie fascination: I found myself staring hypnotically at his hair, which appeared to have a life of its own. Perhaps this was the desired effect, in order to prevent audiences from realizing that a life of its own was precisely what it didn't have, seeing that it looked as if it was kept in a box when it wasn't needed on set. For reasons best known to himself, Cage became the Todd Slaughter of acting, melodramatic when subtlety was called for, and so overtly peculiar that he entered the larger-than-life world of stars like Jack Nicholson who can only play mad people, super-villains and were-wolves.

Cage is much taller than Cruz, but if you look at the UK poster you'll see an optical illusion worthy of M. C. Escher that makes them appear to be the same height. For their appearance on posters, stars have their chins lifted, spots removed, eyes whitened, ears tidied, waists narrowed and legs lengthened until the images bear no resemblance at all to the real-life actors.

Back on Bond, we headed to France to accompany the filming of a Ferrari chase that would take place on the most over-exposed piece of road in Europe, the vertiginous Haute Corniche above Monte Carlo. Unless you are one of the five or six people immediately involved in the process, filming is about as interesting as being a hotel doorman, so it's important to have good scenery to stare at.

As the Ferrari went for another take, shot past us and missed its turn in the tunnel, causing around 100,000 euros' worth of damage, Jim waved his cigarette in the air and smiled at me. 'I like it here,' he said, 'you can—'

'Don't say it,' I warned him.

For a boy from Battersea, he had adapted very smoothly to the excesses of the Riviera. The night before, on the steps of the Hotel du Cap, Harvey Weinstein and Bernardo Bertolucci had both stopped to chat to him.

'What was that about?' I'd asked, looking back in amazement.

'Golf,' said Jim. I didn't know they played. Hell, I didn't know *he* played. You can always figure out what shallow people are thinking but Jim's thoughts ran like silent submarines, and it made him hopelessly unguessable.

We returned to Cannes for the launch of the new Bond film, and on our company anniversary threw a beach party on what turned out to be the wettest day in Cannes's history. The rain fell on the sand so hard that it actually bounced in the air, and we sat glumly staring at the drowning flower-decked tables displaying thousands of pounds' worth of food destined to be uneaten, knowing it would all be thrown out in a few hours. Cannes suddenly seemed profligate and pointless. We vowed never to be so wasteful again.

Once it became apparent that nobody was going to turn up, we shut the party down. The waiters wouldn't let us leave until we had paid for everything. The bill had been obscenely inflated, and we couldn't pay it because our credit cards were maxed out.

My abiding memory of that Cannes was sitting in front of mountains of crimson lobster and smoked salmon canapés without a penny in my pocket, wondering what the hell we were doing.

Back in London, we hosted the first screening of *Goldeneye* in our private cinema for the film's sponsors. The carbon arc lamp projectors had been donated to a cinema museum and replaced with modern equipment. The entire company had excitedly squeezed into the projection booth to watch the first reel changeover. When the projectors switched seamlessly from one to the other, we whooped and applauded like NASA scientists watching a lunar touchdown.

31

B-Movie Heaven

A digression into the world of B-movies, including
what to say to a director, Stuart Whitman's legs,
Miguel Ferrer's kidneys, the mirage of choice,
and the end of an era

'You don't like mainstream movies much, do you?' said
Jim one day. 'Why does everybody else?'

'I don't know,' I admitted. 'I can see why others enjoy
them, but they always seem a bit sort of ordinary.' Writers
are wonderfully articulate.

We had been invited to attend a rough cut of a new
English gangster flick which was so appallingly crass that
we found ourselves no longer able to look at the screen. I
studied the preview room's curtains, the carpet, my fingernails, anything that would take my mind off the clichéd
gibberish unfurling in front of me.

Afterwards, as the lights went up, I saw the director
gleefully making his way down the aisle towards us.

'Oh my God,' I whispered from the side of my mouth.
'He wants to know what we thought.'

'Just be honest,' Jim whispered back.

I racked my brain for something positive to say. We had

built our careers on telling the truth, and here was the acid test.

The director stopped before Jim, puffed with pride. 'Well,' he said, 'I want your honest opinion, what did you think?'

Jim appeared to consider the question for a minute. 'I thought it was a unique experience,' he said finally.

'You rotter,' I whispered, 'you had that answer prepared.'

'Nobody says "rotter" any more,' said Jim. 'Except Terry-Thomas.'

I was always amazed when directors thought they had created a gripping, realistic film instead of a pile of hackneyed clichés squashed into an ancient, third-hand plot. It seemed as if, in the process of editing the footage, they slowly convinced themselves of their own veracity.

By now, this had become an endemic problem in cinema. Despite the protestations of their creators, most action films were about as genuinely real and gritty as the Cottingley Fairies, but such was the adult fear of theatricality (unless clearly labelled) that we had to be presented with angry, sweary pub bores as templates for 'real' people. Action films were about testosterone, of course, and the terror of effeminacy that resulted in endless tales of 'hard men' throughout the 1980s. The heroes of the past were more likely to be original thinkers whose bravery took many different forms, often passive and quiescent. By the time we arrived at the films of Guy Ritchie, the empty posturing of machismo became more closely allied to gay porn than anything genuinely heartfelt and heroic.

Had we simply lost our sense of the surreal, the intellectual, the fantastical, the absurd, because we were frightened of seeming weak? The problem, I supposed, was that in modern society few of us ever got the chance to do anything that impacted upon anything else, so of course we enjoyed the impossible adventures of our surrogate heroes. James Bond didn't really have to jump off an exploding building to help us achieve this sensation; he could simply have prepared a meal from scratch or built a bicycle, because most of us could no longer even manage to provide for ourselves.

The next night I dragged Jim back into our comfort zone, an obscure London double bill of *Wide Boy* and *Never Back Losers*, featuring Benny the Spiv selling black-market nylons from a suitcase and criminal mastermind Patrick Magee in a swivel-chair. At least the films were short.

'Would it be asking too much to see something in colour next time?' Jim suggested as we left for the pub.

'Funny you should say that,' I replied. 'I've got the very thing.'

The excitement level was high when we arrived. Girls with multicoloured braids and Goth boots were queuing on the staircase. Fans in fancy dress had made the foyer impassable. A firestorm of cameras flashed, but there were no press photographers here, only audience members taking pictures. There were no stars, either. The crowds were waiting to see half a dozen low-budget B-movies, including *Piranha*, *Phantasm* and *Dead & Buried* from Gary Sherman, the man who had brought us *Death Line*. These films yielded, in order, the sight of Stuart Whitman's legs being gnawed to the bone, a flying chrome ball drilling holes through victims' heads and a nurse dropping the needle of a massive hypodermic syringe into a patient's eye.

The best thing about B-movie directors was that they usually bit off more than they could chew, resulting in priceless dialogue.* B-movies loved urban dystopias and end-of-the-world scenarios because they were cheap to create. You just needed a few burned-out cars and derelict blocks of flats. That's not the future, that's Nottingham.†

B-movie directors were fond of the horror, SF and fantasy genres, but when they aimed for comedy the results were usually skanky and disastrous. Due to the parlous state of film finance in the UK, B-movies live on. Two of the least amusing English Bs ever made are *Fat Slags*, from the *Viz* comic strip, and the appalling *Three and Out*, in which Mackenzie Crook tries to drive his tube train over a tramp to qualify for early redundancy. It's no surprise they're both English – from the 1950s to the present day we couldn't make Bs without jokes about bad sex and farting, although *Three and Out* also has a nice line in homophobic terror, human misery and making London look like a filthy grey toilet.

But if there's one word B-movies are afflicted with, it's 'edgy'. Why, I wondered, did everything have to be edgy? What did it mean: transgressive? Politically dangerous? Liable to get you thrown in jail? Or just young and a bit rude? When directors told me their next movie was going to be really edgy I always assumed they were still trying to shock their parents. *Irreversible* is edgy. *The Piano Teacher* is edgy. *Donkey Punch* is not edgy. Nor were any of the punk films we endured in the eighties. Quite the

*B-movie dialogue lives on. In *Babylon AD* my favourite B star, Vin Diesel, is told by a doctor, 'We can go back through your memory and fiddle with your brain.' *Fiddle with?* Was that, like, a technical term?
†Lately, France has taken to turning out a nice line in B-movies, with *Two Worlds*, a film about a man who goes to make a pot of coffee and falls on to another planet; *Perhaps*, about a man who falls out of a toilet window and lands in Paris after global warming; and *RrrrRRRRRrrrr*, a film about detective cavemen that features sabre-toothed ducks.

reverse: *Breaking Glass* was the charmingly old-fashioned rags-to-bitches tale of a singer clawing her way to the top and losing her innocence. Jessie Matthews could have starred in it.

If you look back at the great B-movies, very few were genuinely transgressive. Did *The Rocky Horror Picture Show* ever really shock anyone? Its staying power was built around the beauty of its songs, as in any good musical. 'Edgy', in B-movie terms, eventually came to mean depressing and almost unwatchable. After sitting through *Martyrs*, *Hostel 2*, *Inside* or any *Saw* film which dwells on the contents of victims' heads, you may feel nauseous, dirty, vaguely depressed, but not especially elated by the bravery of ideas on display. Perhaps you've been taken to the edge of what you could sit through, but I could theoretically get that by visiting a government old people's home or sitting in on a dental operation. The word we should really attach to B-movies, and make our criterion for judging them, is 'ingenious'.

So *Fermat's Room* was a witty take on an Agatha Christie locked-room mystery. *Timecrimes* had its hero bounced in a time machine, not by years but by less than an hour – just long enough to unpick his mistakes (or make matters very much worse). Likewise, *Retroactive* threw noir tropes (girl, gun, car) into the time-travel mix and came up with every variation you could think of in ninety minutes. One of my favourite Bs was *The Harvest*,* in which writer Miguel Ferrer lost one kidney on holiday and spent the rest of the film trying to outrun gangsters who had come for the other.

In the UK, B-movies started to die out in the late 1960s as main features grew longer and cinemas stopped

---

*I wrote the poster strapline: 'CHARLIE'S LIVING HIS MOVIE SCRIPT. THE GOOD PARTS. THE SEXY PARTS. THE BODY PARTS.'

showing double bills. The subjects we had once considered offensive, shocking, transgressive and outrageous were whittled away as soon as society began to tolerate them. As for sexual perversion, the crack of the crop and creak of the corset now seemed rather passé to anyone who had survived a summer holiday in Ibiza. After inventive swearing and alienated sex, what was there left to portray on-screen? The proper gentleman, English films had told us, was civilized, and therefore free from decadence – at least in Victorian times he had kept it under his hat: spanking the servants, infecting the locals, whipping the rent-boys, then all back to matron for hymns in the parlour. Only toffs were decadent.* Ordinary folk prayed on stone floors and equated backbreaking work with purging goodness.

By the time the 1980s had rolled around, audiences knew better. Now, the nation was changing fast. B-movies about corruption in high places and working-class lads trying to make money from strangers on street corners were no longer shocking – and B-movies needed to shock – because audiences had grown far more cynical, even if a bout of buggery could still turn the viewers of the nation's new fourth channel into a foaming mob. What were mass-market movies to do?

It was a time of excess, so movies became excessive. Thanks to computer graphics, battles are now staged with millions of participants instead of hundreds. Explosions destroy planets instead of buildings. Popular films do this simply because they can, and, because Hollywood endlessly repeats and copies itself, they all give you the same choice: big or nothing. And the bigger it gets, the less effective it becomes.

*This idea was neatly explored in Hammer's *Plague of the Zombies*, in which the land-owning Victorian gentry exploited members of the local workforce even after they were dead. A little like now, in fact.

People who encourage you to buy everything from mobile phones to package holidays preach the benefits of added choice, but freedom to choose only works if you can have something different. A friend of mine who is a television producer sold her channel to a network for a lot of money. Yet she was the first person to admit that hardly anyone watched it. I wanted to know why a company would pay out so much for a TV channel that nobody would watch.

'I don't care how many people watch,' she replied, 'the brand is strong.'

I asked her to explain. 'Well,' she said, 'when viewers buy a package, they want to be able to choose from recognizable brands. They want a lot of choice, so the value of having a great many channels is to do with their perception of extra choice, even though no one will ever get around to actually watching them.'

In other words, we want the promise of more entertainment even though, statistically speaking, we will only watch five channels in the package. In the same way, we'll buy books we'll never read, DVDs of shows we'll never finish, gadgets we won't use, clothes we may never get around to wearing.

As popular television and film fades into a decorative backdrop it becomes ever more excessive, and not such a far cry from the baroque architectural follies of mad King Ludwig II of Bavaria, only with more penis jokes. Genuine decadence is more intellectual than physical, more de Sade than G. G. Allin, more Monaco than Los Angeles. It is not to be found in the seething swill of Leicester Square on a summer night, or among the backstreet snake-handlers and strippers of Bangkok, because it is controlled not by economics but by irrational, perverse desire.

Margaret Thatcher had orchestrated an irreversible change in the national psyche, and in a time when everyone had begun to shout their wares at the tops of their voices rigour, form, emptiness and stillness became desirable once more: calm in a mad world, order from chaos. With this in mind, a lot of the old brigade left the industry for good, and Wardour Street shut up shop, its properties snapped up by developers eager to turn Soho into a bar and restaurant area, not quite as anodyne as the new Times Square perhaps, but not far from it.

London, like New York, had become a place where the young came from all over the globe to make their names. 'English' films, such as they were, finally ceased to exist as a separate indigenous genre, and perhaps that wasn't entirely a bad thing.

1984 brought two films from the same source, but they couldn't have been more different. In a way, they symbolized the end of one era and the start of another.

George Orwell's dystopic view of *1984* was made into a star-driven epic with Sir Richard Burton and John Hurt. The result was relentlessly grim and wearyingly reverential, although to be fair, director Michael Radford pulled off the almost impossible trick of incorporating the book's polemic into the narrative. Even so, it felt like a slow-moving dinosaur of old-school film-making. One suspects that the moneymen realized this when they saw the rough cut, as Virgin insisted on changing the film's colour saturation and replacing Dominic Muldowney's orchestral score with a set of already dated synth-pop tracks from the Eurythmics. Radford angrily claimed that the new pop soundtrack had been foisted on him.

Meanwhile, Terry Gilliam had developed his own vision of 1984 in *Brazil*, but his take on the material was freewheeling, satirical, bizarre, hilarious and thrilling, from its ludicrous opening line: 'Hello there, I want to talk to you about ducts,' to its final heartbreaking image of a tortured man accepting Big Brother. Filled with witty non-sequiturs, jokes and visual paradoxes, it, too, fell foul of

its distributors. In America, the film was famously recut
so that it now had a happy ending, in a version that came
to be known as the 'Love Conquers All' cut. In real life,
it seemed that Big Brother really had triumphed. Gilliam
placed full-page ads in *Variety* accusing Universal of
burying his film, but he had the last laugh: the original
version has become a classic.

It was a stark demonstration of the quandary faced by
the film industry in the eighties.

32

The Neon Flickers Out

Palace, werewolves, *Absolute Beginners* and an almost absolute disaster

I had never seen Jim look worried before. He always appeared relaxed, even when nightmares were unfolding. 'I think we have a problem,' he said, ushering me into his office.

'How big a problem?' I asked. Even through our most disastrous cash-flow crises we had barely discussed financial matters, because Jim told me he expected them to occur in the natural course of running a business. He always saw what was coming just over the next horizon. It was like working with someone who was standing on a chair, armed with binoculars. Jim loved playing chess, and had a chessmaster's grasp on life. He knew that large results in the future came from insignificant acts in the present.

'We may have to stop trading,' he explained.

I knew we had suffered a few ups and downs. The lousy British TV spin-offs and smutfests had now gone, but we had also worked on some big Hollywood stinkers. One of the most disastrous had been *Howard the Duck*, a mega-million epic based on a cult Marvel comic book whose chief appeal had been that it was drawn for a time by fan-worshipped artist Gene Colan. The first cut of *Howard*, who was a potty-mouthed, cigar-smoking extra-terrestrial fowl stranded on Earth, was peppered with off-colour adult jokes (including one about Howard keeping condoms in his wallet, which raised the uncomfortable spectre of inter-species sex) until someone realized that the only way to recoup its $35 million budget was to trim it and make it play to children.

So out went the smut, and the result, with a wonderfully lunatic turn from Jeffrey Jones and a giant go-motion alien being, wasn't too bad. But the failure didn't reflect well on us. Similarly, *Harry and the Hendersons*, a charming and often very funny film about Bigfoot, also had trouble finding its audience. But in the UK we generally got paid whether a film bombed or not. So I couldn't see why Jim was worried.

'What could be wrong?' I asked. 'Everything's going great. We've got a lot of films on. Palace is going—'

'That's the problem,' he said. 'Palace is going.'

Steve Woolley had been at the Scala Cinema. Nik Powell had worked with Richard Branson. Together they started Palace Pictures as a specialist video distributor in the early 1980s. After a series of extremely astute acquisitions they moved into film distribution and production, and Palace became a mini studio. While mainstream films in the UK were represented by companies like Goldcrest, Palace Pictures was the disreputably grungy younger brother who screened alternative cult flicks for teens. Steve and Nik knew what smart kids wanted to see. Their 1980s independent features included films from the Coen brothers, John Cassavetes, John Waters, Fassbinder, Oshima and Bertolucci. They fought the law to screen Sam Raimi's *The Evil Dead*, which local judges were trying to ban, mainly for a scene in which it was suggested that a girl was raped by a tree. This was 1983, when all hints of perceived sexism were being excised from films, even if they involved supernatural botany.

For a while it seemed that nothing could ever go wrong for Palace Pictures. Notoriously tight-fisted, they maintained total control over their productions, then took outrageous leaps of faith. It was a technique that paid off. After Neil Jordan filmed *The Company of Wolves*, a disjointed arthouse horror film consisting of vignettes from Angela Carter's tales of men and wolves that made very little sense, they elected to screen it not in a tiny specialist cinema but in London's largest auditorium, the Odeon Leicester Square, which has a capacity of 1863 seats per performance. The industry took a collective look at them and roared with laughter.

This was the closest you could get to career suicide without being found dead in a bordello. Where would the audiences come from? The Palace team had thought of that: they would create an unimaginable level of publicity for the film, which starred David Warner and the elderly Angela Lansbury, not then known for their ability to pull in crowds.

What happened next remains a mystery to me, even to this day. The movie caught fire and took off, filling show after show, selling out the entire run. It was a vindication of Nik and Steve's belief that the English public had been starved of intelligent entertainment, although I think a lot of people were attracted by a gory scene in which a wolf emerges from inside a human body, exiting through the mouth.

Palace repeated the trick a number of times, and as they rode ever higher we rode with them. They were notoriously late payers but at least they delivered, and our company matched theirs in aspirations. Month on month

Palace expanded, with new films constantly going into production, and everyone made a little money.

Soon Palace were the toast of English cinema, presenting a fresh face to the world that nobody had managed since the heady days of Hammer. But there was a flaw in the gem: they had started allowing their directors to control them. Instead of instinctively turning down certain projects, they trusted the film-makers to deliver big audience pictures. One couldn't blame them: Neil Jordan directed the hooker-with-a-heart flick *Mona Lisa*, and the chick-with-a-dick drama *The Crying Game*,* which became a surprise smash hit in the US. Michael Caton-Jones filmed *Scandal*, a racy version of the Profumo affair of the 1960s.† But for every hit there started to be a flop. Peter Richardson's disastrously unfunny *The Pope Must Die* underwent an absurd title change in the Catholic-sensitive US, becoming *The Pope Must Diet*. Jordan's *High Spirits* was a weak big-budget family ghost comedy that bombed. *Dust Devil*, *Waterland*, *Michael Collins* and *B Monkey* failed miserably.

All of this culminated in the slow-motion car crash that was *Absolute Beginners*, a rock-musical version of the Colin MacInnes book about a young photographer and the new youth culture that climaxed with the Notting Hill race riots.

The signs were bad. The English film industry was faltering once again, after the stinkbomb that was *Revolution*, an ill-conceived epic that audiences had avoided like herpes. A far bigger problem for *Absolute Beginners* was the wrong choice of director, the relatively inexperienced

---

*It had been formerly titled *The Soldier's Wife* until we were let loose on it.

†Caton-Jones failed to fulfil his early promise and switched to television after the appalling *Basic Instinct 2*.

Julien Temple, who made the cardinal mistake of informing the press of his every waking move. Although erudite and quick-witted, he was perceived as arrogant and abrasive in interviews, and quickly undermined confidence in the project.

As the film geared up for production, it seemed that you couldn't throw a stick in Soho without hitting someone who was working on the picture. There were seamstresses and artists, sound recordists and painters and model-makers and dog-handlers and choreographers who weren't sure if their work would ever make the final cut. The budget ballooned, personnel came and went, stars were hired and fired, and at the film's centre, holding this sprawling mess together, were two unknown leads, Patsy Kensit and Eddie O'Connell. At least Kensit had experience, but O'Connell had come from TV sitcoms and had no acting weight. It was his first film, and he was being asked to hold his own against character actors who had sixty or seventy features under their belts.

The production was working without a shot list. The script was in a permanent state of flux. New pages arrived daily, old ones were torn out. Later, Steve Woolley said, 'The costume people spent money like it was going out of fashion. It's always the same on a big-budget movie. Nobody's guilty, everyone gets inspired by the director and wants to make his vision. And spend a lot of money. It was worse here because there was a feeling: "This is a big movie, it's got David Bowie, we can spend money." The producers were in a state of terror, day in day out, because the money was running out.'

Inside the production, *Absolute Beginners* became known as *Absolute Bollocks* and was the punchline of a thousand jokes, but then the jokes spread beyond the set of Soho and out to the press.

The hyenas of the fourth estate scented a wounded

animal and trailed it, tearing the film to shreds while it was still in production – and Temple wouldn't keep his mouth shut. Even character actors playing cameo roles were asked for their opinions.

'I had no idea what I was doing on the film,' veteran performer Irene Handl admitted to me. 'I've got one line of dialogue – "Smell my broom" – what does that mean?'

Throwing more money at the production only made matters worse. The director was barred from the edit suite, and the new editor decided that the shot footage was barely salvageable.

But *Absolute Beginners* might easily have become the year's biggest hit. It boasted great work from Ray Davies of The Kinks, David Bowie, Sade, Charlie Mingus, Gil Evans and Miles Davis, and there are sections that almost catch fire, notably in the Notting Hill riot sequence.

But 'almost' doesn't cut it with the public. The problem was that too much had been revealed in advance about the production, and artificial-looking musicals, no matter how young and hip, hadn't worked with audiences since the days of *Summer Holiday*. Besides, it wasn't really a musical; most of the numbers ended halfway through, as they did in the equally disastrous *One From The Heart*. Despite garnering some rave reviews from respected quarters such as the *New York Times*, the film was dead even before it opened.

The shining neon logo that heralded the start of every Palace Picture cracked and fell – and we went with it. One day I went around to their offices and found the loyal staff all sitting on the floor – the desks and telephones had been repossessed.

The rest of the film industry was quick to follow on the heels of press opprobrium. The general feeling was that Palace had been too arrogant and deserved everything they got. It seemed as if everyone in London was owed money. The producers were cold-shouldered and openly insulted at Cannes. For a while it looked as if Nik and Steve might be lynched in public. The revelling in the company's demise was palpable. I felt differently: everyone had been perfectly happy to try to make money from Palace on the way up, and the company was being kicked very hard on the way down.

Palace wasn't the only English company to face a downturn. George Harrison's Handmade Films had a run of success with films like the superb gangster drama *The Long Good Friday*, *Time Bandits*,* *Privates on Parade* and student cult favourite *Withnail and I*, with its built-in drinking game. Its biggest flop was *Shanghai Surprise*, another lousy Madonna vehicle. Eventually the company folded, leaving behind a string of memorable films, most of which eventually went into profit. Typically, at the time of each film's release, British critics reacted with sniffy insults.

The year after the demise of Palace was a difficult one. We nearly folded, but managed to keep going with extended lines of credit. The home entertainment revolution settled down, and audiences returned to cinema as they always did.

For once, we stayed away from the cash haemorrhage that was the Cannes film market. Instead, we threw a cheap party in London called, with grim inevitability, 'The No-Cannes Do'. The film *Absolute Beginners* was never rehabilitated into the pantheon of great films about London, and remains an outcast despite flashes of brilliance. Its director went on to redeem himself with the excellent documentary *London: The Modern Babylon*.

In my head there's a top-ten list of London films. In no

---

*John Cleese *(as Robin Hood)*: Have you met the poor? They're awfully nice.

particular order, that I constantly revise, often to include
Hue and Cry, Hope and Glory, Dance with a Stranger
and *An Education*, among others.

My Top Ten London Films

1. *This Happy Breed*: David Lean's poignant study
   of the inter-war years seen through the eyes of
   one family in a terraced south London house is
   another attempt by Noël Coward to encapsulate
   the essence of Britishness. This time he succeeds,
   particularly in a shot where Lean's camera
   remains inside a room while news of an off-
   screen tragedy is broken.

2. *Nil by Mouth*: An astonishing one-off from Gary
   Oldman about a deeply damaged working-class
   family in south London that reveals an essential
   truth: they can still find pleasures *in extremis*.
   Visceral and unpatronizing, it's also remarkably
   entertaining, thanks to amazing performances
   from Ray Winstone and Kathy Burke and
   luminous night photography.

3. *The Long Good Friday*: Harold Shand (Bob
   Hoskins) watches his criminal empire collapse
   over the course of one nightmarish day.
   Underpinned by Helen Mirren, the only person
   left who still believes in him, Hoskins represents
   the death of Old London during the Thatcher
   makeover of Docklands, and exhibits wonderful
   gallows humour.

4. *Passport to Pimlico*: The idea of London as
   a collection of separate villages is beautifully
   realized here when a small neighbourhood near
   Victoria Station discovers that it's technically
   part of France and can do what it likes. The

film stars a veritable *Who's Who* of British comedy actors.

5. *Naked*: Mike Leigh's angry, difficult film about a young man too clever and too dangerous to ever find his place in the newly commoditized city. The London streets have never looked less hospitable as David Thewliss roams them, being alternately pitied, shut out and beaten up.

6. *Beautiful Thing*: Lensed on the Thamesmead Estate; two working-class lads fall in love, complicating the lives of everyone around them. The wish-fulfilment ending isn't so very far-fetched thanks to writer Jonathan Harvey's understanding of working-class London's liberal attitudes to class and sex. Great score from the Mamas and the Papas.

7. *Smashing Time*: A controversial choice over *Blow Up* and *Performance*, I know, but this Swinging London comedy, filled with duck-walking dollybirds, helmet-haired hipsters and smarmy record-fixers somehow captures London better, even though the comedy is cringe-inducing. Michael York's photographer ('I love yer boat-race, darlin'') beats David Hemmings hands-down.

8. *28 Days Later*: The one apocalypse movie that shows London to its best advantage, as Cillian Murphy wanders dazed past a double-decker bus tipped on its side. In many ways the opening echoes the start of *Day of the Triffids*, with its blind Londoners blundering across Piccadilly Circus. The litter of the apocalypse looks no different from any Saturday night in town.

9. *High Hopes*: Mike Leigh catches the strange juxtapositions of London lives as a pair of gentrifying opera-lovers in King's Cross fall out with the working-class old dear who lives next door, and a row over lost keys quickly spreads to her suburbanite relatives. Packed with annoying behavioural tics and quotable lines, it exudes the same ghastliness as *Abigail's Party*.

10. *The Sandwich Man*: Completely forgotten now, this picaresque family comedy has Michael Bentine walking around London with a sandwich board, observing slapstick scenes of life featuring dozens of British stars. It's dismally unfunny, but as a snapshot of London on a sunny day is fascinating for all the wrong reasons.

33

Winding Down

**The new ideology, the new epic, the new executives,
a new perspective and a very big family**

When you work on so many films each month, it's inevitable that you start to pick up on trends, and to me the most shocking one was the compartmentalizing of Hollywood cinema in order to fit audience demographic profiles. This division frequently meant dumbing stories down.

To take just one example, in 1954 Richard Matheson wrote a science-fiction novel called *I Am Legend*, about the only man on Earth not afflicted with vampirism. In 1964, AIP made a cheap film version starring Vincent Price, which many acknowledge to be the template for all 'living dead' movies that have followed. 1968 saw the arrival of *The Omega Man*, the second film version of Richard Matheson's story. If you've seen this, you may recall that the war between scientist Robert Neville and the infected was one of conflicting ideologies: Neville's technological determinism was the cause of the world's end. The sick now shunned technology and turned back to faith in order to save the planet. Once the relationship between Neville and his infected opposite number, the intellectually conservative Matthius, had been established, we knew the conflict could not be resolved without Neville's death because he was the last representative of the old guard, the true Omega Man who had to be superseded by religious zealots as the clock of civilization was reset. Complicating this was the fact that Matthius was himself infected, while the scientist Neville was not.

Therefore there could be no real winners. While the virus might be halted, that in itself couldn't eradicate the new ideology, and in this scenario Neville was as extinct as a dinosaur. This was the idea that drove the story and gave it so much resonance.

And so we arrive at the third 're-visioning'* in 2007, starring Will Smith, and in this version the ideological impasse is the first thing to go. *I Am Legend* becomes a triumph of style over ingenuity. Post-apocalyptic New York's return to nature, all buzzing insects and grass thrusting through cracked concrete, is rendered in impeccable detail. Then the CGI zombies arrive and everything ends up in a welter of cheap shocks.

Now the infected weren't real people, but had been replaced by superhuman computer animations. They couldn't even speak, so there was no real conflict at all, except the bog-standard Zombies *v.* Survivors tropes we'd all seen a million times before. When Charlton Heston sat in a cinema and mouthed the dialogue from *Woodstock*, he overturned our preconceptions about him and made a point about free will. Will Smith got to duplicate the scene by mouthing dialogue from . . . *Shrek*. No longer could a simple idea be communicated to a mass audience without fear of alienating them.

---

*Like 'imagineer' and 'quadrilogy', this is a word that should never, ever be used.

More pernicious was the creepy use of the escape to Eden that *I Am Legend* offered. Instead of a white Neville having sex with an independent black woman, we now had a black man chastely hanging out with a God-fearing (and safely light-skinned mixed-race) Brazilian girl. Instead of heading off to live in a flawed, argumentative commune built around new alternative families, something that would replace the traditional failing model of family life, we had the survivors arriving in a heavily guarded fortress town that looked like an isolationist Mormon Disneyland sponsored by the National Rifle Association. SF is required to reflect the era of its creation, which is why *I Am Legend* rankles.

Each remake of a popular film points up the new ideological losses. *The Invasion*, the fourth version of Jack Finney's *Invasion of the Body Snatchers*, went further still, disturbing with its suggestion that it might not be so bad to be a pod-person after all: at least you know who to obey and do what you're told.

When George Lucas and Steven Spielberg ushered in the era of the megabuck tentpole release, subtlety was gleefully hurled aside in favour of sensation, and films became a lot less fun for us to work on. Suddenly there were no more open lines to stars, no more penniless producers hawking dog-eared scripts, nothing to talk about in the pub except special effects. There were no crazy ideas we could use to excite audiences. Control was taken away by Hollywood, who now had the means – and the screens – to do whatever they wanted, and what they wanted most was to sell lots of merchandise.

I wrote a play in which one of the main characters, Billy, gave the following speech, which was very closely modelled on a conversation I'd had with a disillusioned Hollywood executive:

'I take my new job very seriously, and they reward me very well. I'm rising to the top like cream. I watch my back and keep my nose clean. I take my drug tests and do as I'm told. I'm a Senior Vice President. These days, we're in everything. We fake the photographs. We kill the rumours. We leak the sex tapes. We doctor the phonecalls. We edit the interviews. We supply the sunglasses to the celebrity who'll wear them in public so you'll insist on buying them. We've presold all the clothes you'll wear, the books you'll read, the things you'll want next year. We've already chosen the toys your unborn children will beg you to buy. As for the truth – we buried that a long time ago. The only thing that's real now is you handing over money, forever.

'Almost everything you see and hear about a new film apart from its title and trailer is a lie. Everything, good and bad. You only know because we told you, or somebody leaked it online, and how do you know we didn't do that?

'Our best trick? We replaced the journalists with "showbiz correspondents". And we replaced stars with celebrities. We saved a fortune. Now there's just the brand and the franchise. Celebrities are anyone we choose to put in front of you. And us, we've become completely invisible. Perfect.'

It is virtually impossible to produce something that is wholly original, with no reference to anything that has gone before. All ideas for stories are built on interpretations and permutations of existing concepts. But as we rode on through the years and into the future, I realized I had absolutely no opinion about films like the *Transformers* series or *Speed Racer* or *Battleship* (all based on toys), any more than I had an opinion about the kind of fries they serve in McDonald's. The product conformed to its basic definition, but beyond that it was difficult to recall anything at all, because it seemed like a reproduction filtered through someone else's memory; it was what the makers thought a French fry or a film or a pair of trainers should be like in order to sell it painlessly to the broad majority. The one thing they couldn't accurately replicate was genuine human emotion.

I showed my age when I saw the cinema listing for *Hancock* and instantly thought of East Cheam. Then I realized that Tony Hancock announcing 'Does Magna Carta mean nothing to you? Did she die in vain?' wouldn't get a laugh today because many people would think she did.

There's a Victorian *Punch* cartoon that shows two thick villagers watching the arrival of a stranger.

> FIRST VILLAGER: 'E's not from around 'ere – 'eave 'alf a brick at 'im.

We don't like things that aren't from around here, but Hollywood films aren't and the world can't get enough of them. Each year sees higher ticket sales. Hollywood's summer releases are designed to appeal to the universal inner child, the simplest thoughts and emotions, *bang, wow, ouch, aah* and *boo-hoo*. The majority rules because it sells easily, and it needs to sell around the planet because Hollywood needs to break big in international markets. In late autumn it releases its Oscar-worthy films, and for a couple of months we get a glimpse of what it can do when it aims higher.

In the fragmented tribal world that modern technology has created, we can choose to lose ourselves in the strangest back-alleys of culture and anti-culture because we no longer have to be embarrassed about loving something that's truly hard for others to understand. In the same way that Hellboy drunkenly sings a Barry Manilow song without feeling ashamed, I can admit to liking Norman Wisdom films without quite knowing why. I think I like them as cultural artefacts rather than knockabout nostalgia, but that's not the point. It's about having passions, whether they're for folk bands singing in the backs of pubs or the strange little cloth voodoo dolls some Japanese girl is making in London's Camden Market. Admitting to others what you really like can be a cathartic experience that sets you free. You no longer have to pretend to love Clint Eastwood movies just because the critics do.

I like bad English comedies, but it doesn't end there. *Hallowe'en* was not my favourite horror film. I watched *The Funhouse* more often, because it was a stranger, more knowing archetype. *Blade Runner* wasn't my top SF movie, that was *The Fifth Element*, a film in which the future of the universe hangs on a single match. *The Devils* was not my preferred Ken Russell movie;* that honour belonged to *The Boy Friend*, with its freewheeling, half-recalled dialogue segueing in and out of reality. *Amarcord* over *8½*, *After Hours* over *Raging Bull*. Terry Gilliam over Steven Spielberg. *The Orphanage* over *The Shining*. *Barbarella* over *Star Wars*. Sid James over – well, there was no one to compare him to.† *The Railway Children* over *It's a Wonderful Life*. *The Italian Job* over *Pulp Fiction*. Actually, just about anything over Tarantino's *Kill Bill* films, including acute appendicitis. As Pedro Almodóvar

---

*The dour film critic Pauline Kael typically thought the man was mad. Had Russell been Italian he would be as revered as Fellini.
†The most ubiquitous of post-war character actors, James was a Jewish South African former circus clown who reinvented himself as a cockney chancer, in the same way that Mayfair posho Terry-Thomas was actually from Finchley.

points out, many of us prefer films that eschew realism in favour of a happy coincidence of image, emotion and odd dialogue. He said: 'I remember feeling that the less real life there was in a film, the far better for us. The more unreal a film was, the more we loved it.'

Year in, year out we sat through dreadful films because – well, partly because we could do it and get paid for the pleasure of doing so. There on the biggest of big screens we watched endless double bills about killer bats, cats, rats and Joan Collins, talking dummies, mummies and Brad Dourif, and they left marks on us like vampire bites. The itch still exists, encouraging me to collect all kinds of rubbish old movies, and it's nice to know that every single one of them will outlive *Speed Racer*. Until *Speed Racer* becomes someone else's unfashionable little secret.

I realized I had spent decades apologizing for my taste, and Jim had never once questioned it. Instead he had encouraged me and everyone else to do what they enjoyed most, and by doing so brought out the best in them. It was an odd way of running a business, but it seemed to work. I sought his approval and found it in a faint smile, a slight wink, a silent agreement.

Seemingly overnight, Jim fell out of love with cinema, and I realized that it was partly because they banned smoking. I saw *The English Patient* with him, and half-way through I realized he had left his seat. Heading out of the foyer, I found him leaning against the wall quietly savouring a cigarette.

'What are you doing out here? You just missed the big scene.'

He examined the tip of his Rothmans. 'I wasn't enjoying it as much as a fag.' I noticed he was wearing his favourite Gant shirt. He always wore them because you could fit a packet of snouts in the top pocket.

Although he was the least introspective man I'd ever

met, one day, wedged in his customary spot on a pub bar stool, he said, 'I suppose I did something, didn't I?'

'What do you mean?' I asked.

'All those people's lives, the careers and marriages and children.'

'What, our staff?'

'Oh – yes, I suppose so. I never really thought of them as staff.'

I knew what he meant. Jim wasn't a father, but considering the quarter-century of people who passed through the doors of our company, it looked as if he had raised a very large family indeed.

'Funny,' he said, 'Wardour Street not being there any more. It doesn't seem right.'

'It's still there.'

'You know what I mean. All those people out of work.'

'They took early retirement.'

'To do what? Sit on the seafront and watch the seagulls? They lived for films. Okay, most of them were rubbish but at least they were ours. This country doesn't own anything any more. They were *our* bloody films.'

That was his last word on the subject. He hardly ever watched a film all the way through again. The last time the possibilities of film excited him was when we worked on 007. *Goldeneye* foregrounded vast sets and stunt work over computer graphics, and Jim became fascinated with its mechanical effects, although seeing them produced on set is always a disappointment. Even a scene in which a tank ploughed through a truck full of Perrier cans* seemed unexciting because such moments happen in real time and without much noise.

---

*It was going to be Coca-Cola but the product placement deal fell through. Companies don't mind if you smash up their products so long as you show them.

As I watched him fall out of love with something that had been his greatest passion, I knew our partnership had reached a conclusion.

34

How It Ended

'I called because something weird has just happened.' It was an old colleague I hadn't heard from in an age, ringing at four in the afternoon. I thought it odd that he should call out of the blue.

'What do you mean?'

'I was on a bus going up Tottenham Court Road and I think I saw Jim. I recognized that car, the great big old white Mercedes you always called the Vanilla Gorilla. It was stuck right across the middle of the road.'

'You think you saw him?'

'Yeah, there were police, and they were propping him up against a taxi. I think he must have hit it. I thought I'd better call you.'

I had always trusted Jim with my life because he had saved it more than once. The first time, we were going to France on the ferry, but it had been cancelled because of a spectacular sea storm. Even though it was barely possible to stand upright at the shore, I battled my way out of the ferry house and along a jetty to stupidly try to watch the waves colliding with the sea wall. Just then the wind caught a steel door, whipping it back and smashing it into the concrete behind me, removing part of the wall's fascia.

It was where I had been standing a moment before. Jim had seen what was about to happen and had knocked me from my feet.

Everyone needs a guardian angel, and if you don't have one you should either find one or become one yourself, as it's the most satisfying thing you'll ever do. Jim was mine, and I in turn became someone else's. It's a great system. I don't consider myself particularly spiritual, but there were several occasions when Jim turned up miles from where he was supposed to be, on the off-chance that he could help out.

On one such occasion I had just destroyed my car on a blacked-out stretch of night road where someone had abandoned a truck in the fast lane. Ploughing into it, I demolished my vehicle and was dragged to safety by two sturdy old women who ran a nearby Greek restaurant. While they were working out what to do, Jim appeared in the doorway. He had been sitting at home and sensed something bad, so he had jumped in his car and traced my route. As a writer I'm naturally prone to exaggeration, but it happened, and I was grateful.

'I couldn't figure out why there were police standing all around him,' said the guy on the phone. 'I think he might be quite badly injured. He was having trouble standing. I wondered if they were breathalysing him.'

That made no sense. Jim had gone to a business lunch but would never drink and drive, and was brilliantly in-stinctive behind the wheel. I didn't think he'd ever had an accident in his life. I tried his mobile and there was no answer. I guessed that if he had come to any physical harm, they would take him to Euston's University College Hospital, so I headed there.

I lived so near to the hospital that I beat the ambulance into the bay. The medics told me that he appeared to have had a stroke, and would be taken to a specialist unit for tests. Further examination revealed that he had suffered a seizure brought on by a cancer in his brain. It had already spread to his lungs. It was explained to me – reluctantly and belatedly, as I was not a relative in the doctor's eyes – that he did not have long to live.

As a heavy smoker, Jim was sanguine about discovering that he was dying. He said, 'It's a bit rubbish, I'd have liked seven more years.' Then he went back to sleep.

He came round again a few hours later. 'I'm really sorry about this,' he said. 'I'm going to be annoying for a while.'

'That's all right.'

'You know once when we were drunk you said if I died you'd kill yourself?'

'Yes.'

'Well, don't worry, I'm not going to hold you to it.' He fell back to sleep again.

As I left the hospital it began to rain hard. A few close friends went to a nearby café and sat in gloomy silence. Suddenly I felt violently claustrophobic and left, heading up the road to Regent's Park, where I stood in the downpour, utterly lost, not knowing what to do.

For the next three years, the disease drifted in and out of his life like a bad-tempered thundercloud. Every few weeks he would suffer a seizure that would rob him of his memory and his power of speech. Gradually his mind would return, but each time there was a little less of it, and the attacks became more frequent.

After one particularly unpleasant bout, the doctor brusquely told me to come in quickly and say goodbye to him, as my friend was likely to die within the next few hours. The doctor didn't like being unable to work out my relationship to his patient, and I couldn't begin to explain the complexity of it to him. 'Friends and business partners' could not sum up the intensity of our lives together.

When I arrived at the hospital I found Jim sitting up in bed eating fish and chips, watching *The Simpsons*.

'What do *you* want?' he asked, puzzled.

'I was told you were about to die.'

'No, that was just the doctor. He's a real panicker.'

'As I'm here now, is there anything you want?'

'Yeah, can you nip out and get me twenty Rothmans and a pint of Kronenburg?'

Knowing that this would now be the pattern of his life, Jim became increasingly mischievous. One day he assembled his entire family at the foot of the bed, then told them to stand still while he framed his hands around them. 'That's it,' he said, 'I can remember you all like that. You can go now.'

You know you really love someone when they can persuade you to stand on a toilet seat unscrewing an anti-smoking device so that they can have one more killer cigarette without setting off the hospital alarms. I took to smuggling him out of the hospital to a pub opposite and putting him back in bed before the nurses' rounds.

We all took turns looking after him. His blood family and his friends (who by now had termed themselves 'Real Family') lined the trenches on opposite sides, as is common in such trying circumstances. Immediately after each lapse, Jim was vulnerable to the predations of others with financial agendas, so a lawyer had to make sure he wasn't persuaded to add a wobbly signature to some ludicrous codicil. 'Madness,' Rocky Horror had said, 'takes its toll.' People who had been perfectly lovely before the crisis suddenly started behaving wildly out of character. Squabbles broke out as the thought of inheriting money tainted the memory of a man who was, actually, still alive.

There's nothing you can do to prepare for the loss of a loved one that makes a jot of difference. Shortly before he became ill for the last time, Jim and I had a long frank talk about dying. Our accountant was with us, trying to delicately outline what would happen after his death. Tiptoeing around the phrase 'after you die', the accountant used euphemisms like 'when you drop off your twig' and 'when you're pushing up daffodils', inadvertently making things worse.

At the end of the discussion, Jim rose and went out on to the balcony, and stood watching the building site opposite. I left him there for a few minutes, quietly smoking, then came out and stood beside him. I was worried that the conversation had become too upsetting for him.

'Tell me honestly what you're thinking,' I asked.

'I was just trying to figure out how they're going to get that bulldozer out of the pit over there,' he replied, looking down into the building site. Although he was grey from chemotherapy sessions, his eyes remained alive. Something behind them danced. 'I think it's time to do something really extravagant,' he said. 'In the South of France.'

'I'm not going back to the Cannes Film Festival,' I warned.

'No, I was thinking of something *really* extravagant.' He grinned, and an old sun reappeared.

We hired a seriously grown-up yacht with a crew and let them sail us to St Tropez for a few days. At the end of the trip he was exhausted but happy. His family stayed at his bedside, and he drifted into a month-long fugue from which he briefly emerged to grip my hand. His vague smile had become the smile of a child recognizing the face of a friend before wandering off into the dark.

I left him looking out over the sparkling sea in his beloved France, and flew back to London. The next morning, I knew that he had died. In death, as in life, he was everywhere at once: there was a cremation in Monte Carlo, a party for him on the Riviera, a burial in London and a wake in the Pineapple Pub in Kentish Town. Some of him was accidentally left in a duffel bag under the stairs of the house we had bought together in France and a bit more got tipped into a friend's handbag.

As I headed back to Wardour Street, I thought about Jim. He gave everyone time and a second chance. He gave me confidence and made us all stronger. He said, 'Everyone should be someone's guardian angel.' He asked if he'd interfered too much in my life, if I'd have become a better writer without him, and I said no, of course not.

Nobody in the industry knew that he was profoundly dyslexic. When I returned from Los Angeles he sent me a letter. In it, he eventually gave up explaining that he was going to collect me from the airport and drew a picture of himself waving in his car instead. He was an innocent let loose in a toy shop, and glee showed in his face like a spotlight. When he died I was halved, but in ways I was at a loss to explain.

'You know what you should do after I die?' he said. 'Don't get all maudlin and start dumping flowers on my grave. I hate flowers. Go and see some of our favourite films. And get a few beers down you afterwards. No moping.'

So that's what I did.

I sat alone in the almost empty cinema, leaving the seat down next to me, imagining he was there. By some miracle I had found the perfect double bill of black comedies, showing for just one performance. First up had been *The Producers.**

---

*Timid accountant Leo Bloom and ebullient impresario Max Bialystock plot to stage the worst show in the world, raising the money by seducing old ladies, and guaranteeing it will lose a fortune so that they can keep the original investment. But the play is so bad that it becomes Max's first-ever hit and they go to jail, where they get the prisoners to over-invest in a new show. Wilder and Mostel liked each other so much that they worked together again, in the filmed version of Ionesco's surreal *Rhinoceros*.

'Don't let me influence you,' bellowed Zero Mostel, influencing Gene Wilder by gripping him so tightly that he could hardly breathe.

'Kindly tender my compliments to the chef,' said cheapskate Zero to the hot-dog vendor. 'Kindly tender half a buck,' said the unimpressed vendor. 'Everybody's a big shot,' Zero complained as he chewed.

'Well, what do you know, I'm happy!' Wilder admitted before dancing around a blossoming fountain, followed by the man who had just made him commit to a massive fraud.

As the opening number of their appallingly tasteless show *Springtime for Hitler* commenced in front of a predominantly Jewish New York audience old enough to remember the Holocaust, Leo and Max watched happily from the back of the auditorium, convinced of their successful failure, and Leo kissed the top of Max's head. Mel Brooks couldn't really write roles for women, so he effectively made the film a love story for two men.

After this came *Harold and Maude.**

'Would you like some liquorice?' asked concentration camp survivor Maude, picking Harold up at a funeral where neither of them knew the deceased.

'Do you stage these suicides for your mother's benefit?' asked Harold's psychiatrist. 'No,' Harold replied softly. 'I would not say "benefit".'

When Maude announced that she was dying, Harold told her he loved her. 'That's good,' she replied. 'Go and love some more.'

---

*Harold is a rich, spoilt, suicide-staging teen. Maude is a poor, life-affirming 79-year-old. They fall in love, to the horror of Harold's society mother, who arranges ghastly dates for him which he continually sabotages with acts of self-immolation and hara-kiri. The beautiful Cat Stevens soundtrack became the most requested film score of all time.

The only other film that would have made the bill perfect was Paul Mazursky's Ozu-influenced *Harry and Tonto*, a road-trip movie featuring 72-year-old Art Carney and his cat, which Jim could quote line by line.

I emerged from the doorway of the run-down building and wiped my face. I knew that the old cinema would soon be boarded up. But London had plenty more, and now whenever I went to one I'd feel a little less sad.

Outside, Wardour Street had become an alien universe, shape-shifting into its latest transformation as a Soho centre for wining and dining. It was drizzling lightly, and the pink and yellow neon signs of cafés and restaurants were reflected in the pavement puddles. Pedicabs rode past the sushi bars ringing their bells, evoking memories of *Blade Runner.*

Walking up the street in the sifting rain, I could see only the faintest traces of what had once been there – the odd sign above a shop, the old logos of Hammer* House, Film House, Twentieth Century House, Cinema House and Rank Film Distributors.

A student in a tight jacket and a cap set at a jaunty angle passed me, his arm looped through that of a large blonde with kohl-rimmed eyes. Fifty years earlier they might have been Norman Wisdom and Diana Dors. I saw the face of an elderly man who I was sure used to be a projectionist at the Bijou cinema, and the former landlord and lady of The Ship, who had lately taken to wandering Soho hand in hand, as if conjuring up the past might stop them from fading away.

The screening room in which I had first seen a rough cut of *The Exorcist* with Jim and a visibly shaken Sean

---

*The company name was taken from the stage name of comedian William Hinds, 'Will Hammer', after the area of London in which he lived, Hammersmith.

Connery was now a Mexican cantina. The Rialto, the Crown, the Baronet and Coronet were all cocktail bars.

With each passing day, these physical markers were fewer in number. Soon, nothing would be left to show that the nation's film industry was ever based here, in a single unassuming London street.

And in my mind, Jim had joined the rest of these back-room ghosts. They, together with the English cinema stars, Sid James and Kenneth Williams, Joyce Grenfell and Kay Kendall, John Mills and Stanley Holloway, Joan Greenwood and Hattie Jacques and Lionel Jeffries and John Le Mesurier* and Stanley Baker and Dirk Bogarde,† had become part of the dissolving fabric of Wardour Street's history. It was good that things were finally moving on. But on that rainy night, with the past glimmering beneath the present, it felt as if I could see them all again, just long enough to say goodbye.

---

*Hangdog comic actor whose disappointed expression probably arose from the fact that his second wife Hattie Jacques moved her lover into the family home and his third was sleeping with Tony Hancock. When he died, his obituary notice read: 'John Le Mesurier wishes it to be known that he conked out on November 16th.'

†Bogarde was famously 'private' in a time when the word was synonymous with 'homosexual'. The handsome, likeable actor had a male life partner and made three films a year for Rank. He was admired for not 'going Hollywood', and hated America, about which he said: 'I never want to set foot in their immature, undiplomatic, plastic, mutilated land again.'